STATE ADMINISTRATION IN SOUTH CAROLINA

BY

JAMES KARL COLEMAN

AMS PRESS
NEW YORK

COLUMBIA UNIVERSITY
STUDIES IN THE
SOCIAL SCIENCES

406

The Series was formerly known as
Studies in History, Economics and Public Law.

Reprinted with the permission of Columbia University Press
From the edition of 1935, New York
First AMS EDITION published 1968
Manufactured in the United States of America

Library of Congress Catalogue Card Number: 70-76647

AMS PRESS, INC.
NEW YORK, N. Y. 10003

To
My Wife

CONTENTS

5

AUTHOR'S PREFACE

THIS study is an attempt to present a descriptive analysis of existing state administration in South Carolina and to suggest certain changes in the light of modern political science for its improvement. The author wishes to express his deep appreciation to the many individuals who have rendered generous and valuable assistance in its preparation. Grateful acknowledgment is extended to the large number of state officials and citizens of this and other states, who have furnished material and who have given freely of their time and experience.

The author is especially indebted to those who have made the completion of this study possible. Foremost among these is Arthur W. Macmahon, Professor of Government, Columbia University, under whose direction this monograph was prepared. His careful reading and detailed criticism of the manuscript have been of inestimable value. Mr. A. E. Buck, of the Institute of Public Administration, has also read the manuscript and offered many helpful suggestions for the adequate treatment of the subject. Thanks are likewise due to Dr. Luther Gulick, Director, Institute of Public Administration, and Professor of Municipal Science and Administration, Columbia University, who contributed indispensable advice.

J. K. C.

CHARLESTON, S. C.
MARCH 15, 1935.

INTRODUCTION

THE movement toward a simple and efficient form of governmental organization has been the outstanding feature of political progress in the states during the past fifteen years. The necessity for economy and efficiency in the state and local governments of South Carolina was never more apparent than at the present time. It is no less the duty than the right of citizens to insist that the cost of their government shall be in close keeping with the service rendered. Efficient results cannot be expected of inefficient machinery. An unwieldy structure and a divided responsibility for its operation constitute the chief weaknesses to be overcome. The administration must be so simplified and integrated that accountability for waste, extravagance, or incompetence can be definitely fixed.

Public administration has been defined as " the management of men and materials in the accomplishment of the purposes of the State ".[1] Its function is the execution of the will of the State. Its objective is the most efficient utilization of the resources at the disposal of officials. Enormous improvements have been accomplished through scientific management in some industries and the question arises whether or not similar results are possible in government. In any event, it is obvious that the technician in our technological age has aroused vast dissatisfaction with our antiquated methods and machinery, a heritage of decades of neglect. The time-honored practice of adding a new com-

[1] See L. D. White, *Introduction to the Study of Public Administration* (New York, 1926), pp. 2, 13. See, also, Frank J. Goodnow, *Politics and Administration* (New York, 1900), p. 22.

mission or department to deal with each new activity of
government has broken down, and the states are striving for
a more orderly method of organization which will permit a
regular expansion of government to meet new demands.
The present tendency reverses the old current.   The fear of
political concentration of power is yielding to the need of
administrative integration.[2] Nearly a half-century ago
Woodrow Wilson wrote:

> There is no danger in power, if only it be not irresponsible.
> If it be divided, dealt out in shares to many, it is obscured; and
> if it is obscured, it is made irresponsible.   But if it be centered
> in heads of the service and in heads of the branches of the ser-
> vice, it is easily watched and brought to book.[3]

State administration is so broad and so important that it
may profitably be studied from many points of view.   Inasmuch as the economic and social institutions are in large
measure fostered, modified, or restrained by the numerous
administrative services of the states, the subject is of vital
interest to every citizen in every walk of life.   It will be the
task of this inquiry to examine the problems involved in
the administration of the state government of South Carolina, with the view of appraising the structure through which
the state performs its administrative functions.

One of the criticisms usually made of the machinery that
has been built up to fulfill an increasing interest of the states
in the affairs of their citizens is that overlapping and duplication are common.   It is not surprising that this condition
is prevalent.   Legislatures have often provided new agencies
for the initiation and extension of governmental activity,
instead of ascertaining whether the function might not be

[2] See J. P. Chamberlain, "Government", *American Journal of Sociology*, vol. 34, pp. 187-205.

[3] Woodrow Wilson, "The Study of Administration", in *Political
Science Quarterly*, vol. ii, pp. 213, 214 (June, 1887).

properly handled by an existing office. The effect has been deplorable. The multiplication of administrative agencies has not only tended to result in duplication of effort and to involve a state in too great an " overhead " expense, but also has made it very difficult for the General Assembly and the public to apprehend the present structure. Moreover, since the agencies are not sufficiently correlated on a functional basis, it is not easy for the legislature to grasp the relative costs and results of the major services of the state government.[4] Such is the condition that obtains in South Carolina in 1935. It is hardly necessary to suggest the need of change. The nature of that change will be the burden of this study.

It is well at the outset to recognize that there is no stereotyped plan of reorganization that will suffice; for diversities in state governmental problems do not permit of the drafting or adoption of a model constitution for all the commonwealths. Certainly the problems that beset South Carolina are not the same as those of New York or California, except as they may yield to certain fundamental principles applicable in part to any of them.[5]

An efficient government is rendered possible only by simplification and definite responsibility throughout all parts of the complex mechanism. And, with increasing needs to be met by governmental action, it is likely to become increasingly complex. While government itself can never be made simple, the machinery of popular control over it can be simplified through the short ballot principle and the fixing of relationships that center mainly in the governor.

[4] See Griffenhagen and Associates, *Report on the Organization and Administration of the State Government of Maryland* (Annapolis, 1921), pp. 16-18.

[5] For a discussion of problems common to all states see for example W. F. Dodd, *State Government* (New York, 1928), p. 568.

The process of integration is applied to state government in four following ways: (1) by increasing the administrative function of the chief executive; (2) by unification and departmentalization of the scattered administrative units; (3) by the establishment of an effective system of financial control; and (4) by coordination of activities through the cabinet system of administration. It is axiomatic that the governor of South Carolina has very little power. He should have power to appoint and to remove heads of departments, to prepare and present the budget to the General Assembly, to supervise its execution, and generally to direct the administration as a whole.[6]

The practice of diffusion of administration is firmly intrenched and the tradition that supports it is grounded in the minds of South Carolina's electorate. Apparently the belief is yet held by a large number that democracy exists to the degree in which all office-holders are elected at the polls. The individual voter cannot be expected to pass judgment upon the technical problems of government. The " will of the people " does not mean the will that specifically guides. Its function is to determine broad policies or tendencies. When the voters of the state learn that they can more definitely hold their government to account by electing only policy-determining officers, upon whom they can fix responsibility more exactly, they will in fact have moved far in the direction of a democracy.

To what extent it will be practicable to unify and departmentalize the scattered administrative units will depend largely upon the general political condition of the state and the public's interest in the problem of administration. In pursuing this inquiry, answers to the following questions will

[6] In proposing reorganization of the machinery, the writer disclaims any reflection upon the honesty and industry of the public servants who attempt to operate the present archaic set-up.

be sought. Are the various boards well articulated with each other and with the other agencies and departments? Do extravagance and lost motion exist, due to loose organization, duplication and overlapping of function? Have the increases in the expenditures of the state government, making due allowance for increased prices generally, been justified by the service rendered?

It goes without saying that much of the increase in cost has been due to the general rise of prices in recent decades and to the consequent increasing cost of carrying on governmental operations. It goes without saying, too, that the increased cost of government has been due to the assumption by the state of expenditures for new purposes, such as increased state aid to education, charitable administration, and promotion of good roads. But there is ample ground for challenging questions that strike at the heart of state administration.

No intelligent conclusions can be reached without a clear understanding of the facts which, for various reasons, are elusive and difficult to establish when they relate to government. Moreover, the bewildering maze of offices, boards and commissions is likely to cause the investigator to go astray.

There is a vast difference between immediate savings and the ultimate and lasting economies that all good citizens are seeking. Doubtlessly substantial public funds can be saved and efficiency promoted, but economy must not be destructive. Efficiency must not be sacrificed but increased. No essential agency of the state should be starved. Progress of a people is not merely in reducing taxes and attracting wealth, however desirable that may be. A state must not neglect the education of its children, the care of its unfortunates, the health of its people and the development of its public works. Many of the changes that will be suggested cannot be measured in dollars and cents, but it is believed that all of them would be conducive to better service and to more business-like practice in the transaction of public affairs.

It is the intention of this study to view the present complex of state administrative agencies as a going concern, to call attention to the apparent defects of organization, and to invite the interest of South Carolinians in the need for machinery adequate to meet the changing economic and social conditions of a rapidly developing society. While certain proposals are advanced, they are in no sense conclusive. A far more comprehensive and expert survey is required than the limits of this study and the ability of the writer permit.

Detailed information could best be obtained by a study of the state by outside experts whose impartiality could not be well questioned. From a survey so prepared a commission of representative men and women familiar with local conditions could adopt and adapt the recommendations in a manner suitable to the needs of the state.

It is assumed that administration has become, and will continue to be, the heart of the problem of modern government. If this study should stimulate research in behalf of better government in South Carolina, the labor of its preparation would be more than repaid.

CHAPTER I

GENERAL ADMINISTRATION

I. PRESENT ORGANIZATION

THE existing administrative structure of the state government of South Carolina is built around the provisions of the constitution of 1895, which was a rather conservative document at the time of its adoption.[1] The constitution of 1868 had been a well balanced copy of the American state constitutions of that period and the present organic law made no radical departure from its essentials.[2] It followed as an inevitable result of the Haskell appeal to the illiterate negro in opposition to the Tillman Movement of 1890.[3] As Dr. D. D. Wallace has pointed out, the new constitution "was not intended to enshrine the agrarian principles of the 90's or to register the triumph of the social and political revolution led by Tillman. . . . No constitutional clincher was needed to assure their permanence".[4] Nor have amendments affected in an appreciable degree the executive or administrative offices.

[1] For an excellent criticism, see D. D. Wallace, *The South Carolina Constitution of 1895*, Bulletin No. 197 of the University of South Carolina (1927), chap. v.

[2] The principal object of the constitution was the elimination of the negro from politics. This discrimination was effected by the temporary "understanding" clause, *art. ii, sec. 4 (c)*. In practice, the general use of the Primary by 1890 had already accomplished that result.

[3] See F. B. Simkins, *The Tillman Movement in South Carolina* (Durham, N. C., 1926), chap. ix, for history of political events leading up to the constitutional convention.

[4] Wallace, *op. cit.*, pp. 26, 27.

Only eight such officers are provided for in the constitution, as follows: Governor, Lieutenant Governor, Secretary of State, Comptroller General, State Treasurer, Adjutant and Inspector General, and a Superintendent of Education. It further provides that they shall be elected by the qualified voters of the state. All other positions charged with administrative duties are created by statute law. " Public officers " is construed to mean all officers of the state that have been commissioned, and trustees of the various colleges of the state, members of state boards, and other persons whose duties are defined by law.[5]

Every state of the Union recognizes in its scheme of government the principle of checks and balances, and each has established an executive branch, independent of the legislature. The constitutional officers mentioned above, together with the Commissioner of Agriculture, Commerce and Industries, and the Insurance Commissioner, constitute such a branch in South Carolina.[6] A second group of boards, commissions, and offices, created by statute and subject to the control of the legislature, may be regarded as performing administrative rather than executive duties. But, inasmuch as both groups exist for the same fundamental purpose of carrying into effect the public policy, little distinction will be made between the two groups for the purpose of this discussion. Usually, one speaks of the higher offices as executive and the lower ones as administrative.

The constitution of South Carolina declares that " the supreme executive authority of this State shall be vested in a Chief Magistrate, who shall be styled ' The Governor of the State of South Carolina '." [7] He holds his office for

[5] *Code 1932*, secs. 1512 and 3042. " Other persons whose duties are defined by law" does not include guardians, administrators and other trustees, *Sanders v. Belue*, 78 S. C., 171.

[6] *Code 1932*, sec. 3082.

[7] *Constitution*, art. iv, sec. 1.

CHART I

Present Organization of State Administration

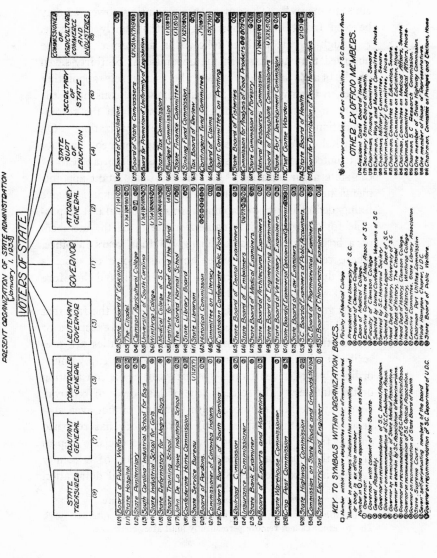

four years and is ineligible as his immediate successor. He is instructed " to take care that the laws be faithfully executed in mercy". The governor's appointing power, as may be seen from the accompanying chart, is fairly extensive. Although no rule has been followed in this respect, it will be observed that he shares in the appointment of thirty-seven of the state's agencies, to wit: he is the sole appointing power in twenty instances; he must have the consent of the senate in eight; and, in nine he appoints upon the recommendation or selection by some outside organization.[8] On the whole, the governor's power of appointment has not contributed materially to strengthen his position as head of the state administration. For the most important appointments he must obtain confirmation by the senate. Laws fixing definite and overlapping terms often make it impossible for the governor to name a majority of the members of a board or commission during his four years in office. These restrictions, of course, limit his choice of officials whose duty is to aid him in law enforcement, and therefore tend to weaken his control over them.

The governor's control is further lessened by the fact that he has little power of direction over the other executive or administrative officials, since most of their duties are prescribed by law. Whatever ordinance power he enjoys must ordinarily be derived from a specific grant in the constitution or the statutes. The same is true of his power of removal. Generally the governor of South Carolina cannot even suspend an unfaithful officer until a grand jury has returned an indictment.[9] He has no power to take a decisive step to protect the financial interests of the state or of a county against an incompetent or corrupt official until defalcation

---

[8] Twelve officers and boards are elected by the legislature.

[9] *Constitution*, art. iv, sec. 22, and art. xv, sec. 4; *Code 1932*, sec. 3098. The governor cannot remove permanently until after conviction.

or other violation of the law has become flagrant. And, in like measure, he is helpless against a sheriff who either wilfully or negligently fails to enforce the law of the commonwealth. The long controversy over the removal of the sheriff of Jasper County in 1931 was sufficient evidence of such impotency. For two full months Sheriff Spivey refused to surrender the keys to the office until the State Supreme Court had affirmed the legality of the vacating proclamation. The removal of the Greenville County supervisor, who stood convicted of a felony, had to await many months during the same year for a ruling of the court *en banc,* i. e., the justices of the supreme court and the fourteen circuit judges. A sad commentary upon the science of government in South Carolina! As one writer has expressed it, " the governor is merely the leading executive with limited supervisory powers over a number of executives among whom there is no organization for concerted conduct ".[10]

The " Chief Magistrate " of the state is one of eight major state officers elected by popular vote. His seven colleagues, so to speak, are his peers in the sight of the law. He neither appoints them, nor removes them; he cannot prescribe their duties, which are covered by law. The constitution provides that " all officers in the executive department and all boards of public institutions, shall, when required by the Governor, give him information in writing upon any subject relating to the duties of their respective offices or the concerns of their respective institutions, including itemized accounts of receipts and disbursements ".[11] But positive power of direction is non-existent. Determination of policy in regard to the state's services, generally, lies beyond his grasp. It is not surprising that consistent and efficient administration is well-nigh impossible.

[10] Wallace, *op. cit.,* p. 42.
[11] Art. iv, sec. 14.

Just how much actual authority the governor can exercise in the general oversight of state administration depends in a large measure upon his personality. If he has public opinion as an ally he may often compel all other state officials to carry out his policy. It must be remembered, however, that under the present set-up, the chief executive's influence can only be indirect and imperfect, and entire responsibility for the conduct of state administration cannot properly be considered to belong to him.

To supervise state finances, the governor has not the treasurer alone to watch; he must watch various independent officers and commissions that play a part in the collection of taxes and fees.[12] Inasmuch as South Carolina has no executive budget, the governor can not assume genuine leadership in the formulation of fiscal policies. The shaping of a financial program must be in collaboration with two members of the General Assembly, selected for that purpose. However, he enjoys the right to veto single items in appropriation bills and can go far in shaping their final form in a negative way.

The veto power now exists in every state except North Carolina. South Carolina is one of only four states that permit their governors, under the usual liability of being overridden by a two-thirds majority of the legislature, to strike out any item or section of a bill of any kind.[13] During the session, the governor has only three days in which to act upon a measure. After adjournment, however, the bill need not be returned until within two days of the next meeting.[14]

In addition to his administrative functions, the governor enjoys the quasi-judicial function of issuing reprieves, com-

[12] Financial control is discussed in detail in chapter ii.

[13] *Constitution*, art. iv, sec. 23. But the common understanding is that this item veto is to be confined to appropriation bills.

[14] *Ibid.* Thirty days would appear to be sufficient time in which to exercise this prerogative.

mutations, and pardons after conviction (except in cases of impeachment), in such manner, on such terms and under such restrictions as he may think proper. Every petition for a pardon or commutation of sentence may be referred to a board of pardons, appointed by him. However, he may act independently of their recommendation.[15] There is much evidence of abuse of this absolute power in the hands of the governor of South Carolina.

Finally, note must be taken of the governor's military authority.[16] He is commander-in-chief of the armed forces of the state and, in case of an extraordinary disturbance beyond control of the regular officers of the law, he may call out the state militia to restore order. As in most states, the privilege of the writ of *habeas corpus* may not be suspended except in times of rebellion and invasion when the public safety requires it.

The administrative departments and agencies are so numerous that they almost defy classification. However, as the real fields of activity of the state government are relatively few, the greater proportion of the state agencies can be grouped according to the principal functions that they are designed to perform. An attempt to do this has been essayed in the accompanying chart which shows these agencies, as of January 1, 1933, with an indication of the method of their appointment or election. They will be discussed individually, and also collectively in their associated activities, in the succeeding chapters.

II. THE REORGANIZATION PLAN

The purpose of the reorganization plan is to throw the administrative machinery into bold relief so that the people and the General Assembly can focus responsibility for the

[15] *Constitution*, art. iv, sec. 11; *Code 1932*, sec. 3436.

[16] *Constitution*, art. iv, sec. 10.

management of the public business.   There can be no doubt of the need of integrating executive authority in the state government of South Carolina.   The problem is what should be the degree of consolidation and correlation of activity, · consistent with local conditions and needs of the state.

Guided by the restraining influences of practicability and adaptibility, an administrative system which would offer reasonable promise of unity, coordination, and singleness of direction and responsibility has been sought.   It is believed that the resulting plan would greatly simplify the state government; that it would remove a large degree of duplication of effort; that it would be an aid in reducing waste and extravagance through a more effective control of expenditures; that it would promote efficiency through a merit system of employment which would largely eliminate the discharge of employees for political reasons; and, in general, that it would result in a better quality of service and economy in administration.

The proposed plan is designed to make the governor the actual and responsible head of the state administration through the adoption of a short ballot.[17]   It embodies the centering of executive authority in the governor through the establishment of a small number of administrative departments under his control and direction, and is similar in general to the schemes that have been successfully carried out in a number of states.[18]   South Carolinians should be especially

[17] See Richard S. Childs, *Short Ballot Principles* (Boston, 1911), *passim*, for an outline of the doctrine and the problems of their application.   Also, see " The Short Ballot ", a brief pamphlet by the same author, National Municipal League, New York.   Also, see J. A. Fairlie, " The Executive ", an explanatory article printed with *A Model Constitution*, pp. 25-31.

[18] For the best summary of administrative reorganization in the several states, see A. E. Buck, *Administrative Consolidation in State Governments*, published by the National Municipal League (5th ed.), January,

CHART II
PROPOSED ORGANIZATION OF STATE ADMINISTRATION

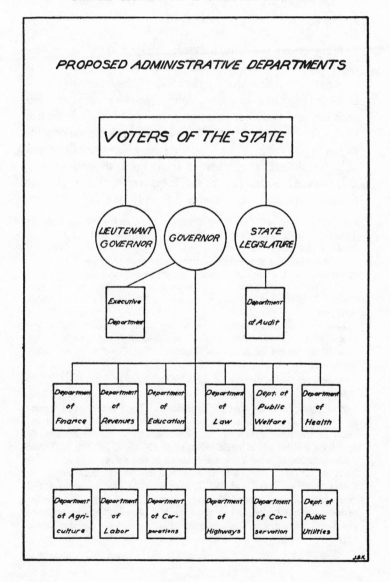

interested in the plan that was instituted in Virginia under
the leadership of Governor Harry F. Byrd,[19] and that in
Georgia under the direction of Governor Richard B.
Russell, Jr.[20]

A complete administrative reorganization should be undertaken in South Carolina.   Such a plan would require constitutional as well as statutory changes.   Minor improvements,
short of organic revision, might produce an increased
economy and efficiency in administration, but they could not
have a far-reaching effect so long as the fundamental organization is defective.   The following constitutional offices and
agencies should be eliminated from the constitution: (1)
Secretary of State, (2) State Treasurer, (3) Comptroller
General, (4) Attorney General, (5) Adjutant and Inspector

1930. See, also, *A Digest of Systems of Government Enacted in
Thirteen States,* issued by the Missouri Association for Economy in
Public Expenditures (St. Louis, 1926).

For an admirable discussion of lines of present progress in reorganization, see Dodd, *State Government,* pp. 573 *et seq.* Also, see Professor
J. P. Chamberlain's articles on "Government" in the *The American
Journal of Sociology,* reviewing the session laws of the several states
each year.

The first substantial contribution to the theory of administrative reorganization is found in the second chapter of the report made by the
New York Bureau of Municipal Research, *The Constitution and Government of the State of New York,* 1915.

[19] See Buck, *Administrative Consolidation,* pp. 42-44.

[20] Following a survey made in 1930 by the firm of Searle, Miller &
Co., of New York, the Georgia Legislature in 1931 reduced 102 departments and bureaus to less than one-fifth of that number. For an account of the inauguration of this program, see *N. Y. Times,* Sept. 6,
1931. As a result of an investigation by the National Institute of Public
Administration of New York, the State of Maine reorganized its administration in 1931. For an account of the drastic changes, see *N. Y.
Times,* April 19, 1931, and W. T. Gardiner, "Maine reorganizes and
saves money", in *National Municipal Review,* Feb., 1933. For a brief
review of recent studies and surveys, see J. A. Fairlie, "Studies on State
and Local Government", in *American Political Science Review,* April,
1933.

General, (6) State Superintendent of Education (7) Railroad Commission, and (8) State Board of Education.[21] In like manner, the constitutional restriction on selection and control of the officers of the State Hospital should be repealed.[22] It is extremely necessary, moreover, that Article X, dealing with finance and taxation, be revised.

With these revisions of the constitution made, it is suggested that the legislature create thirteen administrative departments, as follows: (1) Executive, (2) Finance, (3) Revenues, (4) Health, (5) Public Welfare, (6) Agriculture, (7) Labor, (8) Corporations, (9) Public Utilities, (10) Highways, (11) Education, (12) Conservation, and (13) Law.

The governor would be the head of the Executive Department and the heads of the other departments would be appointed by the governor with the advice and consent of the senate.[23]

The departments of Finance, Revenues, Health, Agriculture, Labor, Conservation, and Corporations would have

[21] *Constitution,* art. iv, sec. 24; art. ix, sec. 14; art. xii, sec. 2; art. xiii, sec. 4.

[22] *Ibid.,* art. xii, sec. 2. The S. C. Council is of the opinion that "many provisions of the State Constitution are so archaic that a convention for the formulation of a new constitution should be held", *County Government* (Cheraw, 1931), p. 17.

[23] Although the office of Lieutenant Governor is retained under this plan, it is of little value and could be abolished without loss. For a discussion of this viewpoint, see J. A. Fairlie, "The Executive", *A Model Constitution,* p. 28. Instead of the election of an officer whose principal purpose is to fill a vacancy, a preferable plan is perhaps that of having the immediate succession in some one of the important officers appointed by the governor. Professor J. M. Mathews has suggested that the office be abolished or else reconstructed into a position of greater usefulness. He suggests that this official might be made a sort of deputy governor to relieve the governor of many routine duties which distract his attention from more important matters. See his article, "State Administrative Reorganization", in *American Political Science Review,* vol. xvi (1922), p. 392.

single heads, known as commissioners, to hold office at the pleasure of the governor.[24]   The Department of Education would be headed by the State Board of Education, consisting of seven members chosen by the governor with consent of the senate for overlapping terms of seven years, who would appoint the Commissioner of Education as the executive officer of the department, to serve at their pleasure.   The Department of Public Welfare would likewise be headed by a board similarly constituted and empowered to appoint the Commissioner of Public Welfare, to serve at the pleasure of the board.   The Department of Highways would be governed by a commission of five members enjoying five-year overlapping terms, instead of fourteen members as at present.[25]   A Public Utilities Commission of three members,

[24] For cogent arguments against applying these principles to all branches of the administration, see F. W. Coker, "Dogmas of Administrative Reform", *ibid.*, pp. 408-411.

[25] Ordinarily it may be said that the performance of the administrative branch is likely to be less efficient in proportion to the extent to which the executive officers are subject to the control of boards.   But certain types of activities which involve duties of planning and supervising, rule-making, and the exercise of quasi-judicial power are not strictly executive functions and may best be performed by a group of well-disposed persons meeting from time to time.   This is especially true in welfare work and in the field of education.   Continuity of procedure and program in handling social problems and in controlling institutions is particularly desirable and necessary and is more likely to be secured through the governing direction of a board with overlapping terms.

The almost total absence of centralized control of the state's penal and charitable institutions and of an active state welfare agency is convincing evidence of the need of a board as suggested.   Comprehensive planning by an interested group will be necessary before there can be said to be a program to be executed.

In the field of education a collective mind is needed to solve the problem of public school finance and to establish a school system above the present standard.

A reconstructed highway commission, rather than a single department head, is proposed because of the building program now in progress.   It is suggested that the commission be abolished when the system of roads is completed and the task becomes largely that of maintenance.

appointed for overlapping terms of six years, would replace the present Railroad Commission of seven members elected by the General Assembly.

It is intended that the board of education, the board of public welfare, and the highway commission would perform no purely administrative duties.[26] It would be their task to formulate the general policy of their respective departments, but the execution of its details should be left to the executive officer. The members should be removable by the governor, but he should be required to make a public statement of reasons for such removal.

Three purely advisory bodies are provided, as follows: (1) Advisory Health Council; (2) Agricultural Advisory Council; and (3) Advisory Commission of Conservation. Agencies of this sort are not open to the same objections as are commissions charged with supervising duties, and often serve as useful aids in performance of executive functions.[27] They do no violence to the principle of the bureau type of organization and, in these three cases, it is believed that they will prove to be valuable adjuncts. South Carolina has found that many of her ablest men and women, who would not accept a salaried position, are willing to serve in a consultative capacity without pay. Moreover, to quote a celebrated English writer, " the use of a fresh mind applied to the official mind is not only a corrective use, it is also an animating use ".[28] However, a body advisory to the policy-

[26] Boards acting as administrative agents cannot render the most efficient service. They may be useful to insure deliberation, and to check work done, but lack initiative and responsibility in the execution of the task itself. Facilitation of prompt dispatch of business requires the action of an individual, solely responsible.

[27] See Dodd, *State Government*, pp. 257 *et seq.*; White, *Public Administration*, p. 189; F. O. Lowden, " Reorganizing the Administration of a State ", in *National Municipal Review*, vol. xv, p. 10 (Jan., 1926).

[28] W. Bagehot, *The English Constitution* (New York, 1884), p. 200.

determining agency should not be clothed with power; its function is to communicate opinion, rather than actually to govern.

Ex-officio boards are particularly objectionable. Either there is considerable draft upon the time and energy of the members, which interferes with the performance of their primary duties, or the real work is actually done by some one member or employee of the board. Consequently, the suggested reorganization proposes the abolition of all such agencies, except a State Finance Committee to be composed of the governor, the commissioner of revenues and the commissioner of finance. The general function of this committee would be that of maintaining a balance in the state treasury. It would be empowered to perform the duties of the present state finance committee. (*Cf. infra,* p. 49.)

The proposed intra-departmental structure requires explanatory comment. Perhaps a few of the suggested bureaus may be regarded by some as being too elaborate from the standpoint of South Carolina's needs and resources. It may probably be argued that this state is after all small as states go and that much must remain rudimentary and simple here. A realistic sense of state government recognizes the soundness of that contention. Nor is it lost in the present search for a logically complete scheme for South Carolina. It is to be understood that the bureau structure as outlined constitutes in many respects an ideal toward which it is believed the state will grow, as it comes to know its responsibilities and possibilities and improves financially.

In this connection, undue statutory rigidity must be avoided in order that an adequate internal flexibility of departmental structure may be maintained. It would be a very serious error to nail down every detail in the statute. On the contrary, the department head should be free to determine the bureau organization below him which is appropriate for the work to be done. He should be authorized to add new bureaus, to merge or abolish existing bureaus, or to transfer functions from one bureau to another. In order to protect subordinate officers and employees, however, it should be provided that the machinery should not be reduced without the approval of the governor. The consent of the legislature should also be required whenever the changes involve additional staff or additional expenditures. Of course the department head can not effect any changes in the internal organization unless he is given supervision over the subordinate personnel. He must have authority to transfer employees and to modify their duties. The proposed establishment of a system of personnel control (Chapter XII) does not preclude a considerable flexibility in administrative management. These two things are not in conflict.

A system of personnel control under the Department of Finance would be established with the view of guaranteeing a reasonable permanency of tenure and a greater degree of competency in the state service. All subordinate officers and employees, the educational institutions excepted, would be employed through this agency. It is believed that centralized personnel management is one of the greatest needs in the state administration today.

According to Professor Leonard D. White, the governor's office should be conceived " (1) as the connecting link between the administration and the legislature, (2) as the center of responsibility for all the administrative agencies, (3) as a vital point at which the tone of the administration can be directly affected by the pitch of public opinion, so far as it is able to make itself articulate on this subject ".[29]

[29] White, *Public Administration*, p. 158. See a very interesting and suggestive article by Harvey Walker, " Theory and Practice in State Administrative Reorganization ", in *National Municipal Review*, vol. xix, pp. 249-254 (April, 1930). Contending that the governor can never be more than a chief administrator in name since his time must be spent

This interpretation of the role of the chief executive as an administrator is in keeping with the intent of the scheme outlined in the plan proposed.[30]

The present disintegrated state administration, with its endless incongruities and absurdities, is due in large measure to the traditional fear of one-man power. Of course, increased power to work effectively means an increased possibility of danger as well. It is believed that under the plan offered here the executive organization, with the governor as its responsible head, will be so conspicuous that inefficiency or corruption cannot hide itself.[31] In the words of Theodore Roosevelt, " you cannot get good service from the public servant if you cannot see him, and there is no more effective way of hiding him than by mixing him with a multitude of others so that there are none of them important enough to catch the eye of the average work-a-day citizen ".[32]

Responsibility commensurate with the governor's increased power would be enforced in part through the simplified machinery and the greater publicity in which the work of the administration would be conducted. The installation of the civil service system proposed should help prevent the use of executive power to build up a political machine and, at the same time, it should serve to maintain efficiency in administration in spite of the unavoidable frequency in the

largely in his executive, legislative and political tasks, the author suggests the creation of the office of " Chief Administrator ", a kind of expert business manager, to attend to the routine business of the state. Such a position is unnecessary in South Carolina.

[30] For discussions of the governor in state administration, consult, for example: Mathews, *American State Administration*, chaps. 3 and 5; J. A. Fairlie, " State Governor ", in *Michigan Law Review*, vol. x, pp. 458-464; Holcombe, *State Government*, chap. x; Dodd, *State Government*, pp. 238 *et seq.*

[31] See Dodd, *op. cit.*, p. 253.

[32] Address before Ohio Constitutional Convention, 1912, quoted in Childs, *Short Ballot*, p. 30.

change of department heads.[33] Another restraint would be the requirement that the governor give publicity to his reasons for removals, as he is required today in vetoing a bill. So far as danger still inhered in concentrated executive power, one of the most effective checks would be found in the department of audit which would be supervised by the state auditor elected by the legislature. This would be responsible solely to the law-making body and would serve as the general critic of the administration.[34]

While the reorganization plan would strengthen the governor in the administration of public affairs, it would simultaneously increase the power of the legislature to call the executive publicly to account. The governor and the heads of departments would be entitled to seats in the legislature and would be required to attend sessions of that body at stated times to answer questions not adequately covered by their budget statements. The members of the governor's cabinet would be empowered to introduce bills and take part in discussions, but would have no vote.[35] Certainly they are best qualified to give information concerning the merit of a proposed measure affecting state administration. The appearance of administrative officials before the legislature for interpellation is thoroughly sound and should throw much needed light upon the operation of the state government.

[33] For a discussion of feasible checks, see Mathews, *American Political Science Review*, vol. xvi, p. 398 (1922).

[34] For a discussion of this role, see Brookings Institution, *Survey of North Carolina*, Introduction, p. xxxix.

The services of the state auditor would probably be more effective should he be made directly responsible to a committee in the legislature similar to the British Committee on Audit headed by the opposition.

[35] See *A Model State Constitution*, sec. 47. The practice of administrative officers appearing at hearings of legislative committees is no substitute for this proposal. The state treasurer and the comptroller general appeared before the South Carolina Legislature in 1932 to give information and advice regarding the state deficit.

Although no American state has yet adopted this practice, no preconceived formulas of government should be allowed to stand in the way of the main objects of state administrative reorganization.

The proposed plan of reorganization is submitted with the full realization that no state can expect to achieve its political and governmental salvation through mere administrative machinery. Organization alone can not insure success, but it can help make it possible for the people to have the kind of government they desire. No plan will succeed in itself, for its successful working will depend in a large measure upon the character and competence of those who administer it. The human element cannot be eliminated, and vigilance is the price of efficiency. But the people will not be able to hold their government to account unless they have a government they can understand.[36] Simplification and reorganization of administration are matters of much importance in the state of South Carolina.

A warning must be sounded against indiscriminate curtailment of essential services at the request of panic-stricken citizens in the name of retrenchment. Constructive elimination of waste and inefficiency is to be had through business-like budgeting and purchasing methods, revision of antiquated tax procedures, establishment of better machinery for financial control, creation of a system of personnel management, and integration of administrative services on a functional basis with definite responsibility fixed. These suggestions are not theories, but are practical, working principles in successful operation in certain of the states that have modern methods in conducting the public's business. The proposed plan is based upon these principles, in so far as they appear to adapt themselves to South Carolina.

[36] See *Report on Retrenchment and Reorganization in State Government of N. Y.*, 1919, p. 12.

No attempt is made to forecast the savings which might result, should these recommendations for simplifying and improving the administrative machinery be adopted. It is sufficient to say that appreciable economies have resulted from similar reorganizations made in other states.[37] It is believed that the merit of the proposals will also lie in the indirect saving reflected through increased efficiency and greater service to the people. These benefits cannot be measured in dollars and cents.

Comprehensive governmental reorganization is very difficult of accomplishment, because the people as a group are not greatly interested in economy and efficiency. As Dr. Howard L. McBain has pointed out, " We are not a thrifty people by nature, habit or economic condition. We are, moreover, extremely complacent ". And, as he further observes, " Efficiency in government is apt to raise a storm of opposition among those who are immediately affected and to leave quite cold the great mass of people in whose interest it is undertaken ".[38] However, it is to be hoped that an efficiency survey, which will be necessary to a scientific solution of our problem, will arouse the citizens of South Carolina to an appreciation of the need of change.

[37] Results in the nearby State of Virginia bear eloquent testimony.

[38] H. L. McBain, " The Problem of Governmental Reorganization ", in Academy of Political Science, *Proceedings*, vol. ix, no. 3, p. 1.

CHAPTER II

FINANCIAL ADMINISTRATION

THERE is scarcely an administrative act that is not reflected in the financial records. Even though government costs be distributed equitably and revenues be made adequate, the state's financial problem cannot be solved without an effective system for the control of financial administration as a whole.

Since economical and effective management of the affairs of the State of South Carolina may not be expected with an unsatisfactory system of financial administration, the present organization requires examination. It is believed that economies and increased efficiencies in governmental operation can be achieved through the adoption of better and more modern machinery and the application of more business-like methods.

I. FINANCIAL OPERATIONS OF THE STATE GOVERNMENT

1. *Expenditures*

The constitution of 1895, Article X, Section 10, provided that the fiscal year should commence on the first day of January of each year. There can be no doubt that this provision tended to cripple the operation of the government in a number of ways. In the first place, it was an obvious impossibility for the administrative departments to close their accounts on the last day of the calendar year and have their complete annual reports ready for the General Assembly when this body convened on the second Tuesday in Janu-

36

ary.[1] Consequently, the legislature was without the full information necessary to an intelligent consideration of the needs of the public service. Secondly, the budget estimates made up before the end of the fiscal year necessarily caused the appropriation for the following year to be based in large measure upon a mixed statement of facts and conjecture. Furthermore, the appropriation bill was not enacted until three or four months of the fiscal year to which it applied had passed, making it difficult for the departments to adjust themselves to any radical change in appropriations or policy.

Although it had been recommended a number of times, dating back to 1900, that the fiscal period be changed to end on June 30, it was not until 1933 that the legislature ratified an amendment to that effect.[2] The appropriation bill can now be passed in a reasonable time before the beginning of the year to which it will apply and, by 1935, knowledge of the actual expenditures of the previous year will be available for budget studies.

Despite valid objections, detailed appropriations are still very popular with state legislative bodies including the South Carolina General Assembly.[3] Dr. F. A. Cleveland condemned the practice in the following words:

The best that may be said for the detailed appropriations of the past is that they are a part of a system that has operated to prevent administrative action premised on infidelity and ignor-

---

[1] In recognition of this fact, the legislature in 1929 directed the annual reports to close as of September 30.

[2] *Acts of 1933*, p. 591. The constitution of South Carolina is amended in the following manner: Any amendment may be proposed by the General Assembly, two-thirds of the members elected to each house agreeing. If a majority of the qualified voters at the next general election, voting thereon, vote in favor of such amendment, a majority of each branch of the next General Assembly may ratify the same. *Art. xvi, sec. 1.*

[3] Exceptions have been made in the case of state institutions since 1931.

ance; that legislative control over administration through detailed appropriations is a device adapted for use of a political institution, in which all the elements essential to administrative efficiency are lacking. Given a responsible government and a real executive, the restrictions which go with detailed appropriations are the first obstacle to efficiency to be removed.[4]

Until the State of South Carolina has set up a responsible system of budgeting and fiscal control, along lines that will be discussed presently, it is hardly feasible to ask the General Assembly to adopt the general practice of lump-fund appropriations. As things stand the authority that is supposed to provide enough flexibility to prevent tie-ups in the operation of the government is vested in the governor, the chairman of the senate finance committee and the chairman of the ways and means committee of the lower house. With the written approval of this committee transfers may be made within departments, or from one department to another.[5]

Turning our attention to the cost of operating the state government, we note that direct appropriations for the ten-year period, 1923 to 1932, were as follows:

1923	$7,297,138.69	1928	$9,558,259.70
1924	9,132,870.87	1929	10,276,901.04
1925	9,380,662.66	1930	10,585,855.54
1926	10,218,247.89	1931	10,371,762.63
1927	9,937,765.06	1932	9,255,343.90

The total amount authorized by the legislature does not always appear in the direct appropriations, however. It is often increased through the authorization of loans to depart-

4 F. A. Cleveland, "Detailed Versus Lump-fund Appropriations", a paper prepared for the annual meeting of Association of Public Accounting Officers, Chattanooga, June 6, 1913. Quoted in A. E. Buck, *Public Budgeting* (New York, 1929), pp. 128, 129.

5 Appropriation Act of 1932, sec. 55, *Acts of 1932*, p. 1625.

ments from the Sinking Fund, which of course must be charged as an expenditure against the year's revenue. In this way, for example, the expenditure actually authorized for the year 1930 amounted to $11,260,796.96.[6]

The following analysis indicates how the appropriations of 1929 were expended:[7]

Departments	Purposes	Amounts	Per Cent
Administrative	Salaries	$676,726.62	5.97
	Operation	657,281.90	5.81
Penal and Charitable Institutions	Salaries	329,757.03	2.91
	Operation	1,480,868.23	13.07
Schools and Colleges [a]	Salaries	1,247,388.77	11.01
	Operation	4,677,676.30	41.29
Legislature, Judicial, and Regulatory Boards	Salaries	228,986.66	2.02
	Operation	393,274.53	3.47
Other Expenditures [b]	Salaries	183,283.16	1.62
	Operation	560,179.06	4.95
Contingent Items	Operation	31,666.38	0.28
Contributions	Operation	861,468.31	7.60
Total		$11,328,556.95	

[a] Of the total under this head, $3,840,519.00 was expended for state aid of high schools.

[b] Comprehends interest on notes and bonds, salaries paid county officers, state elections, and miscellaneous.

[6] See *Report of the Comptroller General*, 1930, p. 4.

[7] The per capita payments for operation and maintenance of the general departments of the state government in 1929 amounted to $8.14 as compared to Virginia, $10.43; North Carolina, $7.29; Georgia, $5.91; Alabama, $8.87; Mississippi, $8.57; Louisiana, $11.12. See U. S. Bureau of Census, *Financial Statistics of States, 1929* (Washington, 1931), p. 60. The statistics for 1929 were the most recently available when this comparison was made. Since then the Bureau of Census has issued similar reports to include the year 1932. For individual states, see, also, *Financial Statistics of State and Local Government: 1932* (Washington, 1934), and *Digest of State Laws Relating to Taxation and Revenue: 1932* (Washingon, 1934).

The constitution charges the General Assembly with the responsibility of making ample provision for the ordinary expenses of the state each year. Article X, section 2, reads:

The General Assembly shall provide for an annual tax sufficient to defray the estimated expenses of the State for each year, and whenever it shall happen that the ordinary expenses of the State for any year shall exceed the income of the State for such year the General Assembly shall provide for levying a tax for the ensuing years sufficient, with other sources of income, to pay the deficiency of the preceding year together with the estimated expenses of the ensuing year.

Nevertheless, for five successive years, 1925-1930, the comptroller general reported a deficit in operations.[8] These deficits were not so much the inevitable result of adverse conditions as the outcome of an absence of legislative policy and administrative financial control. Appropriations were repeatedly made in excess of revenue provided.

Although operating deficits accumulated in prior years did not increase during 1931, the accrued interest brought the total to $4,989,399.90 at the close of that year.[9]

When the General Assembly convened in January, 1932, some definite plan for the retirement of this deficit within a specified time and for balancing the budget was absolutely necessary. There was no market for state bonds and credit was not available until the deficit was refinanced.[10] Gov-

[8] *Report of the Comptroller General*, 1931, p. 4.

[9] For the unique position of Nebraska among the states, see W. Stebbins, "Nebraska Finances on a Cash Basis", in *United States Daily*, June 2, 1930.

[10] The state was unable to borrow $1,750,000 to make the January payment of its obligations to the school districts. Likewise, there was not a a single bidder when the attempt was made to sell highway bonds.

The state finance committee, composed of the governor, the state treasurer and the comptroller general, is authorized to borrow annually so much as may be necessary for the expenses of the ordinary and current business of the state in anticipation of taxes, *Code 1932*, sec. 2206.

ernor Blackwood was quoted as having described the situation in these words: " Every time the State goes to borrow money at present, the deficit looms in its face like a penalty to be added for its financial status ".[11]

The governor proposed that the deficit be financed with bonds " the maturities of which shall begin not later than five years hence and extend over a period of ten years thereafter ".[12] The comptroller general proposed shifting the debt to the counties of the state. His suggestion was that the state should retain sixty per cent of the amount derived from the one-cent tax on each gallon of gasoline sold in the state which is collected by the state for county purposes. He estimated it would amount to $726,000 annually and would retire the deficit, with interest thereon, in a period of eight years.[13]

The General Assembly acted upon neither plan suggested. Instead, it allocated one-half of the state five-mill property levy to the retirement of the obligation in question.[14] Officials estimated that this arrangement would provide approximately $1,000,000 annually, thus retiring principal and interest in about six years.

In an effort to live within expected revenue, the legislature reduced the appropriations of $10,371,762.32 for 1931 to $9,255,343.90 for 1932.[15] Nevertheless, this figure proved to be approximately $1,300,000 above the amount collected during the latter fiscal year. Again confronted with the perennial problem of operating the state government

---

[11] *News and Courier*, Dec. 19, 1931.

[12] *Annual Message*, 1932, pp. 7, 8.

[13] See *Report of Comptroller General*, 1931, pp. 5, 6.

[14] *Acts of 1932*, p. 1227.

[15] *Acts of 1932*, p. 1624. The amount appropriated for the fiscal year 1934-1935 was $6,548,704.33—*Acts of 1934*, p. 1682. Thus the state has reduced expenditures from its general fund about 40 per cent since 1930.

on a cash basis, the General Assembly in 1933 reduced the total appropriations of the previous year about 35 per cent.[16] Moreover, the Budget Commission was empowered to withhold whatever proportion of this amount might appear necessary to maintain a balanced budget.[17]   Consequently, the deficit carried over from 1932 was entirely absorbed during the fiscal period of eighteen months which extended from January 1, 1933 to June 30, 1934.   The state government was at last on a cash basis with a balance of $203,976 in the appropriations fund.

2. *State Indebtedness*

A constitutional check upon contracting public debt is laid down in Section 11 of Article X, which provides:

To the end that the public debt of South Carolina may not hereafter be increased without its due consideration and free consent of the people of the State, the General Assembly is hereby forbidden to create any further debt or obligation, either by the loan of the credit of the State, by guaranty, endorsement or otherwise, except for the ordinary and current business of the State without first submitting the question as to the creation of such new debt, guaranty, endorsement or loan of its credit to the qualified electors of this State, at a general State election; and unless two-thirds of the qualified electors of this State, voting on the question, shall be in favor of increasing the debt,

[16] That is to say, approximately the same amount was appropriated for the period of eighteen months, extending from Jan. 1, 1933 to June 30, 1934 (made necessary to effect the change in the fiscal year), as was appropriated for the previous twelve months. *Acts of 1933*, p. 643.

[17] The appropriation act of 1933 gave the commission "full power and authority to survey the progress of the collection of revenue and the expenditure of funds" by all departments and institutions and authorized this agency "to make such reductions of appropriations as may be necessary to prevent a deficit" during the period. It was provided that "no liability will be imposed on the State for the unpaid portion of any appropriation which may be reduced hereunder". *Acts of 1933*, p. 652.

guaranty endorsement or loan of its credit, none shall be created or made. And any debt contracted by the State shall be by loan on State bonds, of amounts not less than fifty dollars each, bearing interest, payable not more than forty years after final passage of the law authorizing such debt.

Apart from the state and district highway bonds, the state of South Carolina was bonded on December 31, 1932, in the sum of $5,171,060.16.[18] Its capital debt was one of the smallest of the forty-eight states.

Aside from the obligations of the Highway Department which are separately financed, the present state debt is the aggregate of the bonded debt indicated in the preceding paragraph, and the deficit obligation accumulated prior to 1931—a total of approximately $7,500,000.

The sinking-fund system is the customary procedure in South Carolina. This system of handling the state's capital debt has certain defects and it might advantageously be replaced by the serial bond system. As Professor H. L. Lutz points out, " The record of local sinking fund administration in the United States is a rather sadly tarnished one, but the tendency toward serial redemption of local bonds is entirely praiseworthy ".[19] Discussing the advantages of the serial plan, the Brookings Institution recently made the following comment:

If future issues are made upon a straight serial or annuity serial basis, the amount to be appropriated for each year will be definitely known, the burden upon taxpayers will be nearly equal over all the years of the life of the bonds, and there will be no sinking fund installments to be impounded, invested, and safeguarded, thereby saving labor and expense of bookkeeping and coupon-clipping.[20]

[18] *Report of Comptroller General,* 1932, p. 41. The highway bonded debt is provided for under the Highway Bond Act of 1929, which is outlined in some detail in the later discussion of the Highway Department.

[19] *Public Finance* (New York, 1930), p. 649.

[20] *Survey of Mississippi,* p. 339.

II. PRESENT FINANCIAL ORGANIZATION

An examination of the machinery for the administration of finance reveals some interesting facts. Our attention is immediately directed to the fact that South Carolina's fiscal organization lacks integration and responsible executive direction and control. Such wide scattering of organization and functions leads to waste and inefficiency. A private business conducted on a similar basis would surely go bankrupt.

Raising sufficient revenue to meet necessary expenses is only a part of the fiscal problem. An equally important phase of the problem is the proper management of the state's expenditures through a modern system of financial procedure. To this end, the administrative machinery must be reorganized to supply the needed direction and control.

The role of the fiscal relationships in the ultimate problem of efficient government has been cogently stated by the Brookings Institution in a recent report:

. . . It might be said that the government which has worked out and is employing a satisfactory system of financial administration has gone a long way toward putting the administration of its affairs upon an efficient basis, and conversely, that the government which has not done so cannot possibly have that economical and effective management of its affairs to which its citizens are entitled.[21]

More or less duplication of function exists throughout the structure of the executive branch of state government in South Carolina, but the outstanding example is the financial system. The State Treasurer, the Comptroller General, the State Tax Commission, the Tax Board of Review, the Budget Commission, the Sinking Fund Commission, the

[21] *Report on a Survey of the Organization and Administration of the State Government of North Carolina* (Washington, 1930), p. 21.

State Finance Committee, the Board of Claims, the Contingent Fund Committee, and the Joint Committee on Printing, play their respective parts in the administration of the state's financial affairs. In addition, there are numerous agencies that collect fees of some kind or another, some of which are used in whole or in part for the support of the department, board, or commission that gathers them.

In commenting upon organization and operating procedure, the Joint Committee on Economy and Consolidation appointed by the General Assembly in 1921 had the following to say in part:

This duplication of financial agencies has an important bearing upon the fact that large amounts of money collected are never turned into the State Treasury, that the appropriating authorities have no voice as to the manner in which sums running into the millions are spent, that expenditures in many cases are not audited until long after the money has been paid out when it is too late to take effective action in case of waste, extravagance, or fraud, and that in many cases the auditing is superficial. . . . Economy is so closely tied up with effective financial control that the improvement of the State's financial structure must be regarded as one of the pressing immediate needs.[22]

The state treasurer and the comptroller general are constitutional officers, and are elected by the qualified voters of the state for terms of four years.[23] All payments from the treasury, except for interest on the public debt and the pay of the members and staff of the General Assembly, are made on warrants drawn by the comptroller general. All vouchers drawn on the comptroller general, except for appro-

[22] *Report of the Joint Committee on Economy and Consolidation,* 1922, p. 9.
[23] *Constitution,* art. iv, sec. 24.

priated salaries, must be accompanied by a classified and itemized statement of expenditures.[24]

The major problems of treasury administration center around the safe-guarding of state funds and the economical management of treasury balances. As is the case in all states, the bank depository system is used. State moneys are deposited in such banks as are agreed upon by the state finance committee.[25] As a condition prerequisite to a bank being designated as a depository, either an indemnity bond in an approved surety company or certain designated collateral as security is exacted.[26] The treasurer is allowed to keep necessary cash in the vault of one of the banks designated, and is required at the end of every month to report to the comptroller general an accurate statement of all transactions of the treasury.[27] He is further required to make a daily report to the latter officer of all moneys paid out by him, except that paid upon warrants as indicated above. Banks having on deposit state funds are required to transmit monthly statements to the governor and to the comptroller general, and quarterly statements to the state treasurer.[28]

The law requires that " the Treasurer shall raise an account in the Treasury, in every instance, for the annual

[24] Code 1932, sec. 3140, 3141. For a discussion of provision for carrying accounts in state depositories so that the treasurer may issue checks in payment of claims against the State Government, see National Institute of Public Administration, Survey of Arkansas, p. 19.

[25] Hence "honest graft" in pocketing all or part of interest on state deposits is proscribed in South Carolina. Interest on deposits is paid into the treasury.

[26] U. S. Bonds, Federal Land Bank Bonds, Joint Stock Land Bank Bonds, bonds or other obligations of the State of South Carolina, or any political subdivision thereof, are accepted in lieu of surety bond. Code 1932, sec. 2200.

[27] Code 1932, secs. 3167.

[28] Ibid., secs. 3176, 3180, 3182. For requirement that publicity be given to transactions of state treasury, see ibid., sec. 3181.

appropriations made by the Legislature, so that the appropriations of money and application thereof conformably thereto may appear clearly and distinctly on the Treasury books ".[29] This appears to be quite unnecessary. This office should be regarded as an office of deposit and disbursement, and only such records as may be necessary to disclose the accountability of the state treasurer should be kept.[30] The comptroller general is the chief accounting officer of the state.

While it is true that the plan of electing a treasurer is in common use, there is little to recommend it. The function has not representative character. It is largely a ministerial one.[31] It is therefore recommended that the constitution be amended to remove the provision that the state treasurer shall be elected by the people. He should be subject to appointment by the governor, upon the recommendation of the commissioner of a department of finance. As the head of the bureau of the treasury, he should be relieved of all ex officio duties.[32]

The present duties of the comptroller general may be summarized as follows:

1. To keep a record of General Assembly appropriations and of payments made.[33]

2. To examine each month the vouchers in the office of the state treasurer for all payments made by the treasurer during the preceding month; and, at least twice each year, to examine the cash in the treasury at Columbia.[34]

[29] *Code 1932*, sec. 3173.

[30] For criticism of similar practice in North Carolina, see Brookings Institution, *Survey of North Carolina*, p. 25.

[31] See Griffenhagen, "Administrative Organization", p. 12.

[32] See proposed plan of reorganization, *infra.*, p. 75.

[33] *Code 1932*, sec. 3136.

[34] *Ibid.*, secs. 3136, 3137.

3. To prepare annual estimates of the public revenues and public expenditures for the General Assembly; and, at the same time, to render " a true and accurate account of the actual state of the treasury ".[35]

4. To keep a duplicate of the books of the treasurer, as a complete check upon that office, and to report annually a balance of these books to the General Assembly.[36]

5. To record an abstract of all settlements with the county treasurers as to all taxes—state, school, county, and special.[37]

6. To report to the General Assembly a detailed statement of all taxes for which each of the counties is liable under the tax acts of each year, and of the amount of local taxes collected in each county.[38]

7. To examine and report annually to the General Assembly on the accounts of all persons having the distribution of public money.[39]

8. To make an annual report of the names of the pensioners of the state.[40]

As the disbursing officer, the comptroller general audits and pays all claims against the state. The enormous increase in the work of his office is indicated in the increase of total expenditures, from $17,000,000 in 1917, to $64,-693,897.57 in 1931.[41] In spite of this fact, this officer reports that " the personnel . . . is adequate to carry on the work, and the organization experiences little difficulty in dispatching the daily routine ".[42]

[35] *Code 1932*, sec. 3139.
[36] *Ibid.*, sec. 3144.
[37] *Ibid.*, sec. 3145.
[38] *Ibid.*, sec. 3146.
[39] *Ibid.*, sec. 3148.
[40] *Ibid.*, sec. 3149.
[41] *Report of Comptroller General*, 1931, p. 24.
[42] *Report of Comptroller General*, 1930, p. 9.

The State Finance Committee is an important ex officio board, consisting of the governor as chairman, the comptroller general and the state treasurer. This committee was created in 1925 in order to correlate the financial machinery of the state. Its function is to maintain at all times a cash balance in the treasury sufficient to meet the payment of the ordinary and current business of the state. With this in view, it is authorized to transfer appropriations within a department or between departments, and to borrow in anticipation of receipt of taxes and other income of the state for any fiscal year. This committee also supervises the deposit of state funds.[43]

The Budget Commission is composed of the governor, who is the chief budget officer, the chairman of the ways and means committee of the house, and the chairman of the finance committee of the senate. The latter two sit with the governor at all public hearings on any and all estimates to be included in the budget and join with him in all reports and recommendations thereon to the General Assembly.[44]

The Board of Claims consists of the comptroller general, the adjutant general and the secretary of state. It is the duty of this board to examine the correctness, validity, and legality of all claims for the refunding of overpaid taxes, or for payment for services rendered or supplies furnished the state.[45]

[43] *Code 1932*, chap. 98, art. 2.

[44] *Code 1932*, sec. 3217. The office of state auditor was placed under the direction of the commission in 1933. *Acts of 1933*, p. 296.

[45] *Code 1932*, chap. 94, art. 2. The following statute of limitation is contained in section 2073: "All claims against the State except the bonded debt of the State shall be forever barred unless presented within three years after the right to demand payment thereof accrues. And such claims shall also be forever barred if twice presented to the General Assembly or either branch thereof and rejected, or twice presented and withdrawn".

The Contingent Fund Committee is composed of the governor, the chairman of the senate finance committee, and the chairman of the ways and means committee of the house. Disbursement of the civil contingent fund requires unanimous approval of this body.[46]

The Joint Committee on Printing, created in 1916, is made up of two members of each of the two branches of the General Assembly. It has control and supervision of all public printing and the purchase of supplies for the departments at Columbia. Prior to its creation there was almost a total absence of direction of the state's printing.[47]

The Sinking Fund Commission consists of the governor, the state treasurer, the attorney general, the chairman of the finance committee of the senate and the chairman of the ways and means committee of the house. Its principal function is to receive and manage the incomes and revenues set apart and applied to the sinking fund of the state for the purpose of paying off the state's indebtedness. In addition, this agency handles the transfer of surplus supplies from one department to another, and insures the public buildings of the state and of all institutions supported by the state.[48]

State insurance of public buildings is generally commended as a sound policy. So long as the insurance sinking fund maintains a balance of one million dollars, South Carolina undertakes to furnish the insurance free of cost on all such buildings after they have been insured for a period of five years. State insurance has been in effect since 1900. For

----

[46] *Acts of 1933*, p. 641.

[47] *Code 1932*, chap. 95. Evidence of extravagance in public printing before the creation of this committee is reflected in the fact that thousands of useless but costly volumes of state publications were condemned and sold as waste paper in 1916 for the sum of $60.00 by the Library Board, under authorization of the General Assembly.

[48] *Code 1932*, chap. 98, art. 1. State insurance is also in effect in Wisconsin, Pennsylvania and Michigan.

that year, the insurance in force was $10,000 and the assets amounted to 73.75.[49] It has grown to handsome proportions. For the year ending September 30, 1931, insurance in force amounted to $41,448,015.50 and the assets totalled $1,004,895.43.[50]

III. FISCAL CONTROL

A. Budgeting

Every state now has some sort of budget legislation. South Carolina is one of those in which the system is ineffective. The Budget, as prepared in this state, not only has no binding force, but little attention is paid to it. Consequently, each department and institution of the state must fight for its life at each session of the legislature.

There are four general types of authorities charged with formulating the initial plan of the budget, namely, (1) legislative committee, (2) administrative-legislative board, (3) administrative board, and (4) executive. South Carolina shares with three other states the second type, as outlined above. In 1930, Arkansas was the only state in the Union in which a legislative committee formulated the budget.[51] The administrative board type, comprising a group of administrative officers, was employed in ten states. The executive type was decidedly the most popular, being in use in more than thirty.[52]

The governor of South Carolina was made the chief budget officer of the State under the Budget Act of 1919.[53]

---

[49] *Report of the Sinking Fund Commissioners, 1930*, p. 6.

[50] The State Tax Commission and the Tax Board of Review are discussed in Chapter III.

[51] The National Institute of Public Administration has recommended the establishment of a Bureau of Budgeting in a Department of Finance, to have supervision over the preparation of the budget and certain phases of its execution. See *Survey of Arkansas*, pp. 13, 14, 100-104.

[52] See A. E. Buck, *Public Budgeting* (New York, 1929), p. 29.

[53] *Code 1933*, chap. 114, art. 7.

He is empowered to require all agencies receiving aid from the state (forty-five in 1932) to submit to him on or before the first day of November, annually, itemized estimates of their needs for the fiscal year beginning with the first day of January thereafter.

On or before the first day of December, the comptroller general is required to furnish the chief executive an estimate of the financial needs of the state, with full and detailed explanation of all increases or decreases. The law prescribes that these estimates shall be included in the budget without revisions by the governor, but with his recommendations thereon. Presumably, the legislature desires the judgment of the state's chief accounting officer as a check against the amounts requested.

The governor is directed to provide for public hearings on any and all estimates to be included in the budget. Responsible representatives of the several agencies seeking aid are required to attend and give such additional information as may be required of them.[54] It is at this point that the executive feature of the budget system comes to an end, for it is provided that the chairman of the ways and means committee of the house of representatives and the chairman of the finance committee of the senate shall sit with the governor at all public meetings or hearings and join with him in all reports and recommendations thereon to the General Assembly.[55] Not only is the governor relieved of responsibility—there is no responsibility anywhere. Indeed the committee has no power, and it does not appear that these proceedings serve any useful purpose. Duplication of work is

[54] Departmental needs should be continuously investigated throughout the year, and not simply as an incident of budget compilation. Data thus secured are likely to be much more useful in revising estimates.

[55] In 1933 the legislature constituted the State Budget Commission of these three officials and devolved upon this agency the budget duties previously exercised by its members individually. *Acts of 1933*, p. 651.

involved for departmental heads are later required to appear before the finance committees of the two houses of the legislature.[56]

Within five days after the beginning of each session of the General Assembly, the governor is required to submit to each house printed copies of the budget, containing a complete and itemized plan of all proposed expenditures classified by function, character and object, and of estimated revenues. The law further provides that he shall accompany the budget with:

(1) The statement of the revenues and expenditures for each of the two appropriation years next preceding, classified and itemized in accordance with the official budget classification adopted by the Governor.

(2) A statement of the current assets, liabilities, reserves and surplus or deficit of the State.

(3) A statement of the debts and funds of the State.

(4) A statement showing the Governor's itemized estimates of the condition of the State Treasury as of the beginning and end of each year.

(5) An itemized and complete financial balance sheet for the State at the close of the last preceding fiscal year ending September 1st.

(6) A general survey of the State's financial and natural resources, with a review of the general economic, industrial and commercial condition of the Commonwealth.

Under the budget system in South Carolina the governor is the " chief budgeting officer " in name only, for the legislative committees actually handle the details of constructing the so-called budget. Now, it is patent that the com-

[56] The abolition of the " Budget Commission" was proposed by Governor Richards, *Special Message*, Jan. 26, 1927; *House Journal*, 1927, p. 226. Failing in that, he vetoed the appropriation item for that agency, but it continued to operate. The expense, amounting to approximately $6,000 annually, was paid from the governor's contingent fund.

mittees are unable, in the short period of consideration, to determine the needs of departments and to coordinate these needs with available resources. The law-making body is without the necessary technical staff to maintain a continuing contact with the actual detailed operations, necessary to the determination of needs on a basis of fact. Nor should it have such a staff. This is the proper function of those in charge of carrying out the plans decided upon, " who acquire the experience from year to year upon which costs are based ".[57]

American writers, practically without exception, have endorsed the executive type of budget. Most students of government are agreed that it is far better calculated than any of the other types to achieve the desired economy in state administration. The governor represents the state as a whole and the general direction of financial policy may on that account be appropriately committed to him. The governor, of all officers, enjoys the most advantageous view of administrative processes. René Stourm expresses this opinion in the following words:

Situated at the center of the government, . . . the executive more than anybody else is in a position to feel the public needs and wishes, to appreciate their comparative merits, and accordingly to calculate, in the budget, a just appropriation which each of these needs and wishes deserves. Others may know certain details as well, possibly better than the executive, but nobody can have so extensive and so impartial a view of the mass of these details and no one can compromise the conflicting interests with so much competence and precision.[58]

Experience has shown that the budget system is most effective when the agent or agency that formulates the budget

[57] Griffenhagen, "Administrative Organization", p. 8.

[58] René Stourm, *The Budget* (translation of the 7th ed.), pp. 53, 54, quoted in Buck, *Budget Making*, p. 285.

plan is the one that carries it out. This duty, then, logically falls on the executive.[59] It is elementary that when a person is required to execute the plan which he formulates he is likely to exercise more care in making that plan.[60] Therefore, it is necessary, from the budget standpoint, to make the executive's power real and effective.

To have an effective budget, the governor should control the administration. This is necessary in order that he may have the proper information at hand for its preparation and that he may be able to direct the execution of the plan when it has been adopted by the legislature.[61] With numerous independent agencies, the inevitable result is competition and waste, rather than cooperation and economy in carrying on the state's work. Effective and unified financial planning is practically impossible in South Carolina, with the existing administrative structure of more than three score agencies. The matter of a proper budget system is closely associated with the reorganization of this structure into a more compact and integrated system.[62]

In no sense of the word does the procedure under the executive type of budget here advocated usurp the appropriating power of the legislature. It is merely adherence to the principle of executive responsibility of recommendations, leaving to the legislature the right of acceptance or rejection.[63] The General Assembly would still retain its power

[59] See F. A. Cleveland, "Constitutional Provision for a Budget", in *Proceedings of Academy of Political Science*, vol. v, pp. 141, 142 (1914); "The Constitution and Government of New York State", *Municipal Research*, no. 61, pp. 72-83 (May, 1915); "Responsible Government", *ibid.*, no. 69, pp. 1-67 (January, 1916).

[60] See Mathews, *State Government*, pp. 286, 287. Also, see J. P. Chamberlain, "American Budgetary Reform", in *The Nation*, vol. 108, pp. 976-978 (June 21, 1919).

[61] See N. Y. Bureau of Municipal Research, *Survey of Nevada*, p. 14.

[62] See Chapter I for proposed reorganization plan.

[63] See The League of Municipalities, *Administration of the State of Minnesota* (Minneapolis, 1924), pp. 12, 13.

of rejecting or modifying the governor's budget, and the governor would retain his item-veto. In discussing recent budgetary legislation, Dr. W. F. Willoughby of the Brookings Institution makes the following appraisement:

. . . With respect to the three main stages through which the budget passes, namely, formation, determination, and execution, it now appears to be the consensus of opinion that the executive should control the first and third stages, but that the legislative body should dominate the second and be provided with an independent check on the third. This allocation of authority is not only in harmony with our present system of government, but it also seems to be a sound basis for an effective budget system.[64]

An effective budget system is no panacea. It does not compel economy, but it does make the executive conscious of its responsibility and enlightens the legislature with the facts. It encourages careful planning of the year's financial operation and thus seeks to prevent deficits. In addition, a budget is a powerful aid to citizens and taxpayers. When properly prepared and thoroughly discussed before the law-making body, it is a most valuable source of public information.

A budget is not merely a financial document; it is a work and tax program. It should contain a complete plan of proposed expenditures and estimated revenues for the ensuing fiscal year. Dr. Charles A. Beard suggests that this program should embrace among other things:

(1) A summary statement showing the total receipts and expenditures of the previous two years and the estimated receipts and expenditures for the coming year correctly classified.

[64] W. F. Willoughby, *Principles of Public Administration* (Baltimore, 1927), pp. 479-480. See J. M. Mathews, " State Administrative Reorganization ", in *American Political Science Review*, vol. xvi, pp. 390, 391.

(2) Details of the summary statement, including departmental requests for funds (and supporting data from departmental chiefs) with the allowance made by the executive set forth in parallel columns, presenting to the legislative body and to the public the work requirements as viewed by operating officials. This analysis should be linked line by line with the summary statement and furnish the supporting data for proposed changes.

(3) An analysis of all increases over and decreases from the previous year, indicating the purpose for which they are made, such an analysis to present the public policy and work program involved in each material increase or reduction.

(4) Any collateral information necessary to explain the exact financial condition of the government, such as fund balance statement, surplus statement, debt statement, operating statement, and departmental reports of accomplishments.[65]

According to Mr. A. E. Buck, Technical Adviser, U. S. Bureau of the Budget, the budget document should be set up in three parts.[66] Part I should show the financial plan as a summary and balanced statement, explained by a budget message and supported by a few schedules and charts. Part II " should present the detailed plan and all the information upon which the first is based, such as the expenditure and revenue estimates, and comparative expenditure figures, cost data where available and pertinent, and statements of the financial condition and operations of the government ". Part III " should contain the appropriation, revenue, and

[65] Charles A. Beard, *American Government and Politics* (New York, 1928), p. 51.

[66] For a discussion of the budget as a financial plan, see A. E. Buck, *The Budget in Governments of Today* (New York, 1934), chap v; see, also, his *Public Budgeting*, chap iv. As the author points out, a standard form has not yet developed in the United States. Moreover, the technique of presenting the financial plan and supporting information must come from practice.

borrowing measures which are legally required to carry the financial plan into operation ".[67]

Considering now the appropriating function of legislative bodies, we note three general methods of revising budget requests, viz: (1) percentage cuts; (2) study of probable needs; (3) authorization of maximum expenditures. The second method is found in the majority of the states. The third method of fixing the maximum amount and allowing the spending officers to perform the task, assures that the cuts will be made where they least interfere with administrative work. Obviously, the first method of cutting on percentage basis is the simplest and the most unsatisfactory method.[68] It is the most unintelligent and generally results from an insufficient budgetary procedure. Without sustaining information, the legislative body practically has no other choice. Such is the case in South Carolina.[69]

The execution of the financial plan is the most important part of the whole process of budgeting. There is no advantage in having a budget, though carefully prepared by the governor and fully considered and enacted by the legislature, if this budget is not to be enforced during the fiscal year to which it applies. It is a mere " paper plan " unless it is effectively carried out.[70] The term " budget " when applied merely to a consolidated statement of estimates means noth-

[67] Buck, *Public Budgeting*, pp. 56, 57. While the inclusion of these measures in the budget is not widely sanctioned by present usage, the author regards them quite desirable. They are in the budget of North Carolina. For a discussion of operation in that state, see Brookings Institution, *Survey of North Carolina*, pp. 26-33. Also, see A. J. Maxwell, N. C. Commissioner of Revenue, " Complete Executive Control of the State Budget ", in *Tax Digest*, November, 1931, p. 381.

[68] This method usually rests upon the erroneous assumption that all estimates are inflated and " padded " in about the same degree.

[69] See Buck, *op. cit.*, p. 352, for discussion of methods of revision.

[70] See N. Y. Bureau of Municipal Research, *Survey of New Jersey*, p. 56.

ing. Compilation of estimates into a single document, with some revision before it goes to a legislative body, is of some assistance. But, unless there is a single command to make sure that the document as adopted is adhered to, the estimates amount to little. There must be permanent machinery within the state government for the centralized administration of the budget, so as to make sure that money appropriated will be expended throughout the year according to the schedule previously planned.[71]

There is no one in South Carolina between budget periods who is directly charged with the responsibility of studying the work and problems of the various institutions and state departments, to determine the condition under which they operate, the character and quality of the services they render, and to estimate the cost of doing the work or giving the service for which they are responsible.

A balanced plan between income and outgo should be maintained during the entire period of its execution. Under an integrated financial system there are two devices which enable the executive to maintain budgetary balance: (1) current planning and definite allotment of authorized expenditures; (2) careful scheduling of anticipated income.[72]

The rate of outgo is to be determined on the basis of the work program, which has the double advantage of making possible real executive direction and supervision and of enabling the administration to meet changing conditions which

[71] See Dodd, *State Government*, p. 259. In 1928, only six states had adopted constitutional amendments in respect to the budget, namely, Maryland, Nebraska, West Virginia, Massachusetts, California, New York.

[72] See Buck, *Public Budgeting*, p. 452. The General Assembly of South Carolina inserted the following provision in its appropriation act for 1932: " *Provided*, that the authorities of all institutions for which a lump sum appropriation is made shall make a quarterly report to the Budget Commission of all expenditures ". *Acts of 1932*, no. 897, sec. 68.

cannot be anticipated.   Expenditure requirements should be allocated to quarters of the budget year.   Such an arrangement or apportionment has the effect of bringing up all activities for review periodically, thus affording the means of real financial control.

A satisfactory work program cannot be formulated when the appropriations are highly itemized.   The desired flexibility in the execution of the program requires lump sum appropriations which are made practicable under the executive budget system.   Detailed expenditures should be limited to the purposes and objects enumerated in the estimates for a major operation unit.   Best results will be obtained in this way, for this gives administrative officers discretion as to their expenditures in the accomplishment of a specified purpose or object and at the same time places full responsibility upon them for efficient and economical management.[73]

Nor can financial supervision and control be established in a state government unless all moneys are passed through or accounted for by one central office.   When a department or agency collects fees for its services and is legally authorized to spend these fees for its own expenses, treasury supervision over the custody of such funds is rendered very difficult.   Moreover, the practice of segregating state income by placing it in the deposit accounts of the various departments and institutions must be condemned.   While this practice may be regarded advantageous to the agencies concerned, it cannot be defended from the view of financing the state government as a whole.   In the first place, each institution becomes practically an independent unit so far as the handling of finances is involved, for central financial control must be mainly of the post-audit type.   Secondly, when the moneys are scattered around in various deposit accounts, the

[73] See Buck, *op. cit.*, pp. 456-458.   Also, Brookings Institution, *Survey of North Carolina*, pp. 27, 28.

state may be hard pressed to meet a major obligation at a given time.[74]

The state government of South Carolina is being operated partly upon a credit system. For several years it has been necessary annually to borrow approximately $7,500,000 in anticipation of taxes. Interest on these short-term loans has amounted to more than $300,000. While the state has been borrowing these sums, it has had on deposit in the banks of the state, in the deposit account of the various state agencies, far more than the amount borrowed.[75]

In 1930, the General Assembly passed what is known as the "Daily Deposit Act", requiring state funds to be deposited in the state treasury when collected.[76] It provided, however, that in the discretion of the state treasurer each department or institution may be allowed to maintain a revolving fund. It further provided "that the provisions of this Act shall not apply to fees or other revenues, collected by any State institution, which are not required by law to be remitted to the State Treasurer". The state auditor estimated that a sum of approximately one million dollars has been made available for general use by the terms of this Act.[77]

For several years the comptroller general has advocated the pooling of all state funds into a common fund when deposited in the various banks.[78] In 1930 the legislature

[74] To require state institutions to deposit all their fees, such as tuition, rent, board, etc., would hamper their operations. In these cases, a "petty cash" fund for each institution should be provided, from which incidental expenses may be met. This fund would be reimbursed from the general treasury when the bills were turned in and approved by the central accounting office.

[75] See Governor Richards, *Annual Message*, 1931, pp. 23, 24.

[76] *Acts of 1930*, p. 1361.

[77] *Report of State Bank Examiner*, 1930, p. 44.

[78] See *Report of Comptroller General*, 1931, p. 10.

empowered the State Finance Committee to borrow from any department of the state government " for the use of the State any surplus which may be on hand in the office of the State Treasurer to the credit of the Departments of the State Government ".[79]   The law provided, however, that no funds belonging to any particular department could be used by the State Finance Committee " without the written consent of the Department affected ".   The proviso practically nullified the pooling plan.

B. *Centralized Accounting*

The problem of controlling public expenditures is the primary element in the larger problem of governmental costs, for the reduction of taxes can only be accomplished by control and reduction of the amount spent.[80]   There is no more technical problem of public administration than that of devising and operating a system of accounting and reporting through which full and accurate information may be available regarding the financial condition and operating of the government.[81]   It has been aptly said that no business can rise above its bookkeeping.   This might well be applied to government.   Professor Paul W. Wager has made this interesting observation: " Not only does a good system of accounting enable the governing body to know the exact financial condition at any one time, but it makes any irregularity conspicuous.   In fact, most public officials who go wrong do so to cover up a shortage that was not calculated.

[79] *Acts of 1930*, p. 1344.

[80] See H. L. Lutz, " The Control of Public Expenditures ", in *Tax Digest*, November, 1931, p. 368.

[81] For discussion of accounting and reporting, see *Report of Reconstruction Commission on Retrenchment and Reorganization in the State of New York* (Albany, 1919), pp. 8, 9; Brookings Institution, *Survey of North Carolina*, pp. 61-63.

Many a good-intentioned official has been ruined as a result of deficient bookkeeping ".[82]

An effective system of fiscal control must be installed in order to make sure the state actually lives within the appropriations. In addition to the prevention of over-expenditures, such a system should provide information concerning comparative costs and afford a study of comparative competency.

The financial condition of the government is reflected in the general account, but that is not enough. Intelligent planning and direction require detailed data, principally in connection with operating expenditures. This need will be supplied by cost accounting, which is essential to the improvement of the quality of the public administration. Comparative unit costs can be obtained for the various classes of state institutions according to a uniform classification of objects of expenditures. The quantity, quality, or results of governmental performance can be tested by the administrator in this way. Then, and only then, can returns from public expenditures be evaluated. But let it be emphasized here that competency cannot be measured solely by a study of comparative costs. A financial saving cannot be taken as an indication of true economy if it is obtained by lowering the standard of service below requirements.

One controlling set of accounts for the entire state government should be installed under a bureau of accounting in a Department of Finance. In order to show a true picture of the government's affairs, the central accounting system should be established on the accrual basis. No subsidiary accounts should be kept in the departments and institutions except as they are required to complete the central system.[83]

[82] Paul W. Wager, "County Government in North Carolina", in *National Municipal Review*, January, 1929, p. 7.

[83] See National Institute of Public Administration, *Survey of Arkansas*, p. 15; Brookings Institution, *Survey of North Carolina*, pp. 62, 63. A

This bureau would be under the direction of the chief accounting officer of the state, the comptroller general, who would be responsible for supervising the entire accounting system of the state government, for supplying the governor and his budget officer with the information needed in financial management, and for conducting the administrative audit.[84] This officer would be relieved of all other present duties. All disbursements would be pre-audited and settled by the central accounting office before payment.

C. State Auditor

All transactions in public funds would be comprehended by the records kept by the bureau of accounting. This administrative accounting, including such matters as cost accounts and operating accounts, must be distinguished from control-accounting under the direction of an auditor independent of the administration. This independence is generally sought either by his popular election, or by his appointment by the General Assembly. It is believed that the former method has little to recommend it. Making the auditor responsible to the appropriating body has very definite advantages, since it is his primary function to exact compliance with the legislature's will. In this role, he is made the permanent critic of the governor and his administration.[85]

It would be the duty of the state auditor to conduct a continuous post-audit of the financial operation of the administration. He should keep no accounts in his own department, " but only working papers such as a firm of commer-

uniform system of accounts for the several departments is necessary. The state auditor was directed to require uniformity in 1930, *Acts of 1930*, p. 1411.

[84] See Buck, *Public Budgeting*, pp. 529-531.

[85] Virginia, Tennessee, and New Jersey have such an independent auditor.

cial accountants would have in making an audit of the State's business ".[86] Payments made by all disbursing officers should be audited for the purpose of ascertaining: [87] "(1) that public moneys are paid out only for the true value of the goods or services received; (2) that the expenditures are authorized by competent authority; and (3) that the expenditures come within the purview of the appropriation act."

Like most states, South Carolina has no independent audit. The law requires that the state bank examiner " shall make an examination of state officers and institutions at least twice each year and of offices once a year ".[88] The state auditor is employed by this officer to perform this task. In his report for 1930, the bank examiner said in part: " Appropriations for the various activities of the State Government have been carefully checked and reconciliation with the Comptroller General's office effected. It appears that as a general proposition State Funds have been expended for purposes for which appropriations were made, and with a due regard to economy and efficiency ".[89] The law also provides that the auditing clerk in the comptroller general's office " shall visit the various penal, charitable and educational institutions of the State, and report on the conditions of the books of the same, when required by the Comptroller General ".[90] Whatever audit he makes is in reality an audit of his own accounts.

If the accounts and reports of all persons or agencies having the receipt, custody or disbursement of public moneys

[86] National Institute, *Survey of Arkansas*, p. 65.

[87] Brookings Institution, *Survey of North Carolina*, p. 47.

[88] *Code 1932*, sec. 7847. The office of State Bank Examiner was abolished in 1933 and the state auditor was placed under the direction of the State Budget Commission. *Acts of 1933*, pp. 297, 298.

[89] *Report of State Bank Examiner*, 1930, p. 44.

[90] *Code 1932*, sec. 3135.

were continuously examined by an independent Department of Audit, as outlined above, South Carolina would make a most progressive step in state financial organization.

D. Centralized Purchasing

Centralized purchasing is based upon successful methods utilized by business concerns throughout the country. Dr. Russell Forbes, director of purchasing for the government of New York City, has described this means of securing economy in the administration of public affairs in these words: " Centralized purchasing in government is the delegation to one office of the authority to purchase supplies, materials and equipment needed for use by the several branches of the organization. It is neither a fad nor a theory but a combination of logic and economics. It may well be called a sentry at the tax exit gate ".[91]   The fact that thirty-six states have established such an agency indicates conclusively that it has passed the experimental state.   Indeed, centralized purchasing is more uniformly in evidence than any other consolidation feature in the recent movement toward state administrative reorganization.[92]   It is doubtless one of the fundamental steps in reorganization with the view of reducing the cost of state government.

Dr. Forbes gives us some idea of possible savings.   He says, in part:

The average government today spends from 20 to 30 per cent of its current operating budget for material goods.   A quarter century's experience has demonstrated that the centralized

[91] Russell Forbes, *Centralized Purchasing*, p. 5.   A pamphlet distributed by the National Association of Purchasing Agents (New York, 1931).   Also, see his larger work, *Governmental Purchasing* (1929), *passim*, for a comprehensive treatment of the various phases of the subject.

[92] Centralized purchasing was recommended by at least five governors to their respective legislatures in 1931.   See Harvey Walker, "Governors' Messages ", in *American Political Science Review*, vol. xxv, p. 355.

method of purchasing, granting even a reasonable freedom from political interference, can reduce the unit cost of commodities from 10 to 15 per cent, and can be the means of reducing the aggregate expenditure, or for increasing the mileage of the tax dollar which goes for material, by that amount.[93]

A few of the chief advantages of centralized purchasing may be listed, as follows:

(1) Possible economies from quantity buying in large lots and in anticipation of needs.

(2) Standardization of commodities, enabling a larger volume of purchases.

(3) Centralization of available information regarding vendors and prices would make possible dealing with original sources of supplies.

(4) Economy and improved administration through consolidation of orders and generally better control of the buying situation.

(5) Greater efficiency in receiving and inspection—particularly where questions of quality involve intricate physical and chemical tests.

(6) Maintaining stores for anticipation of requirements of all.

(7) Reduction in the examination and payment of vendors' claims, due to the reduction of separate transactions.

There should be exceptions to the procedure, of course. Perishables required by institutions should be purchased locally where it is advantageous to do so. Moreover, little is to be gained by forcing each department to meet its highly specialized needs (material and equipment that no other department has occasion to use) through a central agency. Emergency purchases may also have to be made from time to time, but careful planning should keep these down to a

---

[93] Forbes, *Governmental Purchasing*, pp. vii, viii (Preface).

minimum. Furthermore, attempt should not be made at the outset to purchase all materials and supplies for all state departments, but the central agency should at first confine itself to making general contracts covering the requirement needs of institutions and departments.[94]

The majority of the large number of administrative agencies purchase in small quantities and are unable to take advantage of fluctuating markets, discounts, and quantity buying. It is quite obvious that they cannot buy as effectively as a centralized purchasing agency acting for all. It is likewise true that the efficacy of this instrument of financial control would be facilitated by a properly integrated administrative structure.[95]

While South Carolina is one of only twelve states without centralized purchasing for all of its departments, such an agency was recommended as long ago as 1912 by Governor Blease in his annual message of that year. He contended that " if the officials of the various state institutions who have to purchase supplies would meet together and form an organization to buy their groceries, coal, wood, electrical supplies, and other articles to be used by them during the year, by contract, and by bulk, it would be a great saving to the taxpayers ".[96] He recommended that a law be passed requiring this to be done. In 1920, Governor Cooper urged that a general purchasing agent be authorized, when he said in part: " . . . By buying in bulk, by investigating the markets, a skilled purchasing agent could save much money for the State. This is in line with sound business principles ".[97] More recently, there were definite efforts made

[94] For recommendations covering the needs of an adjoining state, see Brookings Institution, *Survey of North Carolina*, p. 125.

[95] See, for example, White, *Public Administration*, p. 145; and, Dodd, *State Government*, p. 259.

[96] *Reports and Resolutions*, 1912, p. 658.

[97] *Annual Message*, 1920, p. 11.

to gain the approval of the 1932 legislature. The establishment of a central purchasing agency was one of the six governmental revisions proposed by Mr. Neville Bennett, chairman of the house ways and means committee and a member of the Budget Commission.[98]

As already observed, the Joint Committee on Printing purchases office supplies for the departments in Columbia. The Joint Committee on Economy and Consolidation, 1922, recommended the immediate expansion of the function of this committee " to provide for the centralized purchase not only of printing and stationery but also of all staples and some other supplies for departments and institutions and the ultimate absorption of this central purchasing agency in the Department of Finance ".[99]

There are three types of centralized purchasing agencies among the states today: (1) separate department or bureau; (2) division in a department of finance; (3) ex officio or appointive board.[100] From the administrative standpoint, the board type is least desirable. It is here recommended that the purchasing office be established in South Carolina as a bureau in the proposed Department of Finance, because of the close relation between purchasing and the planning and execution of the budget. Professor Holcombe endorses this arrangement: " This step would enable the standard specifications used in centralized purchasing to be readily followed in preparing the budget estimates and would provide the budget authority with accessible data concerning changes in prices of supplies and materials, expenditures for various kinds of goods and the prospective needs of the state departments and institutions in the preparation of the budget ".[101]

[98] See *News and Courier*, Nov. 22, 1931.

[99] *Report*, 1922, p. 13.

[100] See Forbes, *Governmental Purchasing*, pp. 41-44.

[101] Holcombe, *State Government*, pp. 385, 386. See Russell Forbes, " Centralized Purchasing in the Governments of the United States and

It is believed that this bureau would bring about economies not only in the purchase of supplies, materials, equipment, contractual services, but also through its control of
their distribution and ultimate use.   This agency should be
given authority to transfer between departments and institutions commodities and services not needed by one but necessary to the operation of another.

E. Personnel Supervision

Personnel is the most important single factor in government both from the operating and the fiscal point of view.
In the government of South Carolina, expenditures for personal service constitute the greatest single item of expense.[102]
Since the proposed central accounting office is responsible
for payroll control, it should have the cooperation of the
personnel agency, where such an agency exists.

It is suggested that a bureau of personnel be set up in the
Department of Finance, and that it be given the power to
select qualified persons for employment in the various services.   It is proposed that this agency should act not only as
a central supply service for furnishing personnel to the state
organizations, but that it should also be its function to
classify positions, standardize salaries, and work out a just
and suitable method of advancements, promotions and demo-
tions according to certain service ratings.[103]

Canada ", in *Annals*, vol. 113, pp. 272-286. Also, Milton Conover, " Centralized Purchasing Agencies in State and Local Governments ", in
American Political Science Review, vol. xix, pp. 73-82.

[102] According to the comptroller general's statement to the writer, there
are about 1400 on the state's payroll, not including those employed by
the Highway Department.

[103] A separate chapter is devoted to the personnel problem.

See the detailed provisions for the establishment of such an agency
in Arkansas, National Institute, *Survey of Arkansas*, pp. 117-123. Also,
the comprehensive discussion of the personnel problem in North Carolina,
Brookings Institution, *Survey of North Carolina*, chap. iv.

F. *Local Government Finance*

It is a well-known fact that the field of local government is the field of our largest expenditures. This means that the weight of taxation largely results from the activities traditionally conducted by local units. Attention is naturally directed to the almost total lack of unified financial responsibility in these areas. Dr. H. L. Lutz has made the following comment on this condition so general among the states:

This condition is a direct outgrowth of the multiplication of agencies. Each separate unit, whether county, municipality, school district, is busy with its own little part of the general task of supplying a flow of services to the citizens. Each has its authority to levy taxes, to plan expenditures, to borrow money. None is ordinarily obliged to know or to consider what the others are doing, or what the aggregate upon the citizens is to be. The governing body of each unit or district could probably make out a case for spending what it plans to spend, since the subdivision of local functions corresponds to the chaotic subdivision of authorities.[104]

It is imperative that South Carolina shall establish some central agency to supervise the issuance of all instruments of local indebtedness and the investment of the sinking funds of its political subdivisions, instead of being content in passing local bills authorizing the funding of current deficiencies. In 1927, the General Assembly enacted a statute requiring the subdivisions to report and register all bonds with the comptroller general.[105] According to the annual report of this officer for 1931, the total bonded indebtedness of the State of South Carolina and its subdivisions, as of December 31, 1931, was $115,496,056.62, classified as follows: state

[104] "The Control of Public Expenditures", *Tax Digest*, Aug., 1931, p. 370.

[105] *Code 1932*, secs. 7332-7342; *Acts of 1927*, p. 260.

bonds and notes, $41,745,060.16; county and school district bonds, $48,569,166.46; and, city issues, $26,181,830.00.[106] However, the chairman of the ways and means committee of the house, when introducing a bill to create a central agency of supervision,[107] placed the total bonded indebtedness at $156,687,497.00, exclusive of an outstanding note total of $29,245,605.00.[108]

To maintain credit of the state and its political subdivisions, provision must be made for state supervision of means and methods of payment of the principal and interest of such obligations promptly at the time and place provided for. Many of the local units have not made adequate arrangements to do this and these certificates of indebtedness must be refinanced. Strong machinery is necessary to deal with the present delinquency and to prevent its recurrence. Governor Blackwood recommended that a central agency be given the power to compel the local units " to levy sufficient taxes to discharge the maturities with interest promptly ".[109]

It is suggested that a bureau of local government finance be created in the proposed Department of Finance. It would

---

[106] *Report of Comptroller General,* 1931, pp. 79, 145, 151.

[107] H. 1773—"A bill to provide for making effective the means of payment for bonds and notes (other than tax anticipation notes), of counties, townships, municipalities, school districts, etc." The State Sinking Fund Commission was the agency designated. The bill was killed, 56-15. *House Journal,* 1932, pp. 896, 897.

[108] For his statement as reported to the press, see *Charleston Evening Post,* Feb. 19, 1932. This estimate. is perhaps more nearly accurate, due to failure of local units to register with the comptroller general. The U. S. Bureau of Census reported the combined gross debt of the state and its political subdivisions, less sinking fund assets set aside to meet debt, for 1932 as $171,698,350—*Financial Statistics of State and Local Governments: 1932, South Carolina* (Washington, 1934).

[109] *Annual Message,* 1932, p. 9. He had likewise urged state control of local bond issues in his *Inaugural Address,* 1931, pp. 4, 5.

be its general function to advise and assist local financial officers. Specifically, this bureau would have control over the issuance of local instruments of indebtedness,[110] would supervise the investment of sinking funds, and would direct the discharge of all maturities when they fall due. It is contemplated that all bonds would be sold at Columbia after publication of notice of sale, and that all bids would be opened in public with the contract being awarded to the highest legal bidder.

In their efforts to curtail the cost of government, taxpayers have been handicapped to some extent by the absence of budget systems, uniform accounting and reliable audits of local governments.[111] It is therefore suggested that the bureau of local government finance be authorized to install a uniform system of budgeting, accounting and reporting in the several counties. This is designed, also, to avoid expensive audits and to make possible a comparative analysis of the cost of county governments, so essential to efficient and economical government.

The Department of Finance should be charged with the duty of making periodic audits of county accounts, and should have authority to order audits of other subdivisions.[112] There is no doubt that considerable savings will result therefrom. Furthermore, it is believed that substantial benefits will proceed from local knowledge that such facilities exist, as well as through their actual use.

[110] To preserve the principle of local self-government, provision might be made for an appeal from the refused approval of the state agency by submission of the proposition to a vote of the people in the local unit affected. This is the arrangement in North Carolina.

[111] See Clarence Smith (Pres., National Tax Assn.), "Control of Public Expenditures", in The Tax Digest, August, 1931, p. 259.

[112] In any event, contracts for audits of counties should have approval of this department.

If state and local credit are to be maintained in South Carolina, effective supervision and control of local finances must be had. The issue lies between the taxpayers, who must pay the cost of the antiquated system, and those who stand to benefit directly from its continuance.

G. Summary

In concluding a discussion of fiscal supervision and control, attention should be called to the limits of its usefulness. The existence of such machinery is essential in aiding the chief executive to perform adequately his administrative responsibility. The real problem is to fit it into the administrative machine so that it can work effectively and still not vitiate the operating departments. Professor Leonard D. White suggests that fiscal supervision and control " has overstepped its usefulness when it interferes substantially with the freedom of the departments to carry out the program imposed upon them by law. It has overstepped its usefulness when it takes the initiative in preparing departmental plans instead of surveying those submitted by the proper officials. It goes too far in attempting to substitute its judgment on technical questions for the judgment of the department. It operates to the detriment of sound administration when it destroys the sense of responsibility within the department for its work ".[113]

The real value of control lies in coordinating the public services, in creating a sense of unity in the entire administration, in counteracting the narrowness and jealousies of the several departments and institutions, and in maintaining the proper accountability, fidelity, and legality in connection with expenditures. The informed business judgment of a single office in touch with all the departments should be the means of fashioning a financial program for the whole administra-

[113] White, *Public Administration*, p. 61.

tion that will take due cognizance of the relative importance of the several services and their operation within the limits of the resources of the state. It is believed that such procedure will result in constructive economy and in lessening the cost of administration.

IV. PROPOSED REORGANIZATION

The following outlines and summary statements indicate the manner in which the present governmental units referred to in this chapter would be reorganized if the recommendations were adopted.

1. *Department of Finance*

Present Organization	Proposed Organization
I. Comptroller General	I. Department of Finance.
II. State Treasurer	1. Bureau of Accounting
II. Budget Commission	2. Bureau of the Treasury
IV. State Finance Com- mittee	3. Bureau of Personnel
V. Sinking Fund Com- mission	4. Bureau of Purchasing
VI. Joint Committee on Printing	5. Bureau of Local Government Finance
VII. Contingent Fund Committee	
VIII. Board of Claims	

Summary of recommendations:

1. The commissioner of finance, appointed by the governor with advice and consent of the senate, to have general supervision over the work of the department. He would have authority, with approval of the governor, to determine the bureau organization appropriate for the work to be done.

2. Each of the five bureaus to be headed by a director, appointed by the commissioner.

3. The Bureau of Accounting to exercise the powers and duties at present conferred upon the comptroller general in so far as they relate to accounting, and auditing before payment of all bills and vouchers.

4. The Bureau of the Treasury to exercise the powers and duties of the present state treasurer in so far as they relate to the collection, custody, and disbursement of state moneys.

5. The Budget Commission to be abolished and its duties vested in the commissioner of finance. This official would prepare the tentative estimates of total revenues for the ensuing year and classify the requests of the several departments, to be reviewed and revised by the governor.

6. The Contingent Fund Committee to be abolished and its duties transferred to the Bureau of Budgeting.

7. The Boards of Claims to be abolished and its duties transferred to the Bureau of Accounting.

8. The Joint Committee on Printing to be abolished and its duties transferred to the Bureau of Purchasing.

9. The Sinking Fund Commission to be abolished and its duties transferred to the commissioner of finance, assisted by the directors of accounting and the treasury.

10. Bonds for all purposes should be issued only on the annuity serial or the straight serial basis, not to exceed for any purpose twenty-five years.

11. The commissioner of finance to be a member of the State Finance Committee, together with the governor and the commissioner of revenues.

2. *Department of Audit*

Present Organization	Proposed Organization
I. Comptroller General	I. Department of Audit
II. State Budget Commission	1. Office of State Auditor.
1. State Auditor	

Summary of recommendations:

1. The state auditor to be elected by the General Assembly and to be responsible solely to that body.

2. The Department of Audit to be organized in whatever manner the state auditor may deem best.

3. The position of State Auditor, directed by the State Budget Commission, to be abolished.

4. The Department of Audit to perform a post-audit of all accounts and other financial records of the state government, or any department, institution or agency thereof, and report to the General Assembly.

5. The Department of Audit to perform an audit of the county governments of the State, as now required of the comptroller general by law.

CHAPTER III

TAXATION

THERE are no problems encountered in the field of state government more important or more difficult than those pertaining directly to the raising and spending of money. It will be immediately recognized that these two aspects are so mutually related that the revision of either the revenue system or the scheme of controlling outgo alone would be inadequate to solve satisfactorily the state's financial problem.[1] The former will be considered here.

THE SOUTH CAROLINA REVENUE SYSTEM

The widespread complaint which rises throughout the state against the burden of taxation is not unfounded.[2] However, no thoughtful citizen expects to solve the tax problem by drastic reduction in governmental expenditures—and, particularly, when he is informed that the per capita cost of the state government of South Carolina in 1931 was only $7.24. The solution appears to point to simplification of the present revenue system and an improved administration. While reasonable retrenchment must be had in the face of decreased revenue at the present time, it certainly should not be so drastic as to be destructive of the essential services.

---

[1] See The Brookings Institution, *Report on a Survey of the Organization and Administration of State and County Government in Mississippi* (The Research Commission of the State of Miss., Jackson, 1932), pp. 17, 18.

[2] See U. S. Dept. of Commerce, Bureau of Census, *Financial Statistics of States*, 1929, p. 58.

The tax system of South Carolina is something of a patchwork quilt, and each year finds the legislature disposed to add to it. A sound policy is one of the greatest needs of the state today. The present state of affairs is discouraging to business interests, which do not know how or when some special levy may be placed upon them. This condition ought to be corrected. Unfortunately the General Assembly is not free to adjust taxes to meet changing conditions. The disease is organic in basis.

Prior to the adoption of the constitution of 1868, the methods of raising taxes were left entirely to the discretion of the legislative body of the state.[3] None of the preceding constitutions contained any fundamental law in regard to taxation.[4]

As Dr. D. D. Wallace has pointed out, " the proper function of the constitution is not to lay down rigidly supposed principles of taxation, but to guarantee against the insidious favoritism that destroys all equity between individuals or localities ".[5] Instead of confining itself to the enunciation of the safe-guarding principle that taxes must be uniform throughout the state as regards all that fall within the same class, the present constitution imposes unfortunate limitations.

With the exception of the poll tax, the only mode of taxation prescribed by the constitution is the general property tax. All property of every kind and description, except that

[3] See A. S. Salley, Jr., "The Methods of Raising Taxes in South Carolina prior to 1868", *Bulletins of Historical Commission of South Carolina*, no. 7, p. 7.

[4] Three constitutions, viz., 1790, 1868, 1895, virtually cover the constitutional history of South Carolina. The one of 1790 may be found in *Statutes at Large*, vol. i. The one of 1868 is printed in *Code 1922*, vol. ii. All are given in Thorpe, *American Charters Constitutions and Organic Laws, 1492-1908*, vol. 6.

[5] Wallace, *Constitution of 1895*, p. 108.

specifically exempted, is positively required to be taxed at its actual value.[6]   Moreover, all property is required to be both assessed and taxed at an equal and uniform rate.[7] There can be no discrimination between real and personal property.   Moreover, if it were deemed desirable to tax certain classes of property or lines of business upon the basis of income or otherwise in lieu of the ad valorem property tax, such procedure would be in violation of the constitution.

I. Sources of Revenue

The general property tax as a producer of revenue had about reached the breaking point by 1920.   Public revenues for both state and local purposes were still almost entirely derived from that source.   Of the six millions appropriated in that year for state purposes, only one million of special revenues was estimated as forthcoming from all state departments, bureaus, and activities of all kinds, including corporation license taxes and insurance fees.   The tax rate had increased from $6\frac{1}{2}$ mills in 1916 to 12 mills in 1920, and the limit was not in sight.   It was obvious that, if the state's established institutions and governmental activities to which it was already committed were to keep pace with the natural growth of population, the need of increased revenues would grow more and more acute.[8]

To resolve this dilemma the legislature created the Special Committee on Revenue and Taxation whose study continues to be the most comprehensive and intelligent contribution to the solution of South Carolina's financial problem.   As a

[6] *Constitution*, art. iii, sec. 29. In executing this mandate, the legislature has provided by statute that "all property shall be valued at its true value in money", *Code* 1932, sec. 2696.

[7] *Constitution*, art. i, sec. 6; art. x, sec. 1.

[8] See *Report of Joint Special Committee on Revenue and Taxation*, 1921, pp. 5, 6, 11, 12, 16; *Report of Comptroller General*, 1920, p. 26; *Report of Tax Commission*, 1920, pp. 5, 6.

result of its convincing case against the defective tax system, the state entered upon an excursion into the field of indirect taxation.

In levying sales taxes on selected articles, designated as luxuries, South Carolina has perhaps been the most successful state in the Union. These taxes are definitely added to the sale price of these articles and are paid as an additional charge by the purchaser. They do not represent a privilege tax on the dealer. Taxes of this class are levied on manufactured tobacco products, ammunition and playing cards;[9] an admission tax upon all places of amusement, including picture theatres, dance halls, and swimming pools;[10] a documentary tax upon the use and transfer of documents and instruments in the sale of property and transaction of business;[11] and soft drink taxes upon bottled and fountain drinks commonly so designated.[12]

South Carolina is one of fifteen states that levy an income tax. The original levy, approved March 13, 1922, made the state tax dependent upon the amount of federal tax paid. It was rewritten in 1927 and amended in 1930. The tax is levied upon the income of every individual residing in the state; also, upon income earned within the state of every non-resident having a business or agency in the state, or from the sale or rental of, or income from property within the state.[13] The levy upon individuals ranges from one to five per cent on the excess over the amount legally exempted. Every corporation organized

---

[9] *Code 1932*, sec. 2527.

[10] *Ibid.*, sec. 2531.

[11] *Code 1932*, sec. 2521.

[12] *Ibid.*, sec. 2532.

[13] *Ibid.*, chap. 107, art. 1. Credit is allowed a nonresident if the income tax law of the state in which he resides grants a substantially similar credit to residents of S. C., *ibid.*, sec. 2439.

under the laws of the state is assessed the equivalent of four and one-half percent of the entire net income. Every foreign corporation is assessed at the same rate upon the proportion that the value of the real estate and tangible personal property located in South Carolina bears to the total wherever located.[14]

The inheritance tax has now been adopted in some form by all except two states. South Carolina first levied such a tax in 1922.[15] It has not yet served as a large source of revenue because the state has not become sufficiently industrialized to produce large fortunes. This form of taxation permits a state to secure a revenue from intangible personal property which so largely escapes the regular property tax.

In South Carolina every corporation organized under the laws of the state to do business for profit, other than public utility corporations, is required to pay an annual license fee of two mills upon every dollar of paid-in capital stock.[16] Foreign corporations are charged an annual license fee of two mills upon each dollar of the value of the property of such corporation used within the state in the conduct of business.[17] Public utility corporations are assessed an annual license fee of three mills on gross receipts from business done in South Carolina and the supplemental of three mills on each dollar of the value of property owned and used in the conduct of their business in the state.[18]   Among other

[14] *Ibid.*, sec. 2440. For a discussion of the operation of the income tax in other states see, for example, *Report of North Carolina Tax Commission*, 1930, p. 36.

[15] *Code 1932*, chap. 107, art. 2.

[16] See an address by Tax Commissioner Frank C. Robinson, 24th National Tax Conference, Atlanta, October, 1931, " The Tax System of South Carolina as Viewed by an Administrator ", (pamphlet) pp. 4, 5.

[17] *Ibid.*

[18] All properties of public service corporations are treated as personal property to be returned as such to be taxed under general property levy. The value of the movable assets are apportioned to the political sub-

annual licenses required are the tax on contractors, graduated from $100 to $175,[19] and a graduated tax on chain stores.[20]

Every domestic insurance company is required to return all its personal property, moneys, credits, investments, and assets of every kind for taxation at the place where its principal office is located.[21] Every foreign insurance company, except benevolent institutions operating under the Grand Lodge System, is required to pay an annual license fee of one hundred dollars, and also a graduated license fee of three per cent on the total premium receipts from the state.[22] Bank stock and banking associations are taxed locally.[23]

In 1931 an excise tax was imposed upon electric power generated or sold within this state. The rate of this tax is five-tenths of one mill upon each kilowatt hour of hydro-electric power or of electric power generated by steam. The provisions of this law apply to electric power manufactured in other states and brought into this state, when such power has lost its interstate character and immunities.[24]

Revenue accruing from automobiles has now reached a large figure, but it is not paid into the general fund of the state. A license tax of six cents per gallon is levied upon gasoline. Five cents on each gallon is turned over to the State Highway Department for the purpose of said department,[25] and one cent per gallon is distributed to the counties

divisions of the state in proportion to value in each, determined by trackage, etc., *Code 1932*, sec. 2635.

[19] *Code 1932*, sec. 2543.

[20] *Ibid.*, sec. 2556. A retail mercantile license tax.

[21] *Ibid.*, sec. 2655.

[22] *Ibid.*, secs. 7941, 7948, 7969.

[23] *Ibid.*, chap. 108 art. 7.

[24] *Code 1932*, sec. 2558. This is regarded as a license tax.

[25] This revenue has been pledged to the retirement of highway bonds issued under State Highway Bond Act of 1929, *Code 1932*, chap. 127.

of the state to be used exclusively for the construction and maintenance of county roads.[26]

The following table will serve to indicate the contribution of the several taxes to the general account of the state during the three years, 1930-1932: [27]

CONDENSED STATEMENT OF REVENUE RECEIPTS—GENERAL ACCOUNT

	1930	1931	1932
Property Tax	$2,041,327.48	$2,100,293.42	$1,639,238.71
Railroad Assessment		54,883.35	44,844.69
Income Tax	1,921,271.03	1,715,204.01	1,171,350.87
Admission Tax	283,729.65	262,070.25	211,776.39
Business License Tax	1,894,770.59	1,690,543.00	1,398,481.05
Documentary License Tax ...	273,429.82	227,899.36	128,015.37
Contractors Tax	79,040.00	52,700.00	19,578.31
Public Recreation Tax	10,325.00	15,675.00	14,475.00
Soft Drink Tax	1,068,755.78	963,950.92	708,891.08
Fish Stamp Tax	25,514.00	22,041.42	19,984.74
Corporation Fees and Licenses	1,444,373.78	1,475,667.82	1,569,629.16
Tax on Mercantile Estabs ...			243,940.88
Electric Power Tax			530,293.39
Electric Power Tax (1931) ..			261,539.94
Inheritance Tax	260,141.07	131,630.13	309,260.07
General Account Interest	17,742.57	207,996.37	60,693.09
Appropriation Refunds	316,992.30	252,354.68	220,133.86
Departmental Fees	497,346.59	387,507.79	323,213.26
Refunds from Special Accounts			1,227.22
Departmental Refunds			43,351.63
Revenue Receipts	$10,134,759.66	$9,560,417.52	$8,919,918.67

While $8,919,918.67 was collected during 1932, the sum of $2,008,815.97 represented back taxes, leaving $6,911,-102.70 as the amount actually collected as revenue for the year. To this amount $1,257,296.18 must be added as the

[26] Ibid., sec. 2507; Acts of 1929, p. 107.

[27] Compiled from the Annual Reports of the Comptroller General. The years 1933 and 1934 are not cited in this table because of the period of eighteen months, January 1, 1933 to June 30, 1934, incident to the change in the fiscal year.

balance of 1932 assessments, bringing the total 1932 revenues of the general fund up to $8,168,398.88. A similar mode of calculation indicates the total revenue applicable to 1931 and 1930 as $10,435,546.18 and $10,224,719.54, respectively.

II. *Appraisal of the Tax System*

The total state and county tax in South Carolina for the year 1932 amounted to $36,615,848.93, representing $18,-655,146.96 of state revenue and $17,960,701.97 as county taxes. An analysis of the several state taxes reveals the following general distribution as among the several groups of taxpayers:

Gasoline and motor vehicle license taxes	$8,938,131.27
Indirect taxes, licenses and fees	7,977,776.98
Property tax	1,639,238.71
Total tax collections for all purposes.......	$18,655,146.96

To the total collected, $18,655,146.96, must be added the balance of 1932 assessments of $1,257,296.18, making a total revenue for all purposes of $19,912,443.14, or $11.37 per capita. The total revenue collected by the state in 1931 amounted to $25,088,731, or $14.39 per capita.

The total assessed value of all property, real and personal, for the year 1932 amounted to $397,121,407, with a total tax assessment for state purposes of $1,985,607.12.[28] Thus it appears that revenue from this source forms only about 10 per cent of the total state tax. The per capita levy, $1.13, was considerably smaller than the levy of $1.66 in 1917.

The publication entitled " Financial Statistics of States ", compiled by the Bureau of Census, reveals the fact that

[28] The assessment for 1933 was $1,933,150.28. Percentage of loss in collection was less than one and one-half per cent. *Report of Comptroller General,* 1933, p. 5. This tax is equally divided between the general fund and the retirement of the state deficit.

the per capita tax for the support of the state government of South Carolina compares favorably with those of
the Southern States that most closely resemble it.   The per
capita receipts from all sources in 1929, were as follows:
South Carolina, $12.48; Virginia, $20.10; North Carolina,
$13.37; Georgia, $9.68; Alabama, $11.77; Mississippi,
$9.42; Louisiana, $14.85.[29]

The per cent distribution of these receipts is shown in the
following table, which is based on the same statistics.

PER CENT OBTAINED FROM—

	Taxes				Non-taxes		
	General property	Special	Poll	Business and Non-business license	Subven-tions and grants	Earnings of depts.	All other
48 states .	17.0	19.5	0.2	41.6	7.4	7.3	7.0
S. Car. . .	10.3	14.9	—	59.4	7.9	6.7	0.8
Virginia . .	10.1	15.3	1.3	43.6	17.3	8.7	3.7
N. Car. . .	—	23.3	—	53.6	6.5	11.3	5.3
Ga.	24 0	4.0	1.2	53.7	7.0	6.0	4.1
Ala. . . .	25.4	6.6	—	40.5	6.7	13.8	7.0
Miss. . . .	32.3	10.7	—	28.6	10.3	10.6	7.5
La. . . .	32.7	2.5	—	50.2	4.5	5.5	4.6

Perhaps the most interesting fact to be noted about the
income of the state government of South Carolina is the
extent to which business and non-business licenses contribute.[30]   Whereas in 1917 these licenses constituted only
7.5 per cent of the total revenue, in 1929 they represented

[29] Bureau of Census, *Financial Statistics of States, 1929* (Washington,
1931), p. 60.

[30] Receipts from business licenses consist chiefly of taxes exacted from
insurance and other incorporated companies, tax on soft drinks and on
gasoline; those from non-business licenses comprise chiefly taxes on
motor vehicles and amounts paid for hunting and fishing privileges.

more than half of the aggregate.[31] This increase is offset
by the decline of property and special taxes which together
had provided 64.4 per cent of the income in 1917. Nevertheless, due to enormous increases in expenditures during the
period, the per capita of property and special taxes increased
from $1.24 in 1917 to $3.25 in 1930.

As we have already observed, the development of the tax
system in South Carolina during the past decade has been
along the line of supplementing the basic property tax with
other forms of taxation.[32] Consequently, the present system
is largely the result of imposing new taxes as the exigencies
of the moment seemed to require. Obviously, such an un-
ordered and unplanned accumulation of individual taxes,
with the legislature each year pressed to find new sources of
revenue, is not conducive to the building of a tax system
upon a firm foundation.

All will agree that a revenue system should be made as
simple as conditions will admit. The importance of this
universal desire for simplicity is overshadowed only by the
demand that taxation be just. Justice in taxation, however, is
likely to be achieved by emphasizing simplicity. It is particularly appropriate and fitting that South Carolina should
give much thought at this time to the formulation of a system
of revenue based upon sound principles of taxation. The inevitable modification of the present economic, industrial,
social and political conditions will be marked by the tendency
to create an ever-increasing complexity in taxation.

[31] The increase in the amount derived from this source by the several
states during this period ranged from 20 to 42 per cent. See Ogg, F. A.
and Ray, P. O., *Essentials of American Government* (New York, 1932),
p. 475.

[32] Indirect tax collected today is sufficient to pay the cost of operating
all departments and institutions of the state government.

It is indicated elsewhere that the property tax is only slightly more
than half the amount returned to the respective counties out of the
state treasury.

Desired simplicity is not to be found in a single tax system, for no single tax is conceivable that can satisfy the demands of a sound revenue system in a modern state. While the purpose of a single tax is commendable, experience seems to warrant the position that it is an unattainable ideal. No scheme of single taxation has yet been devised for attaining its end without sacrificing the principle of justice. An equitable distribution of the state tax burden can be found only in a multiple system of properly coordinated taxes.

1. The South Carolina Revenue System and the Model Plan

In seeking an outline of a system, both sound in its underlying principles and simple in its operation, we do well to direct our attention to the " model tax system " proposed by a committee of distinguished tax experts selected by the National Tax Association.[33] The report submitted by this committee presented a summary of the trend in the field and proposed a plan for the future. The principles laid down have provided a sound foundation for recent development in state tax systems. Indeed, practically every special agency created since that time to seek a solution of the tax problems in state governments has been largely guided in its deliberations by the plan formulated by this committee.

The plan comprises the following combinations:

(1) A Personal Income Tax at the person's domicile upon all sources of income that can be reached by the state, the rate to be progressive.

(2) A Tax upon Tangible Property levied exclusively at its situs, with a separate classification of tangible personal property.

(3) A Business Tax levied at a moderate rate upon the net income received from business carried on in the state.[34]

[33] *Proceedings of the National Tax Association*, 1919, pp. 429 *et seq.*

[34] Net income was deemed a better index of ability to pay than volume of business or gross sales.

According to the committee, this combination rests upon three clearly recognized principles, namely, (1) " that every person having taxable ability should pay some sort of a direct personal tax to the government under which he is domiciled and from which he received the personal benefits that government confers "; (2) " that tangible property, by whomsoever owned, should be taxed by the jurisdiction in which it is located, because it there receives protection and other governmental benefits and services "; and (3) " that business carried on for profit in any locality should be taxed for the benefits it receives ".[35]

In recommending the model system, the committee maintained that it would satisfy every legitimate claim of any American state. It will be noticed that the system is stated in terms of general principles, flexible and adaptable to the differences in economic, social and political conditions among the various states. Certainly, measures predicated upon these three simple principles contain nothing " wholly foreign to American experience and contrary to the ideas of the American people ".

The South Carolina tax system has fortunately followed in a general way the standards outlined under the model plan. In addition to its property tax and the individual income tax, a system of business taxation includes the corporation license tax and the privilege taxes. To supplement these, however, South Carolina has resorted in recent years to miscellaneous taxes consisting of the inheritance tax, the admission tax and consumption excise taxes on selected articles. As already suggested, these miscellaneous taxes were enacted as a result of an increasing cost of government and a shrinkage in the value of farm property. The tax

[35] *Ibid.*, pp. 429-431. For a discussion of these principles, see, for example, Brookings Institution, *Survey of Mississippi*, pp. 35-37; Beard, *American Government and Politics* (6th ed., 1931), pp. 642-644.

authorities seek to justify the taxes on non-essentials on the ground that they reach a class of people who pay no property taxes. There can be litle doubt that these indirect taxes have become a permanent part of the state revenue system for the people of South Carolina appear to have accepted them without much protest. In any event, they have served as a sburce of great strength in the present emergency.

2. New Sources of Revenue

In the face of recurring deficits, there has been considerable agitation for new sources of revenue. In 1930, the comptroller general recommended the passage of a tax of three per cent on gross sales and collections to defray the entire cost of operating the public schools.[36] He repeated this recommendation in 1932.[37] Citing the fact that the property tax as the principal source of revenue for support of the schools is inadequate and therefore unsatisfactory, he maintained that his proposed sales tax would not only furnish sufficient revenue for that purpose but also would be the means of reducing the property tax throughout the state from one-third to one-half of the present assessment.[38] It was contemplated, of course, that the selective sales tax would be revised so as to conform with the proposed general sales tax.

Attracted by the experience of Mississippi in experimenting with this type of taxation, the governor, the chairman of the Tax Commission and a number of legislators became advo-

[36] Report of Comptroller General, 1930, pp. 6, 7.

[37] Report of Comptroller General, 1932, pp. 5, 6. Such a tax would not apply to merchants only, but to every business activity carried on in the state.

[38] The volume of retail business in the state in 1929 amounted to approximately $300,000,000. It is generally estimated that this volume had decreased by about one-third in 1932. Hence, a three per cent tax should produce approximately $6,000,000 in revenue, depending upon the scope of exemptions.

cates of such a tax.[39] Should it be regarded imperative that
the presented revenue be augmented and should this form of
taxation be resorted to, it is urged that it be regarded strictly
as an emergency measure. A general sales tax violates one of
the basic and fundamental principles of taxation, namely, the
ability to pay. It must not be considered as having a permanent place in the revenue system of the state. It is vastly
different from the so-called luxury tax which, in the experience of South Carolina, is as nearly painless as any tax can
be and at the same time may be relied upon to yield substantial revenue.

Instead of deviating from sound principles of taxation,
South Carolina will do well to maintain with constancy the
effort to build on the basis already recognized a system that
will operate with a minimum of inequality and injustice.
The demand for increased revenue should be met by realizing
more fully the potentialities of the present system through
its simplification and through improved administration.
There is little likelihood that the financial difficulties now
confronting the state can be overcome by the formulation
of any new taxes.

III. The General Property Tax

The state property levy had been reduced from the twelve
mills levied in 1920 to five mills in 1932. As already noted,
it now plays relatively a small part as a source of state
revenue, i. e., about ten per cent.[40] Even so, there has been
a veritable furore throughout the state during the past few
years that it be abolished altogether. This idea has become

---

[39] See the editorial proposal that a federal sales tax be levied on
manufactures and that the revenue so derived be distributed, fifty per
cent to the national treasury and fifty per cent among the states according to population, *The State* (Columbia), Feb. 9, 1932.

[40] In 1928, general property taxes represented less than 10 per cent
of state revenue in only five states.

a sort of fetish. Relief is not to be had here; it must come
through reductions in the county supply bills. If the average taxpayer in his desperate effort to save his farm or home
understood that ninety per cent of his property tax is a
county levy—the inevitable result of the mounting expenditures in support of county government—the prevailing complaint would not be so largely misdirected.[41]

Seldom has the protest against the property tax been so
loud, or the opposition to its payment so determined, as at
the present time. This aroused feeling is made articulate
through the organization of the Farmers' and Taxpayers'
League as a rallying center.[42] Apparently, the taxpayers are
aroused to a willingness to sacrifice essential public services.

As in most states, the administration of the property tax
in South Carolina is a story of inequality and evasion of
assessments. The system has been described by a special
committee as being in a state of anarchy. This committee
reported in part:

The general charge of 'outlawry' against our system as it
exists in point of fact is proved beyond the 'reasonable doubt'
of the criminal courts by the bare statement of the law. . . .
The law requires that property be listed and returned, assessed
and taxed, at its actual or true value in money. That this provision is in practice a dead letter is not only known to and acted
upon by every taxpayer but by every taxing official and law
officer of the State from the local assessor up to the General
Assembly and the Supreme Court. . . . The law requires a
'uniform and equal rate of assessment and taxation'. That the
property upon the tax books is not uniformly and equally

[41] For a discussion of the relative importance of property taxation in
the United States, see Brookings Institution, *Survey of Mississippi*, p. 45.

[42] The League urged the abolition of the five-mill state levy. See note
by the author, " Public School Finance in South Carolina" in *National
Municipal Review*, vol. xxi, no. 4, pp. 264-265 (April, 1932).

assessed and taxed as among individual taxpayers, as among local taxing districts in the same county and as among the different counties of the State, is a notorious fact admitted by all men. The law requires that " all property, real, personal and possessory " shall be assessed and taxed. That a vast amount of taxable property of the State is not upon the tax books at all is not only well known, but is acquiesced in and openly justified by the majority of citizens. All of which can mean but one thing—that the operation of the tax system in South Carolina is in point of fact as much an outlaw business as the gentle art of breaking safes or of distilling moonshine whiskey. Any changes in the law tending either to conform the law to the facts or the facts to the law would seem to be desirable.[4]

Although this general indictment was presented a decade ago, the condition as described has not changed materially. Faced with the further fact that $18,912,810.25, or more than 50 per cent of the $36,615,843.93 collected from all sources as state and county taxes, was levied on property in 1932, we are prompted to extend our inquiry into this field of taxation where state and county are in a relation of interdependence.

1. Assessment and Collection of Property Tax

Inasmuch as the state depends so largely upon the local fiscal officers for the assessment and collection of the state property tax, it is necessary to give attention to the local boards of assessors, the county auditor and the county treasurer.

In most of the counties the township boards function as boards of assessors. In a few, the duties in question have been conferred upon school trustees. The members are generally appointed by the governor, upon recommendation

[43] *Report of the Joint Special Committee of Revenue and Taxation,* 1921, p. 25. This report is popularly known as the " Marion Report ".

of the county delegation in the General Assembly, and their tenure is co-terminal with that of the governor appointing them.[44] The lists and returns of all property, both real and personal, are laid before the local boards of assessors at meetings held on the first Tuesday in March. The law requires that these boards shall fairly and impartially assess the property returned for taxation and they are empowered to increase or lower the valuation of any property fixed by the county auditor.[45] The chairman of the local board, under the direction and supervision of the county auditor, is required to canvass the territory of his board immediately after the expiration of the time for returning property for taxation, for the purpose of discovering and placing upon the tax books all taxable property of every description. For the performance of this task he is allowed only five days and for his services he receives a per-diem of two dollars. Members of the board are likewise allowed the same remuneration for each day actually employed.[46]

The county board of equalization is composed of the chairman of each of the township boards of assessors, with the county auditor as clerk. The board meets on the fourth Tuesday of March of each year to equalize the valuations fixed by the boards of assessors. It hears and acts upon all appeals from the local boards.[47]

That such a system of tax assessment is unscientific is patent. One need not be surprised to find inequitable assessments. It could hardly be otherwise.

[44] *Code 1932*, sec. 2737.

[45] *Ibid.*, sec. 2743.

[46] *Ibid.*, secs. 2738, 2744. The board is limited to three days—except every fourth year, when real estate is required to be returned, the limit is extended to five. The time in increased in proportion to the size of the incorporated town or city. A thirty day limit is allowed for an incorporation of ten thousand or more. *Ibid.*, secs. 2608, 2738.

[47] *Code 1932*, secs. 2737, 2741, 2744.

The root of the trouble is to be found in the law. The absence of definite qualifications of fitness naturally produces inefficiency. Inadequate compensation results in many incompetent men seeking and obtaining the office. The tasks ostensibly required could not possibly be performed thoroughly and efficiently in the time allowed. The property owners virtually act as assessors themselves. Governments have not yet been able to operate on a basis of voluntary support or on a basis of self-assessment.

Nor is that all. The local assessors are without the proper tools. They have no way of checking the acreage of tracts and parcels of land, for careful measurements are impossible without surveys and tax maps. As a consequence, a considerable proportion of taxable property in South Carolina is not on the tax books.

Assessment districts should be large enough to justify the employment of at least one permanent official in each district. The best results would probably be obtained by putting a county assessor on a full-time basis and paying a sufficient amount to attract a competent official. There is no real reason why the value of property should not be accurately determined and fairly assessed for taxation. The proposed county assessor should have a term of office sufficiently long to justify his policy by results obtained.

Too much emphasis can not be placed upon the fact that the assessor should be one of the most important officers in the county. In his present position, however, he has neither the power nor the qualifications to cope with the technical problems of property assessment. The public looks upon it as an office of minor importance and it is generally held by one who is accommodating and easy on influential tax dodgers.

" Opinion is unanimous among investigators of the general property tax that the original assessment must be done well or the whole property tax system will crumble ", runs a recent report.[48]   There can be no doubt that the solution of the problem is to be found not in equalization, but in improving the original assessments.   Such was the opinion of the Joint Special Committee on Revenue and Taxation in 1921, when it reported: " Boards of equalization and review may here and there correct an injustice between tax-payers . . . , but unless the initial assessment is as nearly just and correct as human judgment can get it, there is no possible method of really rectifying the inequality and injustice that follows ".[49]

It will not be enough to increase the power of the assessor and to provide him with the equipment for performing his task—it will be necessary to change his status.   The function of assessing property is not one that is likely to be executed efficiently by elective officers.   It is an administrative task requiring technical competency.   That appointment of assessors is in line with sound principles, no serious student of taxation questions.[50]

The question does arise, however, as to the agency that should make the appointment.[51]   It must be admitted that home rule in the assessment at the present time is an obvious farce.   Nevertheless, cherished sentiment will probably demand that the county assessor be appointed by the county board of commissioners.   This method would be inadvisable so long as these boards continue to be appointed by the governor on the recommendation of the legislative delega-

[48] Brookings Institution, *Survey of Mississippi*, p. 150.

[49] *Report*, p. 55.

[50] Assessors may be appointed under the constitution which provides: " The General Assembly shall provide for the assessment of all property for taxation ".   *Constitution,* art. x, sec. 13.

[51] For a discussion of recommendations on this point made by various investigating bodies in the several states during the past few years, see Brookings Institution, *Survey of Mississippi*, pp. 153-157.

tions. Even should the anomaly of that situation be corrected through the election of the county board,[52] there would remain the question of the necessary supervision.

It is unlikely that an equitable and efficient appraisal of property for taxation may be had while its assessment is left in the hands of local officials without central supervision and control. Furthermore, it must be recognized that this is a state function. Should the county board of commissioners be reconstructed, as suggested above, it might then be given the power to appoint the county assessor—but subject to the approval of the state agency. It is preferable, however, to vest the appointment of all assessors in the hands of the State Department of Revenues proposed in this study.

The county auditor receives the returns and makes the assessment for state purposes at the rate fixed by the comptroller general. It is his duty to list any property that has not been listed, adding fifty per cent to the amount of the return as penalty. The county auditor is appointed by the governor with consent of the senate for a four-year term. He may be suspended by the governor during a recess of the senate, if deemed guilty of misconduct in office, or of crime, or if for any reason he should become legally disqualified to perform his duties. His permanent removal, however, is possible only with the consent of the senate.[53]

County treasurers are charged with the duty of receiving tax payments. When the time expires for the payment of property taxes, this officer issues executions against delinquent taxpayers and delivers them to the sheriff for collec-

[52] See recommendations for reconstruction of county government in South Carolina made by the South Carolina Council, *County Government: A Proposed System for South Carolina* (Cheraw, 1931), p. 3; also, see Columbus Andrews, *Administrative County Government in South Carolina* (Chapel Hill, 1933), pp. 185 *et seq.*

[53] *Code 1932*, secs. 2698, 2701, 2704, 2706.

tion. The law provides that the county treasurer shall be appointed and removed from office in the same manner as that prescribed for the county auditor. In practice, however, both of these officials are nominated at the polls.

The constitution stipulates that the office of sheriff shall be filled by the electorate for a term of four years.[54] Such is the method of selecting these three tax-collecting officials, in spite of the fact that they should be removed as far as possible from political influences.

Attention is now directed to the state agency which has general supervision over the local assessors. The State Tax Commission was created in 1915, " in order to effectively carry into execution the equitable assessment of property for taxation ".[55] This body is composed of three members, appointed by the governor with consent of the senate for overlapping terms of six years. The law requires that the members " shall be such as are known to possess knowledge of the subject of taxation and skill in matters pertaining thereto." While the commission has general supervision over the administration of most of the tax laws of the state, the law places particular emphasis upon the equalization of assessments.[56]

The original purpose of the creation of this agency has not been served satisfactorily. In addition to the fact that inherent weaknesses in the system of original assessments create a condition that makes equalization almost impossible, the Tax Commission is not equipped to achieve desired results. Not only must the state agency have sufficient machinery to maintain close contact throughout the year with

[54] *Constitution,* art. 5, sec. 30; *Code 1932,* sec. 3473.

[55] *Code 1932,* sec. 2419. The State Board of Equalization and the State Board of Assessors were abolished, their powers being conferred on this body.

[56] *Code 1932,* chap. 106.

local assessing and equalization officials, but it is also necessary that it have power to enforce its decisions through the county auditor. This can be accomplished only through authority to remove local assessors for inefficiency or misconduct. Furthermore, if the Tax Commission is to be expected to perform its task equitably, provision must be made for an independently collected body of information relative to property values throughout the state.

In order to carry out what has been suggested in regard to original assessments and their equalization, considerably larger expenditures than at present would be necessary but the results obtained would justify it many times over. Not only would the revenue be increased sufficiently to overcome the added cost in administration but the burden could also be so much more equitably distributed that it would not be a crushing burden upon any one. Proper coordination and control of all assessments by the state are absolutely essential.

Although it is true that thousands of property taxpayers have not been able to pay taxes promptly for the past few years, one of the tax commissioners recently stated than an investigation of the tax rolls of the counties will disclose the fact that "thousands of taxpayers able to pay have not been required to pay the taxes charged because the officials charged with the duty of collecting such taxes have not enforced the collection thereof".[57] No argument is needed to maintain the point that the method of collecting these taxes needs changing. A greater degree of control should be given the comptroller general who supervises their collection.

The comptroller is also required to do county auditing, but the General Assembly has failed from year to year to

[57] Frank C. Robinson, "The Tax System of South Carolina as Seen by an Administrator", p. 6. He cites the case of a taxpayer owning large properties who had not paid his property taxes for a period of eight years, although he had been paying an income tax during that period.

make appropriations sufficient for this purpose. Detailed auditing and regular checking of the county offices are essential to their proper conduct. As the comptroller general has pointed out, these operations would be a help to the collector of taxes as well as a benefit to the government generally.[58]

One of the most demoralizing influences in the collection of taxes in Souh Carolina is the practice of the legislature each year of deferring time for tax payments. This does not solve the tax problems of the individual; it merely rewards the dilatory and is a gross discrimination against those who are prompt. In the meantime, the state is forced to borrow money and pay interest on it until the delinquent taxes are paid. On the other hand, the present unsatisfactory system of borrowing could be obviated in a large measure by authorizing small discounts for early payment.[59]

2. Separation of Revenue Sources

The separation of sources of state and local taxes, which was so much emphasized at one time, has found renewed advocacy during the present emergency as a step toward the solution of the property tax problem. It is argued that so long as the state levies a tax on property the incentive will remain for the counties to compete with each other in reducing essessments; that the removal of the state levy would put an end to the notorious inequalities among the counties.[60]

---

[58] See *Report of Comptroller General*, 1931, p. 9. Detailed audits of a limited number of county officers, made under the supervision of this office from 1925 to 1930, revealed irregularities in excess of $200,000. *Report*, 1930, p. 8.

[59] For like recommendation, see *Report of Comptroller General*, 1931, pp. 8, 9; *Report of State Tax Commission*, 1931, pp. 1, 2.

[60] See, for example, *Report of Joint Special Committee on Revenue and Taxation*, 1921, pp. 83, 84.

This argument places too much emphasis on the influence of the state tax on property assessments. On the contrary, it is only a minor influence in undervaluation, and there is little reason to think that the taxpayers would not continue their present tactics were the state tax removed.

Even if the above claim could be maintained with logic, the state cannot at this time afford to give up the ad valorem tax. Not only are the other revenues of the state government inadequate for its operation, but it is also true that one-half of the state property tax is being applied to the retirement of the deficit already incurred.

Moreover, it is believed that positive harm would result from complete separation of the sources of state and local revenues. The history of property taxation during the quarter of a century of agitation in behalf of reform through separation of sources seems to indicate very strongly that progress lies along the lines of greater state supervision. The recent adoption of separation in North Carolina and Virginia is more than counterbalanced by the cases in which the plan has been abandoned in a number of states. Experience abundantly shows that local tax officials constantly need expert advice and effective state control to the end that there shall be just and efficient administration of tax laws. Furthermore, complete separation would tend to destroy the state's sense of responsibility in the matter of local taxation, and to take from the owner of property the awareness of obligation to the state and interest in state legislation.[61]

3. The Uniformity Clause

Students of taxation are practically unanimous in believing that the shortcomings of the general property tax system

[61] See *ibid.*, pp. 85, 86. For like opinion, see *Proceedings of the National Tax Association*, 1919, pp. 176, 177; Brookings Institution, *Survey of Mississippi*, pp. 111-115. For contrary opinion, see for example, Abram P. Staples, "Operation of the Segregation Tax in Virginia" in *Manufacturers Record*, Jan. 15, 1931.

are traceable to a defect in theory. This defect was pointed out by the Supreme Court of the United States when it said: " A system which imposes the same tax upon each specie of property, irrespective of its nature, condition, or class, will be destructive of uniformity and equality in taxation and a just adaptation of property to its burdens ".[62]

The constitutional requirement of " a uniform and equal assessment and taxation " of property will inevitably result in vicious injustice, for it does not conform to the fundamental principle of distributing the tax burden in proportion to ability to pay and to benefits or privileges derived. One need not be surprised that the general property tax in South Carolina is in fact neither uniform, nor general nor equitable. A uniform ad valorem tax has always failed.

It is a well-known fact that, under a uniform rate, intangible personal property escapes taxation almost entirely. Restrictions on the taxing power of legislative bodies should be removed. This is the trend in constitution-making and constitutes a most desirable feature. As was pointed out in a recent survey, " restrictions on the legislative powers of taxation are vestiges of periods when the arbitrary use of power of rulers removed from the people needed to be checked ".[63] They have no place in a representative democracy. The uniformity clause will inevitably block the development of a modern tax system.

The Joint Special Committee on Revenue and Taxation in 1921 made the following recommendation with unusual emphasis:

The Committee is profoundly impressed with the validity of one conclusion that it desires to urge with all the earnestness at its command. That conclusion is—*that there can be no sound sane, thorough-going reform of the taxing system of South*

[63] Brookings Institution, *Survey of Mississippi*, p. 42.
[62] *Pacific Express v. Siebert*, 142 U. S., 351.

Carolina until the constitutional restrictions upon the power of the General Assembly in relation to the general property tax are removed. . . . The only sensible course is to rebuild the foundation. No sound and lasting foundation for a just, equitable and workable system of taxation can be prepared until the people of the State free themselves from the shackles of the present Constitution and confer upon their representatives in the General Assembly the power to construct such improved system.[64]

On the basis of this recommendation, the committee suggested the following amendment to the constitution:

Subject only to the limitations contained in this Article the General Assembly shall have the power to establish and maintain a just and equitable system for raising State and local revenues for public purposes. Taxes shall be levied on such subjects and in such manner as shall be prescribed by general laws, and all taxes shall be uniform upon the same class of subjects within the territorial limits of the authority levying the tax. All property used exclusively for State, county, municipal, educational, religious, benevolent and charitable purposes, and household goods to the amount of at least one hundred dollars ($100.00) for each family, shall be exempted from taxation.[65]

[64] *Report*, p. 131. This committee made the most exhaustive study of the tax system of South Carolina that has yet been made and its report stands today as the best thought on the subject. In summary, it recommended a "judicious combination of a moderate property tax, a moderate personal income tax and a moderate tax upon business, one mode of taxation dovetailing with and supplementing the other". Obviously, the general program could not be executed under the uniformity clause.

[65] *Ibid.*, Appendix, Exhibit "A", p. 137. To accommodate the program in part, amendment has made provision "for a graduated tax on incomes, and for a graduated license on occupation and business". For a discussion of the various states in experimenting with the classified property tax, see Brookings Institution, *Survey of Mississippi*, pp. 121-129. More than thirty states have constitutional provisions which permit their legislatures to classify property for taxation.

Inasmuch as adequate protection against unjust taxation of individuals is provided under Article I, Section 5, of the constitution, viz., the usual guarantee of due process and equal protection of the law, the uniformity clause might well be eliminated entirely with no substitute in its place.[66]

Taxpayers need not be expected voluntarily to disclose intangibles which they own when the entire return would be taken in taxes. It is also true that a high percentage of tangible personal property does not find its way into the tax lists. This situation exists not only in full knowledge of the public, but also with its consent. It is practically impossible for the tax assessor to discover intangibles, and the steps necessary for the listing of certain forms of tangibles are very objectionable. So long as the public feels that the rate imposed upon personal property is too high, widespread abuses in the administration of this tax may be expected. This condition should be corrected as far as possible, for it results in a baneful administration of all tax laws.

In an effort to bring intangible property from its hiding place, for purpose of taxation, the South Carolina General Assembly in 1932 ratified the following amendment to the uniformity clause:

Provided, Further, That the General Assembly may provide by law for the assessment of all intangible personal property, including moneys, credits, bank deposits, corporate stocks, and bonds, at its true value for taxation by State, County and municipal purposes thereof: *Provided,* That the total rate of taxation imposed shall never exceed one-half of one per centum of the actual value of such intangible property. . . .

[66] If a substitute be deemed advisable, it is suggested that the following provision of the model state constitution (sec. 75) recommended by the National Municipal League be adopted: " The power of taxation shall never be surrendered, suspended, or contracted away ".

In 1933 the legislature exercised this prerogative but it is yet too early to ascertain its effect.[67]   It may be reasonably assumed, however, that it will not serve as a solution of the difficulty involved.   The resort to low rates as an inducement to declare intangibles has nowhere resulted in the listing of a substantial proportion of this class of property. The amount which is placed on the assessment rolls at present in South Carolina is negligible and doubtless will continue to be.   The state would do well to give up the attempt, and exempt this form of property, as such.   Anyway, the personal income tax is far more effective and is a sounder basis for deriving revenue from intangible property.[68]

Attention must now be turned to the question of the best way of dealing with tangible personal property.   Dr. Herbert D. Simpson, tax expert of the Northwestern University, maintains that the controlling consideration is whether it is capable of being taxed as a practical proposition.   He notes the fact that there are many forms of personal property which can be assessed as easily and as accurately as real estate, and cites the automobile as an example.   He indicates the untaxable classes in the following language:

On the other hand, articles of dress and adornment, money in one's pocket, watches and personal belongings, cannot be assessed with any pretense of generality.   Household furniture could be assessed under a system of sufficiently rigid espionage and would presumably be a rough index of the general financial position of its owner.   But as a matter of fact, it never has been assessed, and under any system of administration conceivable in this country never will be. . . . [69]

[67] *Acts of 1933*, pp. 567-582.

[68] For like conclusions, see Brookings Institution, *Survey of Mississippi*, pp. 132-134; also, "Model Tax System", sec. 34.

[69] *Tax Situation in Illinois*, 1929, pp. 86, 87, cited in Brookings Institution, *Survey of Mississippi*, p. 131.

In regard to the automobile, there is no form of property tax that could be so easily and uniformly collected. Yet, according to records in the office of the comptroller general for 1932, there were 43,074 less automobiles and trucks returned for taxation than licenses taken. That is to say, of the 171,126 registered, there were only 128,952 on the books of the county auditors. All cars appearing on the highways are registered and classified. The state successfully collects the license fees. Property tax on automobiles should be required to be paid at the time of issuing the automobile license.

The fragmentary and unequal way in which heads of families return household equipment for taxation constitutes a travesty on taxation. As for personal effects, the value of this class of property as appraised by the owners in 1932 was only about one-third the value of intangibles returned for taxation. Inasmuch as property falling under these two heads can be discovered only through a rigid system of espionage, resented by taxpayers, a just assessment is practically impossible to carry into effect. Nor has any standardized procedure been developed for its valuation, when voluntarily returned or discovered. Wisdom seems to dictate the policy of eliminating these two classes of property from the assessment rolls.

With the exemption of household equipment, personal effects and intangible personal property from the property tax and its improved administration, together with a minimum personal income tax and a tax upon the net income of business, augmented by the inheritance and other miscellaneous taxes now levied, South Carolina could move forward in the knowledge that it was proceeding along sound principles of taxation.

IV. Summary of Recommendations

Recommendations made in the course of the foregoing discussion may be summarized in the general statements that follow:

1. The revenue system of South Carolina should be developed on the basis of a tax system that is sound in its underlying principles and simple in its operation—a combination of separate taxes levied upon income, property and business.

2. All licenses, fees and similar revenues should be charged to the general fund and periodically scrutinized by the General Assembly.

3. All revenues should be brought within a budget system, as outlined in Chapter II, and provision for revenue made before appropriations are voted.

4. The amended uniformity clause of the constitution that pertains to the taxation of property should be repealed, in order that the legislature may be free to bring about a more equitable distribution of the tax burden.

5. Separation of state and local sources of revenue as a reform of property taxation in South Carolina should not be adopted.

6. The classified property tax should be rejected.

7. Household equipment and personal effects should be exempted from the property tax.

8. The effort to tax intangible personal property under the property tax should be given up because the income tax is a more effective and sounder basis for deriving revenue from this source.

9. The assessment and collection of property tax on automobiles should be made at the time of issuing the automobile license.

10. The individual income tax should be made universal by requiring a return and a filing fee from every self-supporting individual.

11. A more equitable distribution of the tax burden on real estate should be sought through the adoption of improved administrative machinery and of modern scientific methods of assessing and collecting the property tax, with particular emphasis upon the initial assessment.

12. County assessors should be appointed by the proposed State Department of Revenue, or by reconstructed county boards of commissioners with the approval of the state agency. In either event, the State Department of Revenue should be given the power to remove the county assessor for cause, including incompetency or inefficiency, and after due notice and hearing.

13. All state taxing functions should be integrated in the State Department of Revenue as proposed below.

V. *Administration of the State Revenue System*

The administration of most of the state tax measures is already consolidated under the present State Tax Commission. The suggested creation of the Department of Revenues does not disturb the existing grouping, except as it seeks to carry it to its logical conclusion. It is intended that assessment and collection of taxes shall be the exclusive function of this department, in so far as this is practicable. The following organization units are suggested:

I. Department of Revenues
  1. Bureau of Property Assessment
  2. Bureau of Income Taxes
  3. Bureau of License Taxes
  4. Bureau of Miscellaneous Taxes

In the establishment of this organization, the following details are contemplated:

1. The present State Tax Commission to be abolished.

2. A Commissioner of Revenues, appointed by the governor with the advice and consent of the senate, to have general supervision over the entire department and to have authority to re-arrange the bureau structure as the needs require.

3. Each of the bureaus to be headed by a director, appointed by the Commissioner.

4. The duties of the comptroller general in so far as they relate to assessment and collection of property taxes to be transferred to the Department of Revenues.

5. The powers and duties of the Tax Commission to devolve upon this department.

6. The duties of the Tax Commission which relate to its activity as a board of equalization to be exercised by a board of equalization established within the department, composed of the commissioner of revenues, the director of the bureau of property assessment and the director of the bureau of income taxes.

7. The duties of the Highway Department with reference to registration and licensing of motor vehicles to be transferred to the bureau of license taxes in this department.

CHAPTER IV

Public Education

Education is the most fundamental and vital responsibility of a democracy. The chief concern of the State is to develop a high type of citizenship. This is recognized and evidenced by the fact that there is no single activity for which so much is appropriated as for education and its related functions. The system of public education is, therefore, a basic thing that challenges our study. It is the purpose here to trace briefly its development in South Carolina, and to attempt a fairly intensive survey of its administration.

Education in the United States is regarded primarily as a state function, conducted locally. This has resulted in the growth of independent school systems that differ from each other in general organization, details of administration, and effectiveness.[1] Varying methods of the several commonwealths allow a high degree of adaptability to local conditions. In considering the state's educational problem, effort will be made to discover the extent to which the present machinery and its administration serve the needs of South Carolina.

I. PUBLIC SCHOOL ADMISTRATION

1. *Historical*

The constitution of 1868 was the first organic law of South Carolina to make mention of education.[2] It provided

[1] See U. S. Dept. of the Interior, Bureau of Education, *Education in the United States* (1927), pp. 6 *et seq.* Partial explanation of relative effectiveness rests in the ability and willingness of a locality to maintain schools.

[2] Art. x.

110

for a state system of public schools to take the place of the one that had crumbled during the Civil War. The schools were to be supported by an annual levy on all taxable property and a one-dollar poll tax. Provision was made for a state university, an agricultural college, a school for the deaf, dumb and blind, and a state normal school. All schools were to be " free and open to all the children and youth of the State without regard to race or color ". And, for the first time in the history of the state, provision was made for a state school fund. This was to be created from the proceeds of all lands given by the United States or by the state.

The school system was established by statute in 1870, but there was practically no growth during the years immediately following.[3] The war had destroyed the thing essential to its success—adequate means of support. Appropriations were insufficient and school funds were diverted to other purposes; school officers were inexperienced; good teachers were scarce; suitable school buildings were wanting. These obstacles, together with widespread opposition, barred the path of progress. The victory of home-rule in 1876 was followed by a period of indifference to education, for the struggle for self-government consumed the public energies for many years. The neglect was almost disastrous, for the state was entirely too poor " to afford the resulting waste of ignorance ".[4]

The real beginning of the public school system dates from about 1877. The first steps in its actual establishment were

[3] For discussions of education during Reconstruction, see Francis B. Simkins and R. H. Woody, *South Carolina during Reconstruction* (Chapel Hill, N. C., 1932), pp. 416-443; Henry T. Thompson, *Establishment of the Public School System in South Carolina* (Columbia, 1927), pp. 9-13; John F. Thomason, *Foundations of the Public Schools in South Carolina* (Columbia, 1925), pp. 184-190; Edgar W. Knight, *Public Education in the South* (Boston, 1922), pp. 328, 374.

[4] Knight, *Public Education in the South*, p. 417.

taken in May of that year. At that time the state superintendent of education, Hugh S. Thompson, and his single
clerk, constituted the entire working force of the Department
of Education, occupying the two offices in the State House
that are now used by the Supreme Court as a reception room
and a consultation room. A new school law was passed in
1878, but as suggested in the preceding paragraph, there was
little improvement for many years.[5]

The basis of the present organization is to be found in
article XI of the constitution of 1895. Section I of this
article provides a state superintendent of education, as was
done by section I of article X of the constitution of 1868.
It is stipulated that " he shall be elected for the term of two
years by the qualified voters of the state, in such manner
and at such time as the other state officers are elected; his
duties and compensation shall be defined by the General
Assembly ".[6] Section 2 provides a state board of education, composed of the governor, the state superintendent of
education, and not exceeding seven persons to be appointed
by the governor every four years. The governor is designated chairman, and the state superintendent, secretary.[7]

It is stated that this board shall regulate the examination
of teachers applying for qualifying certificates, shall award
all scholarships, and shall have such other powers and duties
as may be determined by law. It is made the duty of the
General Assembly to provide a liberal system of free public
schools for all children between the ages of six and twenty-
one years. The legislature is also directed to divide the

[5] The constitution was also amended in 1878, fixing an annual levy for
school purposes at 2 mills. In 1888, the legislature empowered all school
districts to levy an additional tax to supplement state funds, the local
tax not to exceed two mills. In 1893, the limit was increased to 4.

[6] Term of office was increased to four years by amendment, ratified
March 12, 1926. *Acts of 1926*, p. 956.

[7] This was a decided change from the previous state board composed
of the state superintendent and the commissioners of the counties.

counties into suitable school districts, to be as compact as practicable and not to exceed forty-nine nor to be less than nine square miles in area.[8]

Whereas the preceding constitution had opened all schools without regard to race or color, the present one provides that " separate schools shall be provided for children of the white and colored races, and no child of either race shall ever be permitted to attend a school provided for children of the other race.[9] The organic law omits all mention of compulsory attendance.

A state fund for the purpose of maintaining public schools is provided in section 11.[10] A three-mill tax is required to be levied annually on all taxable property the proceeds to be held in the treasuries of the respective counties and apportioned among the school districts thereof in proportion to the number of pupils enrolled in the public schools of the respective districts. Moreover, an annual tax of one dollar is levied on each male, the yield of which must be expended in the school district where collected. In addition, the General Assembly is authorized to levy such supplementary taxes as may be deemed necessary.[11]

During the last decade of the nineteenth century wealth greatly increased in the South. This became the basis of substantial increases in school revenues and the foundation of a new attitude toward public education. Moreover, there was an "awakening of class consciousness" among the people of the rural sections as another influence for improved school facilities.[12] These forces, together with the elim-

[8] Art. xi, sec. 5; see *Constitution, 1868*, art. x, sec. 3.

[9] Art. xi, sec. 7; see, *Constitution, 1868*, art. x, sec. 10.

[10] Section 9 prohibits the use of the property or credit of the state to benefit sectarian institutions of any kind.

[11] Art. xi, sec. 6.

[12] For a description of rural improvements, see Yates Snowden (ed.), *History of South Carolina* (Chicago, 1920), vol. ii, p. 1048.

ination of the race issue, prepared the way for effective educational advance.[13]

The need for organized agencies to carry on propaganda to acquaint the people with actual conditions and needs was met in large part by the " Ogden Movement ", also known as the Southern Conference Movement or the Southern Education Movement.   The work of the Conference for Education in the South,[14] the Southern Education Board, and the General Education Board had a powerful influence in promoting active campaigns for better public schools.[15]   In South Carolina a movement for the improvement of school conditions and interests in the state began in the conference held in Columbia, April 11, 1903, under the auspices of the Southern Education Board.   This conference was the first of a series of similar meetings.

The High School Act was passed in 1907.   It provided state aid for secondary schools and placed them under state supervision.   While the state board of education was given the duty of inspection and classification, the details of management were left to the local high school boards.[16]   The first high school appropriation of $50,000, made in 1907, marked the beginning of direct state financial support of public schools.   Although article XI, section 6, of the constitution of 1895, contemplates the levying of a general tax in order to guarantee a minimum term for every school, this guarantee was not actually put into effect until 1933.[17]   It is not to be understood, however, that school funds were not expanding, even though not uniformly.   By 1909-10, the

[13] See Knight, *Public Education in the South*, pp. 425-428.

[14] At the instance of this conference, the Southern Education Board was organized in 1901.   A year later, the General Education Board was formed and began to cooperate with it.

[15] See Knight, *op. cit.*, p. 432.

[16] *Acts of 1907*, p. 520.

[17] See *infra*.

figure passed the two-million mark, amounting to $2,053,-599.40.[18]

A local option law regarding compulsory attendance was signed February 20, 1915.[19] The school district was made the unit of adoption and operation. When this statute went into effect, July 1, 1915, one hundred and thirty-one districts in thirty counties accepted its provisions—six by election and one hundred and twenty-five by petition.[20] During the same year, a supervisor of schools in textile villages was provided by law. The teaching of agriculture in the public schools was not undertaken until the session of 1915-16, when three itinerant agricultural teachers were employed.[21]

The legislative session of 1919 resulted in many progressive laws.[22] Some of the most significant features deserve specific mention. All children between six and fourteen years were required to attend school for eighty days during each year. Schools for adults were permitted to be organized in any school district. Summer schools or county institutes were to be conducted under authority given the state superintendent. The Equalizing Act guaranteed a seven months school in any district voting an eight-mill tax, enrolling twenty-five pupils under each teacher, maintaining an average attendance of fifteen pupils in each classroom, and using the schedule of salaries fixed in the law.

Thus an attempt was made to set up a working standard for rural communities.[23] This act was a landmark in rural

[18] See "Report of State Superintendent of Education", 1909, *Reports and Resolutions*, 1910, vol. iii, p. 840.

[19] *Acts of 1915*, p. 108. See *Code 1932*, chap. 122, art. 6.

[20] *Report of State Superintendent of Education*, 1915, pp. 22, 23.

[21] *Ibid.*

[22] These new laws were issued in pamphlet form as " School Laws of South Carolina, Edition, 1919 ".

[23] *Acts for 1920*, p. 1137. This law supplemented and extended the rural Graded School Act, *Acts of 1917*, p. 100, and as amended, *Acts of 1919*, p. 236.

school development and was extremely important, for South Carolina's problem was and remains essentially rural. The legislature appropriated certain sums of money for special purposes, such as the transportation of children, the erection and improvement of school buildings, the establishment of school libraries, the support of high schools, and instruction in agriculture. The General Assembly also complied with the provisions of the Smith-Hughes Law for vocational training. However, as the state superintendent pointed out, three fundamental needs still awaited consideration: " A state tax for schools, professional supervision, and a proper standard of certification and examination of teachers ".[24]

State appropriations increased at a tremendous rate. By 1923, they had reached the figure of $1,859,336.53, but this sum did not fulfill the state's pledged obligations to the schools.[25] It was seen that the system must be changed. To replace the state aid laws, which were too complex, the state superintendent urged a general law which he maintained would be " more simple, equitable, constructive and progressive ".[26]

By the time the General Assembly convened for its annual session in 1924, sentiment favored making the state the principal school unit, for it was generally conceded that the local unit was wholly inadequate for the purpose. For the first time in the history of South Carolina, the legislature passed a law that guaranteed something like equal educational advantage to the children of the state. No longer would some schools run as little as forty days in some localities and as long as two hundred days in others of the same or neighboring counties. Under the operation of the law enacted

[24] *Report*, 1919, p. 9. The thirteen acts authorizing and governing state aid, 1917-20, are listed in this officer's *Report* for 1920.

[25] A total of $1,998,386.03 was received from outside sources.

[26] *Report*, 1923, p. 15. See the plan advanced by him, *ibid.*, chap. iii.

at this time, commonly known as the 6-0-1 Law, no white child in the state was to have a shorter term than seven months.

This law stipulated that the state would appropriate a sufficient sum each year to pay the salaries of all public school teachers under a prescribed schedule for the first six months, provided the district or county ran its school or schools an additional month. A four-mill tax was levied upon all taxable property of each county, in addition to the constitutional three-mill tax, to supplement the appropriation from the state.[27] In this way a considerable part of the financial burden was to be shifted from the district to the state, and provision was made to run even the weakest school for a minimum period. The local district board of trustees was authorized to run the school for a period of time longer than seven months and, within its discretion, to pay salaries in excess of the fixed schedule, but such excess salaries were required to be paid out of the funds of the district or county in which the school was located. Nor could the salaries paid by the state be in excess of those paid locally for the additional period.[28] In a word, the 6-0-1 Law may be described as an effort to levy school taxes where the wealth existed and to spend the revenues where the children were.

Under the old laws the state appropriated $2,253,400 for the scholastic year, 1923-24; under the new law, the appropriation for 1924-25 amounted to $3,009,800 or an increase of $756,400.

The length of the school year for both races in 1923-24 was 119 days while that of the following year was 142 days. This represented an increase for the white schools from 148

[27] *Acts of 1924*, p. 916; *Code 1932*, secs. 5473-5493.

[28] Power W. Bethea, auditor and statistician of the State Department of Education, estimated that South Carolina's school system was about thirty-nine per cent more efficient in 1924 than in 1914. See his *School Progress*, p. 97.

to 167, or 19 days.   The negro schools increased from 87 to 114, or 27 days.[29]

" The passage of the Equalizing Law has greatly fostered the consolidation of schools.   Its enactment has meant the death knell to the one-teacher school ", wrote the state superintendent in 1925.[30]   Within the first year of its operation the white one-teacher schools in the state decreased from 693 to 564.   The same type of negro school was reduced from 1,868 to 1,721.

The school law was materially modified in 1933.[31]   In effect the 6-0-1 law became a 6-0-0 law as the legislature removed the obligation of local school authorities of providing an extra month of the school term in order to qualify for state aid.   Under the new law the state assumes the responsibility of providing funds sufficient to pay an average salary of $60 per month to all elementary and high school teachers for a term of six months.   In addition, each school is allowed for supervision or incidentals seven per cent of the amount payable to it for salaries.   State aid is based on enrolment and average attendance of the previous year.   As under the old law, longer school terms and excess salaries are permitted at the discretion of the board of trustees or county board of education and at local expense.

With the view of lifting a part of the tax burden on property, the legislature repealed the four-mill school levy. Furthermore, local authorities were authorized to reduce all existing special levies in their respective counties.[32]   In lieu

[29] *Report of State Superintendent of Education*, 1925, p. 20.

[30] *Ibid.*, pp. 20, 21.

[31] *Acts of 1933*, pp. 567-582.

[32] This authority was to be exercised by " local boards of trustees and the county boards of education and by the Senator and half of the members of the House of Representatives of the respective counties; *Provided*, that no tax levy for retiring any bonds or other indebtedness of such school district shall be affected hereby ". *Ibid.*, p. 571. The law

of revenue so removed a new plan of finance included increased taxes on income, a tax on intangibles, additional business license fees, and a license tax on beverage (beer and wine) permits. From income thus provided the sum of $1,823,000 was specifically allocated for support of schools and was to be in addition to $1,124,000 appropriated in the regular appropriation bill for the school term of 1933-1934.[33]

2. Relative Position

The explanation of South Carolina's relative position in education among the states is not far to seek. First and foremost is the fact that she must provide two systems of education with limited funds. She has a relatively greater number of children than any state in the Union. In 1930, for every thousand males in the state there were 1,757 chil-

stipulated that additional local taxes could be levied by submitting the proposal to qualified electors, or by county delegations through legislative enactment. In 1931 the school bonded indebtedness in South Carolina was $19,753,112 or $11.36 per capita. This was approximately fifteen per cent of all bonded indebtedness reported for the entire state (state, county and municipality). In 1934 it was $18,474,752 and represented about forty-five per cent of the estimated value of school property.

In 1930 the total for 48 states had reached the amount of $2,425,796,439, or $19.84 per person. See State Department of Education, "School Bonded Indebtedness in South Carolina," *Statistical Research No. 15* (February, 1935), pp. 1, 10.

[33] The State Finance Committee was authorized to issue notes not to exceed $2,087,748, bearing five per cent interest, to pay 1932-1933 state aid and the deficit of 1931-1932. Unable to obtain credit from any financial institution, the state was forced to borrow from the school teachers through the issuance of so-called teachers' notes, in lieu of cash payment of overdue salaries.

The grand total of school expenditures for 1933-34 was $12,350,881, to which sum the state contributed $3,421,009. Federal aid amounted to approximately $400,000. See *Report of State Superintendent of Education*, 1934, pp. 3, 65, 113.

In February, 1935, South Carolina applied for a federal grant of $425,767 to enable the rural schools to complete the 1934-35 term.

dren of school age for whom education had to be provided. To maintain two systems of education for a large number of children scattered over a wide area with an extremely low property value per capita is the task that challenges South Carolina at a time of general economic retardation.[34]

Illiteracy among the states ranges from 0.8 per cent in Iowa to 14.9 per cent in South Carolina. During the last census decade the white illiteracy in this state was reduced from 6.6 per cent to a 5.2 per cent, while that of the negroes was brought down from 29.3 to 26.9 per cent. Only six states had a greater proportion of white illiterates than South Carolina, namely, Tennessee, North Carolina, Kentucky, Louisiana and New Mexico. Illiteracy among the negroes, who represent 45 per cent of the total population of South Carolina, was the highest in the Union. Perhaps the most disappointing feature of the census report was that illiteracy of day school age in this state, from ten to twenty-one years, showed a decrease of only eight-tenths of one per cent. But one need not expect more until an effective compulsory attendance law is enacted and sympathetically enforced.

The brighter side of the picture is seen in the progress made in adult education.[35] Illiteracy among persons over twenty-one years of age, upon whom the fight was begun fifteen years ago, has decreased 4.4 per cent.[36] In 1930, there were 1857 adult schools in which 23,925 persons were taught to read or write, or both. It is estimated that South Carolina has appropriated over a half million dollars since

[34] See Mitchell and Mitchell, *Industrial Revolution in the South*, pp. 297 et seq.

[35] Reference here is not to continued study for educated adults, but to elementary instruction of the illiterate.

[36] *Report of State Superintendent of Education*, 1931, p. 85. During 1934 the Federal Relief Administration contributed approximately $175,000 to adult elementary education in South Carolina. See *Report of States Superintendent of Education*, 1934, pp. 51-57.

1916 for this purpose. These state funds have been supplemented by county appropriations, donations from cotton mill interests, and from educational foundations. Such public-spirited citizens as Dr. Patterson Wardlaw, the veteran educator in the University of South Carolina and a pioneer in the campaign against illiteracy; Miss Wil Lou Gray, the active and inspiring adult school supervisor; and Mr. Alex Long, a cotton manufacturer who has given liberally, have carried forward a state-wide campaign.

Unfortunately, however, adult education in South Carolina has been too largely restricted to a campaign against illiteracy. Of course, that necessarily must constitute the first step in many cases, but merely to teach an individual to read and write is only a beginning. The state is dreadfully in need of a comprehensive program, particularly in the rural sections, that will include teaching principles of child hygiene, intelligent home management, and good citizenship. Such a program has been promoted by the South's leading agriculturist, Mr. David R. Coker, in Darlington County with marked success. The Extension Department of the State University should be re-established and should function in close cooperation with the extension services of Clemson College and Winthrop College in this important work. With the view of precipitating a veritable revolution in the promotion of a state-wide plan, a committee of county teachers might well be appointed on each of the local boards to operate a program in each of the several communities.

Public education is comparatively young in South Carolina and the idea of education for all the children has not yet entered the minds of some of the people. This is clearly evidenced in the absence of an effective compulsory attendance law. In 1930 there were 673,613 children in the state within the public school age (6-20): 339,736, white and 333,877, negro. The percentage of school population enrolled was 73 per cent for the whites and 64 per cent for the negroes.[37] For years the state superintendent has pleaded for compulsory education for both races. Though this question had been agitated and discussed for a quarter of a century, it was not until the closing days of the 1928 session of the legislature that such a bill was passed. But it was vetoed by Governor Richards. He held it to be unnecessary on the ground that the present local option law was sufficient, and maintained that South Carolina's educational system was "as fine as any in the country". Was he not refusing to face the facts and, like so many others, did he not resent the suggestion that the educational system of this state was not what it should be? Perhaps the real reason of the veto was the racial question and is expressed in the following paragraph: "South Carolina has a condition that is peculiarly her own, and while it is not necessary to discuss this phase of the question, it should be evident to every one that this condition of itself makes a state-wide compulsory law both impracticable and inexpedient ".[38]

3. Operation of Present System

The state superintendent of education is the executive officer of the State Department of Education. He has general supervision over the public school funds, and it is his duty

. . . to visit every county in the State as often as practicable for the purpose of inspecting the schools, awakening an interest favorable to the cause of education, and diffusing as widely as possible, by public addresses and personal communications with

[37] *Report of the State Superintendent of Education*, 1931, p. 96. In 1934 the population of children in public school age was 677,587: white, 344,697 and negro, 332,890. The percentage enrolment was 75 and 69, respectively. *Report of State Superintendent of Education*, 1934, p. 66.

[38] *House Journal*, 1929, p. 59. See recommendation of Joint Committee on Economy and Consolidation, 1922, *Report*, sec. 7, p. 67.

school officers, teachers and parents, a knowledge of existing defects and of desirable improvements in the government and instruction of the said schools.[39]

He is required to prepare and transmit to the several county superintendents of education school registers, blank certificates, reports, and such other suitable blanks, forms and printed instructions " as may be necessary to aid school officers and teachers in making their reports and carrying into full effect the various provisions of the school laws of this state ".[40] By and with the advice of the state board of education, it is his duty to secure uniformity in the use of textbooks throughout the state. As the secretary of the board, he is the custodian of its records, papers and effects, and keeps the minutes of its proceedings.[41] The county superintendents' reports are consolidated by the state superintendent and forwarded to the General Assembly as a part of his own annual report.[42]

In his annual report to the legislature, this officer must show:

(1) The whole number of pupils enrolled in the free common schools of the state, and the number in each county.

(2) The number in attendance, according to race and sex.

(3) The number of free schools in the state.

(4) The number of pupils studying each of the branches taught.

(5) The average salary paid teachers and administrators, of each sex.

(6) The value of public schoolhouse, grounds, equipment, etc.

[39] *Code 1932*, sec. 5273.
[40] *Ibid.*
[41] *Ibid.*, sec. 5282.
[42] *Ibid.*, sec. 2125.

(7) Information in regard to teachers' county institutes.

(8) Such other information as he may deem important in regard to the general condition and growth of the public schools of the state.[43]

The personnel and certain powers of the state board of education, as have been noted,[44] are fixed by the constitution. The governor, the superintendent of education, and seven persons, one from each of the old congressional districts appointed by the governor for a term of four years, constitute the board. This body meets on the call of its chairman, or upon the request of a majority of its members. It has power to adopt rules and regulations not inconsistent with the laws of the state for its own government and for the government of the free public schools; to prescribe and enforce rules for the examination of teachers; to prescribe a standard of certification of teachers; to prescribe and enforce the course of study and the use of a uniform series of textbooks in the public schools; and to review on appeal decisions of the county boards of education.[45]

The state board of education functions as an advisory body to the state superintendent in the performance of his duties.[46] It also operates as the state board of vocational training to cooperate with the Federal Government in the administration of the Smith-Hughes Law.[47] The state board appoints, upon the recommendation of the state sup-

---

[43] *Code 1932*, sec. 5274. This office has grown from a staff of two in 1877, to one of twenty-eight in 1934. Through generosity of the General Education Board, in 1929, two noteworthy divisions were added: (1) Schoolhouse Planning, (2) Research and Information. The writer is greatly indebted to Dr. H. L. Fulmer, Director of the latter division, for much information and many helpful suggestions.

[44] See chapter I, General Administration.

[45] *Code 1932*, sec. 5289.

[46] *Ibid.*, sec. 5288.

[47] *Ibid.*, sec. 5283.

erintendent, two examiners as a state board of examiners for a term of four years.[48] The board is also authorized, as a part of its function, to provide for teachers' institutes and summer schools in its discretion.[49] Finally, the law wisely provides that the state board of education shall act as a board of appeal, in so far as the alleged grievance may relate to law or fact, for " any person or persons who may feel himself aggrieved by any action of any board of trustees, ..."[50]

At the head of the county school system is the county superintendent of education. The law provides that " there shall be elected by the qualified electors of the county a County Superintendent of Education for each county, who shall hold his office for a term of four years and until his successor is elected and qualifies ".[51] There are no legal qualifications required as professional training for the office. By the terms of the law, it is the duty of this officer: [52]

(1) To visit the schools, note the course of study and method of instruction, and make such recommendations as may be necessary to the end that uniformity may be secured as far as practicable.

(2) To acquaint himself as far as possible with the character and condition of each school, and make such suggestions in private to the teachers as to him shall appear necessary to the good order of the school and the progress of the pupils.

[48] *Ibid.*, sec. 5292.

[49] *Ibid.*, sec. 5294.

[50] *Ibid.*, sec. 5304.

[51] *Ibid.*, sec. 5308. Exceptions to this rule: Georgetown County, appointed by county board, *Acts of 1931*, p. 184; Dillon County, appointed by governor on recommendation of county board, *Acts of 1927*, p. 254; Charleston County, appointed by popularly elected county board, *Acts of 1931*, p. 323.

[52] *Code 1932*, secs. 5310, 5312, 5313, 5321, and 5324.

(3) To note the condition of the schoolhouse and furniture, and make suggestions to the several boards of trustees.

(4) To aid the teachers in all proper efforts to improve themselves in their profession by conducting teachers' institutes, etc.

(5) To keep a complete and full record of school district funds.

(6) To file with the state superintendent of education within two months after the end of the scholastic year a full and accurate report of all schools under his supervision.

(7) To make an annual report of all claims filed, audited and allowed and ordered paid by him during each fiscal year to the presiding judge of the Circuit Court.

(8) To attend the annual settlement of the county treasurer with the comptroller general.

(9) To report to the county treasurer, on or before the fifteenth day of July each year, by school districts, all claims approved by him for the school year last preceding.

(10) To keep a register of all claims approved by him and of such other matters as the state superintendent may require of him, in the form prescribed by that officer.

(11) To examine and approve in writing each application and accompanying program of daily classroom work before state aid is granted.

The manifold duties of the county superintendent of education preclude the possibility of any great degree of personal supervision or real direction of the schools of the county. At best, it must be done by indirection. The overwhelming amount of office and other administrative work required of him causes the rural schools to suffer in particular. As the state superintendent of education has observed, " a county superintendent who can do efficient work in supervision in all the schools of his county and who can do besides all of the clerical work and other work demanded of his office, is truly an ideal servant of the people." [53]

The next most important administrative agency of the county school unit is the county school board. The law provides that this board shall be composed of three members, one of whom shall be the county superintendent of education, and the other two members to be appointed for a term of four years by the state board of education.[54] This board is constituted " an advisory body with whom the county superintendent of education shall have the right to consult when he is in doubt as to his official duty, and also a tribunal for determining any matter of local controversy in reference to the construction or administration of the school laws. . . ." [55] Its decisions are not final, however; either party has a right to appeal to the state board.

The county board meets at least twice a year for the purpose of examining applicants for teachers' certificates and for the transaction of other business. Other meetings are held during the year, subject to regulations prescribed by the state board of education. Any certificate granted by a county board may be revoked by the state board " for immoral or improper conduct, or evident unfitness for teaching ".[56]

[53] *Report of State Superintendent of Education*, 1925, p. 2.

[54] *Code 1932*, sec. 5335. The following are exceptions: Berkley County, 2 appointed by the governor and 2 by state board; Charleston County, 5 popularly elected; Dillon County, 2 popularly elected; Florence County, 6 appointed by governor on recommendation of county legislative delegation; Georgetown County, 3 appointed by district board of trustees, and 3 by governor and legislative delegation; Greenville County, 4 by state board on recommendation legislative delegation; Marlboro County, 4 appointed by state board; Spartansburg County, 2 appointed by state board on recommendation legislative delegation; and, Dorchester County, 4 by governor and legislative delegation. *Ibid.*, secs. 5335-5337.

[55] *Ibid.*, 5348.

[56] *Ibid.*, sec. 5349.

It is the duty of the county boards to divide their counties into convenient school districts,[57] and to appoint for each of these districts three school trustees for two-year terms.[58] State aid for the erection of school buildings must have the approval of the county board, which agency also regulates the opening and closing of the school terms of the several schools of the county.[59]

Before devoting special attention to each of the several phases of the administration of the public schools and attempting to evaluate the present system as a whole, it seems appropriate at this point to discuss existing conditions in regard to the negro. Without special comment on negro schools, any discussion of public education in South Carolina would be misleading. The proper education of the negro is one of the most confusing problems facing the South. Intelligent and sympathetic attention is imperative.[60]

South Carolina can hardly boast of its education of this unfortunate race in the past. The idea early arose that it was dangerous to educate the slaves. In 1834, the legislature forbade anyone to teach the slave to read or write. This law, however, was passed over the protests of many of the leading citizens of the state and was often disregarded.

During Reconstruction the schoolmaster followed the soldier and the constitution of 1868 removed the difference between the legal rights of whites and blacks. The Freedmen's Aid Society of the Methodist Episcopal Church and the American Missionary Society, in particular, were active around Saint Helena and Beaufort and the tidewater section

[57] *Ibid.*, sec. 5350.

[58] *Ibid.*, sec. 5369.

[59] *Code 1932*, secs. 5389, 5401. The scope of this study does not admit of a discussion of the organization and administration of the separate school districts.

[60] For a discussion of this problem, see Knight, *Public Education in the South*, p. 455.

generally. Yet the progress of benevolent societies was slow. They accomplished little more than to establish schools in widely distant points. For generations, a majority of the white people in South Carolina believed that if a negro were educated his usefulness as a worker would be lessened. It was not that they placed positive obstacles in the administration of the law; they simply withheld their moral support.[61]

It is claimed by many that one of the most serious difficulties encountered in educating the negro is the attitude of the race toward education. It is maintained that " the mass of negroes do not look upon education as a preparation for work, but as a means of enjoying honor and profit with little labor ".[62] A misconceived objective of education does exist in a measure but it would certainly be corrected through adequate facilities for proper training and development.

The figures reveal the fact that the colored child is yet far from receiving an equal opportunity with the white child. This relative position will continue to exist so long as the negro's relative economic condition continues to be what it is. His standard of living and his low wage scale are a challenge to his own initiative and to the development of the proper kind of leadership among his race; he also stands as a challenge to those who formulate the policy of the state. This retarded race needs more schooling, not only for their own sake but also for the sake of the communities in which they live. As Dr. G. Croft Williams has reminded us, " where there is a mass of ignorant folk, with low standards of living and cultural demands, the community is bound to lag ".[63]

[61] See Meriwether, *History of Higher Education*, pp. 123, 124; Snowden, *History of South Carolina*, vol. ii, p. 1155.

[62] *Ibid.*, p. 1156.

[63] Williams, *Social Problems in South Carolina*, pp. 32, 33.

The reader may conclude that South Carolina does not believe in schools for the colored race. On the contrary, there are signs that public sentiment for their proper education has been gaining in recent years. It is more and more recognized that a properly educated negro is a more efficient worker; that he is a more useful and contented citizen than the uneducated or improperly trained one.

The State Department of Education first attempted to supervise the work of the negro schools in South Carolina in 1917. Until 1924, this work was done by a single individual, whose salary and expenses were contributed by the General Education Board of New York. In July of that year, this board loaned the state another staff member for this purpose, and since 1925 has regularly contributed two full-time men.

Without the stimulus of assistance from outside the state from such sources as the General Education Board, the Rosenwald Fund, the Slater Board, and the Jeanes Foundation, the results accomplished would have been quite different. There were employed during the session, 1930-31, eighteen special teachers in as many counties of the state, a part of their salaries being paid from the Jeannes Fund and a part from the public school fund. These supervising teachers are worth many times the amount spent for their services. The county superintendent has little time for the supervision of colored schools and many of the rural teachers are so poorly trained that, in the opinion of the state superintendent, " much of the money today used in paying teachers in small rural schools is practically wasted ".[64]

This state officer reports that during the last ten or twelve years (prior to 1932), approximately five hundred negro schools were erected in the state, ranging all the way from

[64] *Report of State Superintendent Education*, 1931, p. 70.

the one-room building up through the modern high school.[65] These buildings cost nearly $3,000,000. Of this, the Rosenwald Foundation contributed practically $450,000; the negroes themselves, more than $500,000; the white people, more than $200,000; and the public school funds, the balance. There are yet, however, between 125,000 and 150,000 negro pupils attending school in tenant houses, lodge halls, churches, and other buildings of similar nature. The withdrawal of the State Building Fund at the 1931 session of the legislature halted progress in this field.[66]

It is generally believed in South Carolina that better results are obtained by placing colored teachers in charge of negro schools. The absence of sufficient facilities for training instructors of the same race is perhaps the most fundamental weakness in the education of the negro in this state at the present time. The teacher-training departments of the negro colleges are stressing preparation of high school teachers and are not furnishing elementary teachers fast enough. For several years, the State Department of Education has been successful in organizing eight or ten summer schools for this purpose. Unless the assistance of the General Board of New York is continued, or some other source is found, the operation of these summer schools will fall

[65] In 1931, of the 2,237 school buildings for negroes, 1,302 were one-teacher schools. Thus, a large proportion of colored children were attending schools of this type. There were only three negro high schools whose graduates received state high school diplomas, namely, Booker T. Washington High, at Columbia; Mayo High, at Darlington; and Sims High, at Union. See *ibid.*, pp. 68, 71. This number had increased to seven in 1934 by the addition of Emmett Scott High, at Rock Hill; Finley High, at Chester; Sterling High, at Greenville; Wilson High, at Florence. *Report of State Superintendent of Education*, 1934, p. 36.

[66] *Ibid.*, pp. 70, 71. Payment of Rosenwald Aid was discontinued at about the same time. Therefore, no aid except from the national relief agencies was available for the construction of buildings in 1934.

mainly upon the teachers attending them.[67] It is very un-likely that state appropriations can be had for this purpose for some time, on account of the demoralized conditions at-tendant on economic depression.

The grand total value of all negro school property in 1931 was $5,007,179, as compared to $36,593,581 of white schools. The total expenditures for negro and white schools for the session, 1930-31, were $1,695,606 and $12,990,632, respectively. Though the figures do not reveal the fact, some of the money charged to white schools should be as-signed as an expenditure for negro institutions—probably about fifteen per cent may be accounted for as cost of white supervision of negro schools.

In South Carolina, practically all negro children walk to school. In the entire state during the session of 1930-31, only $660.00 in public funds were spent in transportation of colored children. During the same period, transporta-tion of the white children cost the state $921,122. It might be added, however, that the money spent in the last instance was from the saving in the consolidation of white schools. Another of the explanations of this difference is that the negro schools lost state aid by failure to run seven months. Apart from these considerations, the figures speak for them-selves.[68]

In no other phase of our educational system do such gross inequalities exist as in the buildings and equipment provided for school children (white and colored) among the various districts. Thousands of the state's children are attending school in buildings that are totally inadequate to protect their

[67] *Report of State Superintendent of Education*, 1931, pp. 72, 73.

[68] Where no references are cited the facts in regard to the present operation of negro schools were gathered from conversations with the state superintendent and the director of the bureau of information and research of the Department of Education. Of course, the writer is re-sponsible for all errors of deduction.

health. Since the type of school plant is governed largely by the taxable wealth of the district, the capital outlay for buildings and equipment varies greatly from one locality to another. Beautiful consolidated schools grace the country-side in South Carolina today in some districts, while in others sufficient accomodations are notoriously lacking.

Under the school-building program the communities are required to furnish an equal amount to match state aid. During the quadrennial beginning in 1926, the sum of approximately $3,000,000 was spent annually for buildings and equipment. During the three preceding years, the average annual expenditure for new buildings was less than $100,000. Thus at the end of 1933 the physical plants were about $11,000,000 behind the standards of 1929. It was hoped that more favorable business conditions would soon warrant restoration of state aid.[69]

For several years the State Department of Education has been urging higher standards for teacher certification. This standard has been steadily raised. Approximately 2000 college graduates enter the teaching profession every year, and an increasing number of teachers are expending for their improvement a sum of money far out of proportion to that justified by their salaries. There is no dearth of well-trained teachers and there should be no difficulty in developing a professionally prepared personnel. Brighter prospects in this regard are comprehended in the new requirements that were adopted by the state board of education, December 4, 1931. These new standards became effective July 1, 1934

[69] See *Report of State Superintendent of Education*, 1933, pp. 62-63. With the aid of the Public Works Administration, approximately $1,500,000 worth of school buildings were constructed during 1934. *Report of State Superintendent of Education*, 1934, p. 29.

On February 9, 1935, the state ERA administrator announced that the South Carolina relief administration would conduct a comprehensive survey to determine the condition of school buildings in the state.

and are a result of the report of a committee that had made a study of the problem for six months.

As Dr. Fulmer has pointed out, " School consolidation is chiefly a rural problem and cannot be solved without transportation ".[70] Figures on file in the office of the Department of Education show that the pupil cost in average daily attendance for current or operative expenses in one-teacher schools is greater than that in the five or more teacher elementary schools. These figures also show that, in some cases, the difference in the cost of these two types of schools is greater than the average cost of transporting an elementary pupil. These figures are cited by Dr. Fulmer, who also reminds us that " in the one-teacher school, not only is the efficiency lowered, but the educational value of the investment per class period is greatly reduced ".

During the year 1930-31, the average cost of school transportation to the state per elementary pupil was $16.99, and $27.52 for the high school pupil.[71] A total number of 1669 buses was reported in operation, hauling a total of 43,958 white children or 17.64 per cent of those enrolled. The daily average bus cost per mile was $0.15 and the daily pupil cost per mile was $0.0057. The total cost of transportation represents 7.07 per cent of the total of white school expenditures for that period.[72] An interesting fact revealed, also, is that the daily pupil cost of district-owned buses was $0.022 less than that of the contract buses. The following

[70] "A Statistical Study of School Transportation in South Carolina", prepared by Dr. H. L. Fulmer, Director, Division of Information and Research, Department of Education. (Dec., 1931.)

[71] *Ibid.*, p. 1. Difference is probably due to lighter bus loads of the latter. For 1933-34 the average cost was $13.14 per elementary pupil and $21.07 for the high school pupil. *Report of State Superintendent of Education*, 1934, pp. 72, 118.

[72] *Ibid.*, p. 10.

comparison of the annual pupil cost of transportation with certain other states is also enlightening: [73]

1925-26, Florida	$26.73	1930-31, Georgia	$13.55
1924-25, Alabama	21.38	1928-29, North Carolina	11.67
1930-31, Maryland	25.60	1930-31, South Carolina	20.95
		1927-28, United States	31.90

The foregoing statistics are cited in such detail because of certain impressions that prevail in the state in regard to school transportation. In the first place, rumor has attached considerable graft to contract buses. The figures do show a slight discrepancy in favor of the district-owned buses. Therefore, wisdom suggests that a county-wide organization of operation and supervision be established. The variation among the districts within the same county is too great, and direction should be by the county board of education on a county unit basis. In the second place, transportation, as such, has been attacked in the newspapers under such facetious captions as, " Taking the State for a Ride ", " Ride the Riders ", and " How we Ride ". These editorials are often so reactionary as to attempt to measure conditions of today by standards of the age of the horse and buggy. Such arguments do not deserve comment. However, the present writer hastens to add that perhaps South Carolina has been too ambitious concerning this matter. For the present, general conditions being what they are, economy must be practiced to an abnormal degree. The state can ill afford to spend nearly a million dollars in transporting pupils while the schoolteachers themselves must go without pay. Nor has it been explained why it costs almost twice as much to transport a child in South Carolina as in North Carolina or in Georgia.

[73] *Ibid.*, p. 9.

4. Public School Finance

The promise of adequate educational opportunity demands a satisfactory program below which no community in the state shall be permitted to go. In an effort to realize this objective, however, it is necessary for the state to provide a system of finances that will distribute the burden of this minimum program upon the people in all localities according to their taxpaying ability.[74]

There is little doubt that we have far to go before these principles can be satisfied in South Carolina.[75]

State funds are commonly distributed on the basis of enrolment or attendance at schools. Since this distribution is generally made, wholly or in part, with relation to the ability and effort of the local units to support schools, such funds are known as equalization funds.[76]

All funds collected in any county under the 6-0-1 Law were retained and expended in the county where collected, and payments made from the state treasury to supplement this amount were paid from funds collected largely from indirect taxation. The law provided for the distribution of the 3-mill constitutional tax in the county where it was collected, on the basis of the enrolment of the preceding year. The statutory 4-mill tax was distributed in the county where it was collected, on the basis of the number of white teachers of the preceding year. The negro teachers were not included, in determining the latter allocation, because of the

---

[74] For a discussion of public school finance, see, for example, Paul R. Mort, "The Financing of American Schools", *South Carolina Education*, vol. xii, no. 5, p. 134 (1930).

[75] In 1931, the North Carolina General Assembly assumed complete state responsibility for the public school system of that state. See Gov. O. Max Gardner, "One State Cleans House", *Saturday Evening Post*, vol. 204, no. 27, p. 73 (Jan. 2, 1932).

[76] U. S. Dept. of Interior, Bureau of Education, *Education in United States* (1927), p. 9.

variation in the negro school terms from four months up. The difference in the amount raised in this way by these two county taxes and the amount which the state pledged as a guarantee of six-month salaries under the fixed minimum salary scale, was the amount to which the county was entitled as state aid under the 6-0-1 Law. The sum appropriated by the state for this purpose in 1932 was $3,394,329.[77]

This law constituted the most forward step in the education of all the children in South Carolina that had ever been taken, but serious defects are clearly discernible. In the first place, it failed as a plan to equalize school facilities throughout the state. Instead of rendering the major portion to the more backward districts, the aid went principally to the most prosperous counties. Five of the piedmont counties having white majorities, rich in factories and power installations, and large producing counties, received over a fourth of the total 6-0-1 appropriation. Spartanburg was the chief beneficiary, with Greenville a close second. These two counties received about $600,000 under the "equalizing" law. Such an arrangement can hardly be regarded as serving to equalize educational opportunity in the state.[78]

This situation resulted from two forces at work. The law was so administered that, for the most part, teachers were its beneficiaries. Inevitably the bulk of the state aid

[77] *Acts of 1932*, p. 1585. This law provided that the schedule of salaries for teachers as provided in secs. 5480 and 5481 of the *Code of 1932* would be reduced twelve and one-half (12½) per cent at the close of the scholastic year, 1931-32, *ibid.*, p. 1629. For a specific illustration of the method of distributing the 6-0-1 funds, see *Report of State Superintendent of Education*, 1928, pp. 6, 7.

Act No. 791, *Acts of 1932*, p. 1379, provides that high schools seeking state aid under the 6-0-1 Law may substitute 900 hours of work a year for the required nine-month session.

[78] See *Report of State Superintendent of Education*, 1931, p. 140.

fund went to the counties of preponderant white population, where the white teachers were. The second factor was the unequal and unfair property assessment.[79] This unfair advantage is clearly described by State Superintendent Hope, as follows: [80]

It is obviously true that the district which assesses its property at a high percentage of its true worth is penalized when it pays the State taxes. It again suffers a penalty when state funds are apportioned under the law. It will be seen, therefore, that districts which are assessed at a higher percentage of true valuation will receive a much smaller quota per teacher than they would if all districts were assessed at true value or at least on the same basis. They are penalized twice; first, when taxed for the State school revenue, and second, when this fund is apportioned as a basis of 6-0-1 support.

It is interesting to note that many of the districts assessing this property at a very low percentage of their true value for State purposes, experience no difficulty in voting a sufficient local levy to provide the necessary local funds. By pursuing this twofold policy of lowering its local valuation and increasing its local tax rate, it is guilty of actually defrauding the State at the expense of other districts and counties.

In repealing the four-mill school levy in 1933 the legislature removed the most obnoxious element of the 6-0-1 Law. Although the change was championed as an economy measure, it eliminates the advantage of unfair property assessment as a factor.[81]

The state's financial aid should be given to schools in proportion to the number of children who attend them, and without any relation to the number on the rolls. It is easy

[79] Inequitable evaluation of property for tax assessment is dealt with at length in Chapter III.

[80] *Report of State Superintendent of Education*, 1931, pp. 18, 19.

[81] See *supra*, p. 93.

to see how a system based on the latter lends itself much more readily to waste and extravagance. Each of the three governors since the passage of the present school law has urged this change. Governor McLeod sought reduction of appropriation for public schools on the basis of average attendance, plus ten per cent allowance for legitimate absences.[82] Governor Richards urged the change on the ground that it would create a stronger incentive for greater effort on the part of our local school authorities, not only to see to it that all of the children are in school, but that they are kept there for the full term.[83] Governor Blackwood estimated that it would net an annual saving of $500,000.[84]

The Bush Amendment to the 6-0-1 Law in 1931,[85] sponsored by the State Teachers' Association, was designed to increase the teaching load by increasing the enrolment and average attendance requirements of the preceding year as a basis for state aid. The teachers offered it as an economy measure and estimated that it would net an annual saving of $350,000 from the $3,500,000 appropriation.

The "load" of a first-rate teacher is already too heavy. To effect economy by crippling the efficiency of an experi-

[82] *Annual Message*, 1927, pp. 7, 8.

[83] *Annual Message*, 1928, p. 7.

[84] *Inaugural Address*, 1931, p. 5. As early as 1910, State Superintendent Swearington recommended apportioning the proceeds of the 3-mill constitutional tax on basis of average attendance. See his report for 1910, *Reports and Resolutions*, 1911, vol. iii, p. 845.

[85] *Acts of 1931*, p. 310. See proposed revision of 6-0-1 Law, suggested by Farmers' and Taxpayers' League in *News and Courier*, Jan. 19, 1932. Among other things, the League proposed that the present county taxes, levied in the counties for the support of schools, be retained as a county school fund to be distributed by the county board of education so as to assure each school a term of at least seven months. As a basis of distributing state aid, the total enrolment and the average attendance of the year immediately preceding would be added and divided by two, the result being the number of pupils to be taken into consideration.

enced and well-trained teacher is unintelligent and is lacking in a scientific approach to the school problem. Nor is there either logic or justice in attempting to solve the state's financial straits by cutting all salaries alike. A constructive program demands a plan for developing a high quality of professional teachers, who have prepared themselves for their life work. With approximately two teachers available for every position in South Carolina, there are too many apprentices in the school system of whom only a small minority expect or desire to spend their lives teaching. The best teachers are being driven from the state while the temporary recruits are being cared for.

In 1930, the average expenditure for current expenses per child enrolled in the nation was $71. Approximate expenditures in the Southern states on the same basis were: South Carolina, $30; Alabama, $25; Georgia, $23; Virginia, $35; Mississippi, $26; North Carolina, $32.[86]

It is interesting to note certain comparative statistics over the decade, 1922-1931. The per capita cost of public schools in South Carolina during that time increased from about $5.60 to $8.50. The total cost per pupil of both races on the basis of enrolment in 1921-22 was $19.86. For 1930-31, it amounted to $31.83. For the former year, state aid of $1,350,000 was 12.67 per cent of the public school funds; in the latter year, the amount appropriated by the state was $3,500,000 or 24.52 per cent.[87]

What South Carolina can do within the limits of her resources to improve public school finances involves consideration of the methods of taxation for schools, the distribution

---

[86] See *New International Year Book*, 1930.

[87] *Report of State Superintendent of Education*, 1922, pp. 19, 20; 1931, pp. 96-99. For 1933-34, the cost per pupil of both races on the basis of enrolment was $23.61. The amount appropriated by the state was approximately 27.7 per cent of the public school funds. *Report of State Superintendent of Education*, 1934, p. 71.

of school revenues, and the relation of school taxation to the
system of state and local taxation in general. In dealing
with taxation for schools, it is necessary to consider fairly
the demand for support of other functions of the state, as
well as the efficiency with which public moneys are expended.[88]   Economic conditions in 1933 emphasize the need
of an educational survey to the end that South Carolina can
the more intelligently approach the solution of her public
school problem.[89]

5. Administrative Reorganization

Rural education is the greatest problem in South Carolina's public school system today.   There are about 1,800
districts with approximately 6,000 persons having a hand in
the expenditure of school funds.   Under such an arrangement, economy is practically impossible.   Petty politics
abounds as in no other field of public activity.   That there
is need of a fundamental reorganization and redirection of
rural and small village education, is not even debatable.

The district system is extremely backward and is far behind administrative reform in other states.[90]   There is a
marked inequality in district lines, for property values are
vastly different in the several districts.   " District systems
as a rule are expensive, inefficient, inconsistent, short-sighted,

[88] Administration of finance in general, is the burden of Chapter II.

[89] A Joint Res. to authorize a survey and to appoint a commission was
rejected by the legislature in 1932, *House Journal*, 1932, p. 24.

In 1933, Governor Blackwood appointed a school commission of
eighteen educators and legislators to make a survey of South Carolina's
laws and to make recommendations to the 1934 legislature. This report,
however, was not completed in 1934.

For educational surveys and investigations recently undertaken in other
states, see *Biennial Survey of Education in U. S., 1928-1930*, U. S. Office
of Education, Bulletin, 1931, no. 20, pp. 2, 3.

[90] For a discussion of the rural school situation, see *Report of State
Superintendent of Education*, 1933, pp. 40-44.

unprogressive, penurious.   They lead to great and unnecessary multiplication of small and inefficient schools; they lead
to marked inequalities in schools, terms and educational advantages ", writes State Superintendent Hope.[91]   In line
with the best thought on the subject, he recommends the
county unit as the natural unit for this organization.   Centralized administration under this plan would provide an integrated administration with a county-wide budget and
county-wide buying of supplies.   Even a larger administrative unit would be preferred, but this is not feasible until
the forty-six counties of the state are consolidated into a
smaller number, as they should be.

Moreover, the county system should provide for a board
of education consisting of five members elected by the
people.   This board should appoint a county superintendent
of education, selected on the basis of merit as a teacher and
as an educator.[92]   This is designed to remove the county
superintendent from politics, to secure professional administrators for the position, and also to effect economy by
reducing the overhead from duplicated efforts of the various
school districts.[93]   Dr. Fulmer has expressed the following
opinion:

[91] *Report of State Superintendent of Education*, 1931, p. 17.   See Fred
Engelhardt, " The Future School District ", *American School Journal*,
vol. lxxxi, pp. 51, 52 (July, 1930).

[92] As long ago as 1901, State Superintendent John J. McMahan maintained that the county superintendent should be the " head teacher " appointed by the county board.

[93] See address of Dr. H. L. Fulmer before a state-wide public school
conference, held in Columbia, Dec. 29, 1930, as reported in *Charleston
Evening Post* of that date.   Also, see a study made by South Carolina
Council in 1931, *Report on Education*, p. 5.   This organization includes a
large number of the state's most intelligent citizens in a study of the
most important problems in South Carolina and is making a splendid
contribution of enlightened leadership.

In order to improve school affairs in general over the State, there should be a reorganization which would take the County Superintendent out of politics and establish a county unit plan of school administration and finance on a strictly business plan. In this way, the children of the county would receive equal educational opportunity under a plan supervised by trained persons operating under a strict budget system. As a result, there would be a great saving as well as a great improvement in our school efficiency.[94]

The ideal county board of education would not include teachers. As a governing board, it would be their function to apply business principles to county finance and formulate the general policy. However, administration of the professional details should be left entirely in the hands of the county superintendent chosen by them and well-trained for that purpose.[95] There should be only one superintendent in the county and he should be superintendent of all the schools in fact.

Recent legislation shows a tendency toward placing greater responsibility upon the county as a unit in educational administration. Generally counties are authorized under certain conditions to form county unit systems. Such administrative units are fairly well developed in the following Southern States: Alabama, Florida, Kentucky, Louisiana, Maryland, North Carolina, Tennessee and Virginia.[96]

The growth of educational systems is marked by a progressive shifting from local to central authorities. The office of superintendent of public education is found in every

[94] In a letter to the present writer.

[95] North Carolina requires the county superintendent to be a college graduate with two years of successful teaching and a person of good business qualifications and executive ability. See *Biennial Survey of Education*, 1928-1930, U. S. Office of Education, Bulletin no. 20, p. 14.

[96] *Ibid.*, p. 11.

state. While the title may vary somewhat, the duties are similar and demand a high order of business and executive ability as well as professional skill.

The importance of this office is so great as to require the highest type of leadership available.[97] Therefore, this individual should be a recognized leader in educational work, with broad scholarship and a large vision of the educational and social needs of the state. It is very doubtful whether popular election is the method best calculated to secure this result. If South Carolina is to be assured always of a real leader, the method of selecting him must be changed from popular election to appointment by some responsible authority.[98] He should be freed from politics. The present superintendent recognizes the soundness of this contention and is in accord with it.[99] Popular elections have no place in filling such an office.[100] It is recommended here that a state commissioner of education be selected by the state board of education and that he serve at the pleasure of the board. Nor should he necessarily be chosen from this state.

It is intended that the commissioner of education would be the executive officer of the department, having direct charge of the administration. To this end, he should have authority to establish such bureaus within the department as

[97] See Knight, *Public Education in the South*, p. 450.

[98] No reflection is intended on the incumbent, who is splendidly equipped for his position.

[99] Interview with the writer. See recommendations of the South Carolina Council, *Report on Education*, p. 5. See, also, the Brookings Institution, *Report on a Survey of the Organization and Administration of the State Government of North Carolina* (Washington, 1930), p. 161.

[100] The old method of election still prevails in the majority of states, but those that have reorganized their departments of education have changed to appointive methods. See W. F. Dodd, *State Government* (N. Y., 1928), p. 227. A Joint Res. (H. 1357) to amend the constitution to this effect was introduced in the South Carolina Legislature, 1932. *House Journal*, 1932, p. 378.

he may deem necessary for its efficient and economical operation.

The state board of education should consist of seven members, appointed by the governor with consent of the senate for overlapping terms of seven years.[101] It would determine the general policy of the department and would continue to act as the board of vocational training.[102]

II. INSTITUTIONS OF HIGHER LEARNING

South Carolina maintains five institutions of higher learning for the white race.[103] These are the University of South Carolina at Columbia; The Citadel, The Military College of South Carolina, at Charleston; Clemson Agricultural College at Clemson College; The Medical College of South Carolina at Charleston; and Winthrop College, The South Carolina College for Women, at Rock Hill.

The General Assembly elects the governing boards of the State University, of the Citadel, of Winthrop College, of the State Medical College, and six of the members of Clemson College. Seven members, a majority, of the last-named college are self-perpetuating by the terms of the bequest to the state. Incidentally, the Clemson College board alone is not served by the governor and the state superintendent of education in ex-officio capacities. Other ex-officio members are as follows: the chairmen of the education committees of the senate and the house serve on the board of the University and that of Winthrop; those of the military committees on The Citadel Board of Visitors; and the chairmen

[101] The fourteen judicial circuits might well serve as a territorial basis by selecting one member from two circuits grouped for that purpose.

[102] See recommendations of the National Institute of Public Administration, *Survey of Arkansas*, pp. 60, 61. For changes recently suggested by several governors, see Harvey Walker, "Governors' Messages" in *American Political Science Review*, vol. xxv, p. 359 (May, 1931).

[103] The Colored Normal College is discussed *infra*, p. 149.

of the committees on medical affairs on the Board of Trustees of the Medical College.[194]

Ordinarily, state appropriations are itemized. However, since 1931 the legislature has found it expedient to make its appropriations for the maintenance of these institutions in lump sums.[105] The pall of the economic depression made it necessary to cut the several requests to such an extent that the General Assembly wisely allowed the governing boards to decide how the funds should best be spent. As a check upon the exercise of this discretion, the authorities of the institutions were required to make a quarterly report of all expenditures to the Budget Commission.[106]

With the rapid growth of each of the state-supported colleges, the matter of permanent improvements has become quite a problem. In recent years, the General Assembly has allowed tuition fees to be retained for this purpose. This mode of procedure has been criticised by some,[107] but it appears to be the only available source under present conditions. In any event, financing of permanent improvements can not be made by direct appropriations from current taxation.[108]

As early as 1899, Governor Ellerbe urged "a better organized and a more properly correlated school system from the primary grade to the collegiate degree".[109] He regarded the coordination of the collegiate institutions as the most necessary step in that direction. A legislative committee that investigated conditions in 1910 reported in part: [110]

---

[104] *Code 1932*, chap. 123.

[105] Deposit of these funds in banks is protected by law. See *Acts of 1932*, p. 1629.

[106] *Acts of 1932*, p. 1628.

[107] For example, see Governor Richards, *Annual Message*, 1928, p. 7.

[108] In 1934 the legislature refused to consider the possibility of financial aid under the public works program of the National Administration.

[109] *Reports and Resolutions*, 1899, vol. ii, p. 178.

[110] *Reports and Resolutions*, 1911, vol. iv, p. 448.

Your committee is impressed with the idea that the lack of system of higher education in this State is such that the State's educational energies and resources, instead of being concentrated, are too much scattered and dissipated for the want of a general head and a definite plan.

A joint legislative committee in 1921 arrived at the following conclusion:

The State supported colleges on the whole have been reasonably successful despite the fact that each is managed separately and little conspicuous attention has been paid to the development of a rounded out system of higher education. Nevertheless wide variations in the per capita costs of educating students, in the form of internal organization, in the costs of similar buildings, in the efficiency of maintenance operations, and in the effectiveness of the accounting and record keeping systems exist. Some of the colleges undertake without adequate teaching personnel and with inadequate equipment to give courses that others can give much better and more effectively because they are well prepared to do such work. . . . When requests for appropriations are made to the Legislature the various colleges are in effect competitors with each other and there is little opportunity to consider the State's educational system as a whole. The time may not be ripe immediately to place all of the State supported colleges under one management; it can hardly be questioned, however, that some unification is highly desirable in order that there may be a common recognition of the place of each institution in the educational system, that the money available for State supported colleges may be distributed in accordance with the needs of the various institutions, and that the forms of organization and administration found efficient in one may be extended to others less successful in the same matters, while as soon as the State's finances permit the centralization of administrative control seems essential.[111]

[111] *Report of Joint Committee on Economy and Consolidation,* 1922, pp. 10, 11. Niels Christensen, the present president of the Farmers' and Taxpayers' League, was chairman of the committee. The firm of Griffenhagen & Associates made the expert investigation.

While the report of the Joint Committee on Efficiency and Consolidation, created under a concurrent resolution approved March 25, 1925, made no recommendation in regard to the consolidation of the administration of state colleges, the question has been revived during the present economic distress. A bill was introduced in the house during the 1931 session, seeking " to reorganize the State institutions of higher learning, to readjust their divisions of labor and coordinate their activities for economy and efficiency, . . ." [112]   In 1932, a commission was created " to study and report upon plans looking to the co-ordination along general lines of the activities of the Higher Institutions of Learning ".[113]   This commission, at its meeting in Columbia, June 15, 1932, announced its decision to withhold its recommendation to the General Assembly until education experts could make a detailed study.[114]

The extent to which it is advisable to consolidate the control and direction of South Carolina's colleges is a question the answer of which should not be attempted until after an intensive study has been made by impartial experts. Considerable profit is also to be derived from the experience of neighboring states whose problems and conditions are similar to those of South Carolina.[115]

[112] *House Journal*, 1931, p. 1208. Governor Blackwood in 1934 recommended the consolidation of the University, the Medical College, The Citadel and Winthrop College. See his *Annual Message*, 1934, p. 4.

[113] Created under Joint Res. no. 1972, approved March 7, 1932, *Acts of 1932*, p. 2108. See recommendations contained in a proposed bill by the " Committee on Consolidation of State Offices ", *House Journal*, 1932, pp. 1295-1297.

[114] See *Charleston Evening Post*, June 15, 1932.

[115] In 1931, North Carolina consolidated and merged its three major educational institutions, and appointed a commission to work out the details of a plan for the enlarged institution. Survey staff was headed by Dr. George A. Works, University of Chicago. See O. Max Gardner,

All of the state-supported colleges are expanding rapidly and this growth presents delicate and practical problems. What should constitute the proper lines of development is a problem that calls for a definite program that will place each institution in its proper setting in the picture of higher education. It is believed that appropriate functions are fairly definitely fixed, as things now stand. Moreover, it is possible that the value of their unique characteristics more than outweigh whatever financial advantages might accrue from consolidation. Should careful study suggest the wisdom of control of all by a single board, however, it is suggested that advisory boards for each institution be provided.

III. OTHER STATE SCHOOLS

The Colored Normal, Industrial, Agricultural and Mechanical College is located at Orangeburg. It is under the management and control of a board of trustees, composed of seven members, six of whom are elected by the General Assembly for terms of six years. The governor is ex officio the seventh member and chairman. The law provides that the faculty shall be of the negro race.[116]

This school teaches all the trades, both for men and women, and trains teachers for the high school field. The character of work done is described by the governing board in the following words:

The general education program of this institution is based upon a conception of the needs of the colored race in South Carolina, the most important of which is the training of teachers and the training of negro youth in agriculture, home eco-

---

"One State Cleans House", *Saturday Evening Post*, Jan. 2, 1932, p. 33.

In 1931, Georgia supplanted the various boards that formerly controlled the University of Georgia and its twenty-four branches, by a single board of regents. See art. 10 of act, approved August 28, 1931.

[116] *Code 1932*, chap. 123, art. 7.

nomics, and mechanic arts. The College occupies a prominent position in the educational field of South Carolina and possesses exceptional opportunities for the development of negro leadership and service. It occupies a place of front rank among the seventeen negro land grant colleges of the South.[117]

The South Carolina School for the Deaf and the Blind is located at Cedar Spring, near Spartanburg. The institutional care of these individuals was long regarded as an act of charity, as the public failed to distinguish them from the mentally deficient, but this school is correctly looked upon today as an educational institution for those who cannot be properly educated in the ordinary public school.

Supervision and control of the affairs of this institution are vested in a board of commissioners of five members. The state superintendent of education is a member, ex officio, and four members are appointed by the governor for overlapping terms of eight years. All deaf mutes and blind of the state who are of proper age and mental capacity, each case to be decided by the board, are admitted to the institution. The whole or part of their expenses is borne by the state, according to the pecuniary condition of the applicants.[118]

The colored school is situated a short distance from the white school, under the supervision of the superintendent and the principal of the latter. The teachers are all colored, but are especially trained for their work. Indeed, so far as possible, the same methods are used in the two schools.

The School for the Deaf and the Blind is reputed to be one of the best of its kind in the country. There is no doubt that this institution merits the support of the people of the state. When economic conditions permit, funds should be provided for an industrial building, which is badly needed.

[117] *Report of the Colored Normal, Industrial, Agricultural and Mechanical College*, 1930, p. 3.

[118] *Code 1932*, chap. 122, art. 8, secs. 5684-5693.

The John de la Howe Industrial School, located near McCormick, is the oldest manual training school in America. It is operated as an agricultural and mechanical school for training normal dependent boys and girls of the state. It is governed by a board of seven members, appointed by the governor for overlapping terms of five years. An advisory committee of three women is appointed by the board to advise as to the management of the institution.[119]

IV. OTHER STATE EDUCATIONAL AGENCIES

The Historical Commission of South Carolina is composed of the heads of the History Departments in the State University, The Citadel, Clemson and Winthrop, and three others selected in the following manner: one member by the South Carolina Historical Society, one by the United Confederate Veterans, and one by the American Legion, Department of South Carolina. The three last named are elected for terms of ten years. It is the duty of the commission to procure and preserve for inspection and examination documents and other significant material relating to the history of the state. The commission selects a full-time executive secretary who serves at their pleasure.[120]

The State Library Board serves as the executive committee of the State Library Association. Its five members are appointed by the governor on recommendation of the state superintendent of education. The board is empowered to accept gifts and endowments.

The governor, the secretary of state and the state superintendent of education constitute the ex officio Board of Trustees of the State Library. This library was established primarily for the General Assembly, but is open to the

[119] *Code 1932*, chap. 122, art. 7.
[120] *Code 1932*, chap. 98, art. 4.

public.   The state librarian is elected by the legislature for a term of four years.

The custodian of the Confederate Relic Room in the State House is selected by the Wade Hampton Chapter of the South Carolina Division of the United Daughters of the Confederacy.

The Committee on Literacy, which operates under the leadership of the state superintendent of education in correlating the organized efforts against illiteracy in the state, is composed of twenty members appointed by the governor.

V   REORGANIZATION OF DEPARTMENT OF EDUCATION

Attention has already been directed to the need of the establishment of a single line of responsibility through an integrated department of education.   To recapitulate, the educational policy of South Carolina should be formulated by a state board of education of seven members, appointed by the governor with consent of the senate for overlapping terms of seven years.   The office of the popularly-elected state superintendent of education should be abolished and a commissioner of education, with wide administrative authority, should be appointed by the state board of education. For the purpose of local administration and supervision, the county superintendent of education should be appointed by the county board of education, to consist of five members elected by the qualified voters of the county.

The historical commission, the state library board, and the committee on literacy should be abolished, and their powers and duties devolved upon the Department of Education.   In this connection, too much emphasis cannot be placed upon the importance of the building which is being erected for housing the thousands of priceless records and books that are scattered in the cellar and other places in the State House in Columbia.   In their present condition, they are not accessible and are not being properly preserved. The construction of the Memorial Building, authorized by the General Assembly in 1919, should serve as a valuable contribution to historical research and as the center of public library facilities for the state. The Confederate relic room should find its place there also.[121]

It is also proposed that a bureau of professional registration be established in the Department of Education, for the purpose of centralizing the records and office work of the professional examining boards. A thoroughly qualified director would be required to handle all secretarial and clerical work. It is believed that higher standards of administration will result through grouping all activities in one office, directed by a full-time officer. Should this bureau be established, the examining boards should be appointed by the commissioner of education from lists furnished by the professions, trades, or occupations directly interested.[122]

[121] The appropriation of $100,000 for it was conditioned upon a like amount being raised by private subscription. The S. C. World War Memorial Commission, appointed for that purpose, has reported a total in excess of that amount. See *News and Courier*, August 10, 1932.

[122] See National Institute of Public Administration, *Survey of Arkansas*, p. 62. Also, Brookings Institution, *Survey of North Carolina*, pp. 167, 168.

CHAPTER V

Agriculture and Natural Resources

I. AGRICULTURE

THREE-FOURTHS of the population of South Carolina remain rural and the chief industry of the state continues to be agriculture. However, there are definite signs of fundamental changes, for agriculture has been in a state of transition since the period of the World War and rural South Carolina has experienced constant adjustment and re-adjustment.[1] The boll-weevil invasion, poor prices for cotton, and mortgages resulting from post-war inflation of values have helped create the prevailing picture of hard-times and discouragement. Many farmers are land-poor and in dire need of relief.

Inasmuch as the colored race contitutes a large proportion of farm-labor in South Carolina, an alteration in the relative number of this group should be noted. It appears that during the thirty-year period 1900-1930, the proportion of negroes in the total population decreased from 58.4 in 1900 to 45.6 in 1930. During that time the whites increased over thirty times as fast as the negroes in the state: a gain of 386,233 whites and 11,360 negroes. A negro majority of 46,000 in 1920 was converted into a white majority of 150,000 in 1930.[2] This shift is sure to change the economic and political aspect of the problem.

---

[1] For a description of the change taking place in South Carolina and the character of the problem, see Williams, *Social Problems*, p. 1.

[2] *Fifteenth Census of United States: 1930*, population bulletin, second series, South Carolina.

Of particular interest in the decade last recorded was the trend from the farms of the state.[3] While the rural population showed a decrease of only 1.6 per cent, the " rural-farm " population decreased 14.8 and the " rural non-farm " population increased 43 per cent. In 1930 South Carolina had an urban population of 21.3 per cent, " rural farm " population of 52.6, and " rural non-farm " population of 26.1. Including both farm owners and farm laborers, agriculture employed 344,641, or slightly more than one-half of the total gainful workers of the state. Of the 190,884 farm laborers, however, 108,598 were unpaid family workers. During the last census decade the number of farms in South Carolina decreased 34,799, or 18.1 per cent.[4] In 1930, of an approximate landed area of 19,576,800 acres in the state, there were 10,393,113 acres in farms.[5]

Deplorable conditions in towns and cities of the United States since 1930 have caused a general drift back to the farms, at least temporarily, but this reverse movement has not been so noticeable in South Carolina on the contrary, an additional influx to the centers of population in search of " relief " from governmental agencies is observed. The extent to which farm-labor is being demoralized in this manner cannot be definitely determined. It should be regarded as a temporary factor only, however, since aid from this source is coincidental with the national recovery program.

While it is true that farm relief must come largely of the farmers' own initiative in better farm management, diversi-

[3] In loss of farm population, this state was second in the nation, Georgia leading.

[4] U. S. Dept. of Commerce, Bureau of Census, *Population Bulletin, South Carolina: 1930*, pp. 3-5; *Report of Department of Agriculture Commerce and Industries* (S. C.), 1931, p. 44.

[5] A study of rural depopulation was made in 1932 of Santuc township in Union County by Dr. Wilson Gee, *The Qualitative Nature of Rural Depopulation in Santuc Township, South Carolina, 1900-1930.*

fication of crops, development of market facilities, and production of foodstuffs sufficient to sustain themselves,[6] it is also true that the state could render tremendous service by establishing a well-organized department of agriculture to promote the economic interests of its agricultural population. The state can ill-afford to defer action in seeking some fundamental policy in relieving the plight of its primary industry.

The long depression in agriculture is clearly no transitory distress to be relieved by the usual process of general liquidation. Much of the land that has been vacated is not fit for cultivation at all. Among the salient features of a policy formulated and directed by the state should be a survey of the agricultural land, its classification according to fertility and uses, and governmental reforestation of large areas. Such an undertaking would receive aid and support at the hands of the Federal Government.

Free discussion of the state's social and economic problems has suffered beyond measure. Too long have we fought public consideration of those subjects that shock our sensibilities. A defense-mechanism that operates through self-praise and boasting of past glories creates a public attitude that shrinks from dissemination of facts. Highly sensitive of criticism, we have continued to feel our problems—not face them. Such a condition is a challenge to courageous leadership of unclosed minds. Guidance of this sort is necessary to develop an informed public opinion which will overcome the inertia that has resisted the adoption of efficient and economical organization in the administration of the public business.

[6] *The News and Courier* in 1932 was contributing valuable front-page editorials to promote a live-at-home campaign. According to figures released to the press by the U. S. Dept. of Agriculture (Feb. 11, 1935), farm income increased from $46,219,000 in 1932 to $78,606,000 in 1934. The latter amount does not include $11,457,000 received as AAA payments.

1. *Development of Present State Agencies*

Having indicated that the State of South Carolina is yet essentially agricultural in its general economy, we now address our attention to the state agencies designed to protect and promote the agricultural pursuits of the commonwealth.

The movement to correlate the activities of all state agricultural authorities first appeared in the South, starting with Georgia and Tennessee in 1874 and 1875, respectively. In 1880, South Carolina established a department of agriculture, which operated under a state board of agriculture and a commissioner of agriculture. Like other agencies of this kind, this board was largely confined to advisory functions. In 1890, its powers and duties were devolved upon the Board of Trustees of Clemson College, except as to the control of the phosphate interests of the State.[7]

In his first annual message, 1904, Governor Heyward urged the establishment of a bureau of commerce and immigration. He called attention to the fact that in many states such bureaus were attracting desirable settlers with " a most telling effect ".[8] Accordingly the general Assembly created the Department of Agriculture, Commerce and Immigration under a commissioner having " the qualifications of a competent knowledge of agriculture, manufacturing and general industries, commerce, chemistry and publicity ". He was charged:

. . . with all work looking to the promotion of agriculture, manufacturing and other industries, cattle raising, and all

[7] *Acts of 1890*, pp. 705, 706; *Code 1932*, secs. 5741, 5743.

[8] *Reports and Resolutions*, 1904, vol. i, p. 279. Nearly all the Northern and Western States had such bureaus, as well as Maryland, Alabama and North Carolina. The U. S. immigration laws did not permit advertising of a state's resources and advantages abroad, or any act tending to induce immigration, except by an official act of a state. See first annual report of the department, *Reports and Resolutions*, 1905, vol. i, p. 649.

matters tending to the industrial development of the State, with the collection and publication of information in regard to localities, character, accessibility, cost and modes of utilization of soils, and more specifically to the inducement of capital by the dissemination of information relative to the advantages of soil and climate, and to the natural resources and industrial opportunities offered in the State.[9]

It was provided, however, that nothing in the legislation that created this department should be construed as giving to the commissioner " the right to do scientific, educational or extension work in agriculture " or " to repeal or interfere with the duties or work of the chemist or faculty of Clemson Agricultural and Mechanical College, or any other department of the State Government of South Carolina ". The head of the new department was to be elected by the qualified electors for a term of two years.[10]

From the beginning, the department stressed the advertising of the state's resources. On the one hand, it sought desirable immigrants from sections of Northern Europe. At the same time, strenuous efforts were made to direct attention of investors in the Northern States to South Carolina's mineral resources.[11] This agency, in its early

---

[9] *Code 1932*, sec. 3227; *Acts of 1904*, p. 449.

[10] *Acts of 1904*, p. 449. As in the case of all state officers popularly elected, this term has been extended to four years, *Acts of 1926*, p. 1055.

[11] See report of the department for 1905, *Reports and Resolutions,* 1906, vol. i, p. 889. Thousands of pieces of literature, printed in several different languages, were sent to homeseekers. The first official map since 1883 was issued in 1905. See *South Carolina* (Handbook of 1927), pp. 36, 27. The law provides for the publication of a handbook of the state, but carries no appropriation providing funds. The Department of Agriculture, Commerce and Industries attempts to carry this information in its "Annual Report and Year Book" and in " The Industrial Directory and Labor Report ". Handbooks were published in the following years: 1882, by Major Harry Hammond; 1907, by Commissioner E. J. Watson; 1922, by Commissioner B. Harris; 1927, by the Department and Clemson College.

years, has been described " as a kind of State chamber of commerce, or bureau of information ". Indeed, it does not appear that serious attention was given to agriculture during this period.

In 1908 a bill was introduced in the legislature to establish a separate department of labor. But Governor Ansel opposed the idea and succeeded in having a labor division created within the existing department. The immigration feature, which had been pushed with such vigor at first, had encountered strong opposition. Consequently, in 1909, the law was amended to substitute " Industries " for " Immigration ", and the commissioner was directed to cease seeking immigrants.[12]

" The State Department of Agriculture, Commerce, and Industries was created to care for, protect and advertise the natural resources of the State and to protect its citizens from exploitation and selfish oppression ", wrote the commissioner in 1931.[13] In addition to gathering agricultural and industrial statistics and furnishing information upon subjects placed under its care and regulation, it undertakes the enforcement of all regulatory legislation in this field. Among the particular acts to be enforced are the child labor law, weights and measures law, agricultural seed law, oil inspection law and feed-stuffs inspection law.

The activities of the department fall into four divisions of administration: [14]

1. Superintendence and Records: concerned with general supervision and compilation of statistics. It is through this office that the resources and advantages of the state are advertised. The " Market Bulletin ", containing agricul-

[12] See Governor Ansel's "Annual Message", *Reports and Resolutions,* 1909, vol. i, p. 1032; *Acts of 1909,* p. 191.

[13] *Report of Department,* 1931, p. 3.

[14] See *ibid.,* pp. 3, 4. Also, *South Carolina* (Handbook of 1927), p. 35.

tural, livestock and other items of interest to farmers, is published weekly as an aid to marketing of farm produce.

2. Chemical Laboratory: tests gasoline, kerosene, commercial food-stuffs, and agricultural seeds.

3. Bureau of Inspection: maintains a staff consisting of chief inspector and twelve assistants. Of these, two are assigned to manufacturing plants and all matters connected with the employment of labor.

4. Warehouse Division: [15] operates the state warehouse system which provides a medium whereby the farmer can carry his crop until market prices advance. Under certain restrictions the commissioner is given power to acquire property by lease for the warehousing of cotton and non-perishable farm products. The material stored is insured and the receipt given therefor is negotiable. A revolving fund is also provided from which this official is authorized to aid the farmers in securing the proper fertilizer and farm seeds. It was the declared purpose of the state to operate the warehouse system at cost without profit to the state.[16]

It is believed that the Department of Agriculture, Commerce and Industries should be abolished. The needs of the state, both agricultural and industrial, far exceed the service being administered. Created nearly a generation ago to perform both services, today it does neither sufficiently and satisfactorily. The Joint Committee on Efficiency and Consolidation of 1926 spoke with a fair degree of accuracy when it reported: " This office has long since ceased to have anything to do with agriculture. Years ago this branch of state government was taken over by the Extension De-

[15] This division was created in 1933 when the powers and duties of the state warehouse commissioner were transferred. *Acts of 1933*, p. 95.

The Natural Resources Division was likewise established in 1933 when the duties of the Natural Resources Commission were conferred on this department. See *infra*, p. 162.

[16] *Code 1932*, chap. 138, art. 3; *Acts of 1912*, p. 707.

partment of Clemson, and since then it has been nothing more than an inspection and tax collection bureau ".[17] However, the committee failed to recommend the creation of a department of agriculture to perform the service which it appeared to recognize as necessary. It was in error in recommending that the entire agricultural functions of the present department be transferred to Clemson College. There are certain agricultural activities that, by their nature, have no place in a college.

Every two years the Board of Trustees of Clemson College designates not over five of its members to serve as the State Crop Pest Commission. This body is empowered to make and enforce rules of quarantine against carriers of plant diseases and to enforce regulations designed to prevent fraud and misrepresentation in the sale and dissemination of trees and plants.[18]

The Board of Exports and Marketing, composed of five members, was created in 1919 to exercise general supervision over the operation of corporations organized for the purpose of engaging principally in the business of exporting commodities. The law specifies definite qualifications for three members who are appointed by the governor with the consent of the senate. The commissioner of agriculure, commerce and industries is a member *ex officio*.[19]

The 1933 legislature abolished two independent agencies that deserve mention. The first of these, the Natural Resources Commission, was composed of ten members appointed by the governor for ten-year terms. In addition, the governor, the chairman of the commission for the analysis of food products, one member of the state highway commission and one member of the house of representatives,

[17] *Report*, 1926, p. 7.
[18] *Code 1932*, chap. 114, art. 9; *Acts of 1912*, p. 748.
[19] *Code 1932*, chap. 140; *Acts of 1919*, p. 265.

served as *ex officio* members. It was the duty of the commission to advertise the chemical and other contents of food products grown in the state. The statute provided that it should "promulgate information furnished by the South Carolina Research Laboratories and other educational institutions and such other information as has bearing upon value of South Carolina products". These duties were transferred in 1933 to the Department of Agriculture, Commerce and Industries.[20] The second, the Commission for Analysis of Food Products of the State, consisted of six members, as follows: The president of the University of South Carolina, the president of Clemson College, the dean of the State Medical College, and two members appointed by the governor. The secretary of the state board of health was an *ex officio* member. This Commission was constituted "to have exclusive charge of the analysis of all products grown or produced in this State used as food for human beings or animals". It was directed to issue a bulletin "setting forth an accurate analysis of all such products". The legislation of 1933 provided that "the properties and duties of the Food Research Laboratory, at Charleston, South Carolina, shall be associated with the State Medical College".[21]

2. Proposed Department of Agriculture

The agricultural functions which are concerned with regulatory and promotional work should be brought together in an integrated department of agriculture. The educational and experimental work in connection with agriculture properly belong under the direction of Clemson College, where

[20] *Code 1932*, chap. 114, art. 10; *Acts of 1929*, p. 254; *Acts of 1933*, p. 634.

[21] This agency was often referred to as the Food Research Commission. *Code 1932*, secs. 3274-3276; *Acts of 1927*, p. 253; *Acts of 1933*, p. 653.

the extension director has at his command not only a full-time service but also the benefit of the experience and study of the faculty.[22] This line of demarcation between the control, regulatory and administrative work of the department and the educational and demonstratory work of the college should be carefully maintained to avoid overlapping and duplication of effort, but close cooperation at all times is required for best results.[23]

The head of the Department of Agriculture should be the commissioner of agriculture, appointed by the governor with consent of the senate. It may be desirable to create a non-paid agricultural advisory council of five members with overlapping terms, appointed by the governor with proper regard to the agricultural sections of the state. If set up, its functions should be purely advisory on matters of policy, and it should serve as a liaison agency in maintaining the desired coordination of the work carried on by the department and by Clemson College, respectively.

The commissioner of agriculture should be given the power to distribute the functions of the established bureaus of the department in the manner that would be most advan-

[22] The public service activities of Clemson College have increased tremendously as it has collaborated with the Federal Government in accordance with the terms and conditions expressed in the several acts of Congress. It is the consensus of opinion in South Carolina that splendid work is being done today by the Extension Department. For an account of its activities, see *Report of Clemson College*, 1931, pp. 77-8 and 97.

For the support of this service in 1934, the General Assembly appropriated $210,350. *Acts of 1934*, p. 1669.

[23] This arrangement is generally regarded as being sound. See Edward Wiest, *Agricultural Organization in the United States* (Lexington, Kentucky, 1923), pp. 326, 327; New York Bureau of Municipal Research, *Survey of New Jersey*, p. 137; Brookings Institution, *Survey of North Carolina*, p. 241; Institute of Public Administration, *Survey of Arkansas*, p. 29.

tageous and economical from an administrative standpoint.[24] The following bureaus are suggested:

1. Bureau of Plant Industry
2. Bureau of Animal Industry
3. Bureau of Feeds, Seeds and Fertilizer Control
4. Bureau of Markets and Statistics.

In general, it should be the duty of the Department of Agriculture:

1. To encourage and promote in any practicable way the interest of agriculture, including horticulture, livestock industry, dairying, poultry raising and allied industries;

2. To promote and to improve methods of conducting agricultural industries in order to exercise or balance production and to facilitate the distribution of products at minimum costs;

3. To control the standard quality of chemical feedstuffs, seeds and fertilizers by inspecting and testing the same;

4. To inquire into the causes of contagious, infectious and communicable diseases among domestic animals, and the means for the prevention of the same;

5. To collect, publish and distribute statistics relating to crop production and marketing, so far as such statistics may be of value to agriculture and allied industries of the state;

6. To assist, encourage and promote the organization of farmers' institutes, the holding of fairs and stock shows, and other exhibits of the products of agriculture;

7. To cooperate with Clemson College and the Federal Government in all matters pertaining to agriculture.[25]

[24] Also, with the approval of the governor, to re-arrange the bureau structure as the needs require.

[25] The duties listed here were largely adapted from the administrative code recommended by the National Institute of Public Administration for Arkansas. See, *Survey of Arkansas*, pp. 132-134.

In order to avoid duplication of activity and with the view of improving administration and establishing responsibility, it is suggested that the following agencies be abolished:

1. Department of Agriculture, Commerce and Industries.
2. State Crop Pest Commission.
3. Board of Exports and Marketing.

The weights and measures law should be continuously enforced. Inasmuch, however, as its effective enforcement can be brought about only through the exercise of adequate police power, this duty should be transferred to the bureau of state police, set up in the proposed Executive Department. The inspection of gasoline and kerosene might likewise be transferred to this bureau. Although a continuous inspection of these commodities is hardly necessary today under changed conditions, the state police might well be required to take samples from time to time.

It will readily be recognized that the duties and activities of the contemplated Department of Agriculture comprehend the services now rendered by the present state agricultural agencies and that, consequently, there would be no need for their continued existence. In regard to the Natural Resources Commission and the Commission for the Analysis of Food Products, which were abolished in 1933, the research work of these two agencies should be performed in the laboratories of Clemson College and the data resulting therefrom disseminated through the Department of Agriculture. The food inspection law should properly be the function of the Department of Health.

II. DEPARTMENT OF CONSERVATION

Consolidation of all state services having to do with conservation of natural resources is contemplated in the proposed establishment of a Department of Conservation.

Proper correlation of these activities will conduce to more intelligent supervision and control and to a greater efficiency of service. Moreover, it is believed that, if the problem of conservation is presented as a single major project, a greater degree of both public and private support will be forthcoming. It is only logical to place the protection and development of forests and the protection and propagation of fish and game in the same department with the conservation of other closely allied natural resources.

The execution of the bird and game laws of South Carolina is under the direction of a commissioner, known as the Chief Game Warden, who is elected by the General Assembly for a term of four years.[26] This official has charge of the warden force, composed of at least one salaried warden in each of the several counties who is appointed by the governor upon the recommendation of the legislative delegation of the respective county.[27] The department is more than self-sustaining, being financed by collections from the sale of licenses and fines.

Game preserves from 15 to 22,000 acres in size have been established in eighteen counties about the state. The largest sanctuary is that set aside as a national park at Camp Jackson in Richland County.[28] The state force of 75 paid game wardens and 90 special wardens has special instructions to protect the wild game refuges in the state which now total over 75,000 acres.

[26] *Code of 1932*, sec. 3285. This official was for many years named by the Audubon Society, which was recognized by the legislature in 1907. The impropriety of the delegation to a private organization of authority to name a state official was clearly demonstrated in the many wrangles under this arrangement. See Governor Manning's *Annual Message*, 1918, p. 8.

[27] *Code 1932*, sec. 3286. The game wardens may be removed either by the governor or the chief game warden at his discretion.

[28] Conditions required by the U. S. Government for the acquisition of Jackson National Forest were authorized under Act No. 995, *Acts of 1928*. See *Code 1932*, sec. 3293.

Under the " Coastal Fisheries Act " of 1924, the State
Board of Fisheries was created and given supervision of
commercial fishing in the tidal waters of the state. The
law provides for a board of three members " having expert
knowledge of coastal fisheries and related subjects and not
engaged in the same for profit nor interested in any firm
or corporation ", appointed by the governor for overlapping
terms of three years.[29]   The field force consists of the chief
inspector and five assistant inspectors.   Like the Chief Game
Warden's office, this board operates at no net cost to the
state.

In 1927, the General Assembly created the State Commission of Forestry, consisting of five members appointed
by the governor.   It was provided that " two members shall
be practical lumbermen, one member shall be a farmer who
is a landowner, one member to be selected and appointed at
large, and one of whom shall be the President of Clemson
Agricultural College ".[30]   Other than the last named, the
members are appointed for overlapping terms of four years.
It became the duty of this commission " to inquire into and
report upon forest conditions in South Carolina, with reference to the preservation of forests, the effect of the destruction of forests upon the general welfare of the state, and
other matters pertaining to the subject of forestry and
tree growth, including recommendations to the public generally as to reforestation ".   This agency was directed to
use means to prevent and control fires; to give assistance to
private owners; to promote through educational means an
appreciation of the advantages of forestry; and to cooperate

[29] *Code 1932*, art. 13, secs. 3301, 3304.   The provisions of this article
do not apply to fish or fishing in the fresh waters of the state.   The
members are paid a per-diem, in addition to all actual expenses incurred
in attending meetings.

[30] *Code 1932*, art. 11, secs. 3277-3279.

with the federal government in the distribution of funds allotted the state.

The duties outlined above indicate definitely that South Carolina has only recently given attention to a state service of forestry. With that in mind it is interesting to note a few facts in regard to the problem and what is now being attempted.

Of a total area in the state of 19,576,800 acres, approximately 12,800,000 or about two-thirds are in lumber growth. It is reported that only about 5,000,000 acres of these forest lands are owned by individuals or companies who are sufficiently interested in forest protection to pay a certain percentage of the total cost of protection.[31] It appears, therefore, that one of the major problems of the state agency is to educate the public to an appreciation of its value. During 1931, approximately 148,000 attended lectures on prevention of forest fires; approximately 100,000 pieces of literature were distributed; exhibits were placed at state and county fairs; and forestry was added as a study in one vocational school in each of the counties.[32]

The State Forest Service includes the state forester, the assistant state forester, four district foresters, and a nurseryman. The district foresters are located at Columbia, Spartanburg, Florence, Walterboro and at Aiken. The forestry tree nursery is near Camden. At the close of 1931, there were over a half-million acres of wooded lands under protection of this service, with as many more ready to be served as soon as economic conditions would allow sufficient

[31] See *Report of Forestry Commission*, 1931, pp. 13-15. It is estimated that the cost of property owners at the beginning is about two cents per acre per year. About one-half of the operating costs are borne by property owners, with approximately one-fourth contributed by the state and a like proportion by the federal government.

[32] *Ibid.*, pp. 16, 17. In 1934 an intensive campaign was being carried on in the Civilian Conservation Corps camps with federal funds.

funds.[33]   The expenditures for the year amounted to $70,-
638.53.   Of this amount, $16,952.32 or less than twenty-
three per cent were state funds.

Department of Conservation Proposed

The head of the Department of Conservation should be
the commissioner of conservation, appointed by the governor with consent of the senate.   The commissioner should
appoint the directors of the bureaus and have direct supervision over their work, to the end that the objectives sought
may be more fully realized through coordinated effort and
that responsibility may be definitely fixed.   With the view
of obtaining economy and efficiency in service, the field
forces of the entire department should be consolidated and
supervised by the commissioner's office.   Here, too, would
be the medium of educating the public through the gathering and distribution of information concerning the activities
of the entire department.

It might be well to attach an advisory commission to the
department concerned with conservation—at least for the

[33] *Ibid.*, pp. 8, 9, 14. By the close of the fiscal year 1934 the protected
private lands had risen to a million and a half acres. Meanwhile important
changes in forestry had taken place following the launching of Emergency
Conservation Work in 1933. Under this program seventeen Civil Conservation Corps camps were assigned to South Carolina and placed under
the supervision of the state forestry organization. This expansion of
activities with the addition of new duties made it impossible for the state
agency to perform its tasks efficiently. Consequently, when the legislature in 1934 failed to appropriate sufficient funds for administration,
five camps were removed from the jurisdiction of the commission. It
was evident that the state would be required to display a determination
to man and to maintain Emergency Conservation Work improvements
if the remaining camps were retained. The State Commission of
Forestry, moreover, has agreed to assume responsibility to the extent
of its ability for the administration of the " sub-marginal land program."
In the fall of 1934 four projects, varying in size from 15,000 to 150,000
acres, had already been outlined, to be used as state forests, game sanc-
tuaries, public shooting grounds, and place of recreation.

present, until a program is well mapped out.[34] Should such
a body be created, it might appropriately consist of five
members appointed by the governor for overlapping terms
of five years.   Its personnel should be selected on the basis
of their active interest and competence to give advice in
this field, but it should have advisory powers only.

The following internal organization of the department
is suggested:

  1. Bureau of Forestry
  2. Bureau of Game and Inland Fisheries
  3. Bureau of Commercial Fisheries
  4. Bureau of Geology.

The State Commission of Forestry should be abolished,
and its duties devolved upon the bureau of forestry, headed
by the state forester.   South Carolina has already made a
beginning in the protection, restoration and conservation of
trees and forests.   This program should be expanded and
energetically pushed.   In order to preserve fertility of the
soil and maintain the natural waterways, a state park program of forfeited public lands should be extensively formulated.[35]   In this connection, a readjustment of the state's

---

[34] A plan for a conservation commission to administer all natural
resources in the state was presented to the General Assembly in 1932 by
the Conservation Society of South Carolina and the South Carolina
Forest, Game and Fish Association. See *House Journal*, 1932, p. 487,
and *News and Courier*, Jan. 24, 1932. In the opinion of the writer, the
trained naturalist proposed as adviser should have been advanced as the
administrator and the commission as the advisory body.

The House Committee on Consolidation of State Offices, 1932, recommended establishment of " Department of Conservation and Resources "
under direction of a commission. See *House Journal*, 1932, pp. 1292, 1293.

[35] The Sinking Fund Commission is already authorized to convey
waste lands to the Forestry Commission. *Code 1932*, sec. 3280. Of
course, some equitable arrangement should be made with the counties and
school districts involved, to compensate them for their lost revenues from
taxes. See Institute of Public Administration, *Survey of Arkansas*, p. 38.

taxing policy should be made to encourage the growth of new forests on private lands. Taxes on lands devoted to growing young trees might be abolished or reduced until owners begin to receive financial returns.[36]

The functions of the Office of Chief Game Warden should devolve upon the bureau of game and inland fisheries. What has been written in regard to the development of a state park program applies here with equal emphasis. South Carolina has been entirely too slow in setting up reservations whereby its wild life will have a chance to survive. The state ought not to leave the perpetuation of game to private preserves, for it is the property of the people and not of individuals. In the coastal section vast areas have already fallen into private hands. What has been done in other states can be done here. Establishment of additional state fish hatcheries is needed to replenish the stock in the streams. The Cleveland Hatchery near Greenville appears as a worthy example to be followed by other citizens in contributing lands for that purpose.[37] However, due regard should be paid to the distribution in the streams according to their needs, and more stringent fish laws should be passed.

The functions of the State Board of Fisheries should devolve upon the bureau of commercial fisheries. Efforts should be continued toward replenishing the coastal waters with shad, clams and oysters. The culture of oysters is a particularly promising industry, now that South Carolina is receiving aid and cooperation from the United States Government in this development.[38]

[36] A study of forest land taxation is being made by the United States Forest Service.

[37] Established under Act No. 225, *Acts of 1931*. See *Report of Chief Game Warden*, 1931, pp. 5, 6.

[38] The Board of Fisheries and the U. S. Bureau of Fisheries are operating three experimental stations, one in Charleston County and two in Beaufort County. *Report of Board of Fisheries*, 1931, p. 9.

The bureau of geology is suggested because it is felt that South Carolina should formulate a definite policy looking toward the ultimate development of the state's potential water powers.[39] This bureau should be vested with the duty of compiling data on water supply, stream flow, and stream conservation. Geological and topographical surveys and mapping should be done in cooperation with the U. S. Geological Survey. At the present time only slightly more than one-third of the state has been accurately mapped. While South Carolina is not important as a mining state, there is work to be done in the field of mineral resources, looking towards the development of clay products and the output of granite.[40]

Conclusion

While separate departments of agriculture and conservation of national resources have been recommended, it may be felt that the functions of the agencies gathered together in the latter division are not sufficiently important to constitute a separate department. Perhaps economy does suggest the wisdom of consolidating all activities considered in this chapter into a single administrative organization, for they are closely related at numerous points. However that may be, it is believed that the arrangement outlined would prove a vast improvement over the present disintegrated machinery.

---

[39] See *Report of South Carolina Power Rate Investigating Committee,* 1932, pp. 42, 43. Also, *South Carolina* (Handbook, 1927), pp. 42-54. South Carolina now stands sixth in the Union in the production of electricity by water power.

[40] *Ibid.,* pp. 77-83. The office of State Geologist, created under Act no. 395, *Acts of 1901,* has received no appropriation since 1912. The act was omitted from the *Code of 1932,* and is now inoperative.

The Board of Phosphate Commissioners is known to the law, *Code 1932,* chap. 98, art. 3. Inasmuch as phosphate rock is no longer mined, this article should be repealed.

CHAPTER VI

Labor

DEVELOPMENT of manufacturing interests in South Carolina was long retarded by two factors, namely, the adaptability of the state to agricultural pursuits, and the obstacle raised by the fact that slavery created a monopoly of labor for the slave owners. Within the last fifty years, however, a factory proletariat has emerged. Capitalism is now crowding upon the older culture. The dangerous gauntlet of industrial adjustment must be run.[1]

Before proceeding to discuss the part the state government might advantageously play, it is deemed necessary to note briefly certain attributes of the problem. The "big-four" industries of South Carolina are textiles, cottonseed oil, fertilizer and lumber. Of these, in 1931, the textile establishments represented about 55 per cent of the total investment, and about two-thirds of the value of the manufactured product. Some indication of activity in this field and of its relative position in the industrial life of the state may be seen in the following tables:[2]

[1] See Broadus Mitchell and George S. Mitchell, *The Industrial Revolution in the South* (Baltimore, 1930), p. 164.

[2] Department of Agriculture, Commerce and Industries, *Reports*.

A comparison of the industrial growth in South Carolina and North Carolina may be seen in an article of R. W. Edmonds, "The Workshop of the Carolinas", in *Review of Reviews*, vol. 80, pp. 71-74 (Oct., 1929).

1. Textile Manufactures

	Number of Spindles	Number of Looms
1910	4,088,782	99,126
1915	4,708,414	113,168
1920	4,997,406	115,801
1925	5,311,888	125,566
1930	5,689,642	134,710

	1921	*1931*
Capital invested	$145,290,056	$201,834,665
Value of product	$158,965,179	$168,070,207
Number of employees	55,085	66,032
Total wages (not salaries)	$ 34,848,358	$ 40,694,667

2. All Industries

	1926	*1930*	*1931*
Capital invested	$308,651,800	$385,532,502	$366,691,089
Value of products	$322,851,975	$305,304,886	$256,696,989
Number of employees ..	102,863	90,659	86,102
Total wages (not sal.)..	$ 66,165,462	$ 61,637,693	$ 55,023,186

An industrial revolution, wherever it makes its advent, repeats much of the same familiar story as it moves through three rather definite stages of its progress. During the first period attention is largely absorbed in technical problems of mechanical production and expansion of markets. The second period is marked by a recoil of labor against exploitation. This is characterized by the formation of labor unions and an intensive program of protective legislation. Industrialism may be said to have reached the third stage of its development when a certain balance between human and mechanical forces has been established.[3] Cotton manufacture in South Carolina is passing through the second of these stages at the present time. The explanation of the tardiness of this progress is to be found in the feudal atmosphere of the cotton plantation which has lingered over the factory system in this section.[4]

[3] Mitchell and Mitchell, *op. cit.*, Preface.

[4] For a vivid portraiture of the "Southern Textile Picture", see Howard W. Odum, *An American Epoch* (New York, 1930), pp. 243-248.

The mill workers were drawn from two main sources: (1) tenant farmers, many of whom had been under lien law; (2) mountaineers, who had been subject to abject poverty. These two groups may be classed together as the Poor Whites who had long endured life at a minimum. The factories came to deliver them from their unfortunate condition and employment was received with gratitude. Long hours and little pay were naturally accepted as a matter of course.

The passiveness of the Southern cotton mill laborer was further induced by the policies of the employers and by public opinion.[5] The factory builders maintained the traditional responsibility felt by the dominant whites of the Old South for their dependents. Exploitation was somewhat offset by paternalism, as the employees were provided with the principal facilities for life. Mill villages were built, affording homes, schools, churches, stores, health centers and even forms of recreation.[6] Inasmuch as the establishment of cotton factories was the salvation of cotton culture, the general public was enthusiastic in its support. The press, the pulpit and the platform promoted the building program by advertising a plentiful supply of cheap, non-union, native operatives, proximity to raw materials, abundance of power and ideal climate as advantages to be exploited. This campaign brought in new industry and new capital; it also crystallized opinion against labor agitation.

[5] The presence of the negro, willing to take his job, also delayed the worker's self-help.

[6] This welfare program became the most completely developed system of any great industry in the nation. It is not implied that this solicitude was prompted by unmixed motives. The writer is of the opinion that the early factory builders were sincere, in the main, and that their policies harmonized with the heritage of the Old South. The extent to which the second generation has deliberately used a welfare program as a tool of exploitation and profit, however, is an open question.

The lower labor standards prevailing in the South and the depression in industry following the post-war lapse of 1920-21 were potent influences in causing many of the New England mills to drift to the South. The wave of strikes in 1929, however, can not be attributed solely to objectionable practices imported when this migration took place. The absence of labor unions and strikes prior to the recent invasion can not be construed as evidence of the fact that conditions were good and that labor was contented before the influx of new capital. Contrarily, it has been indicated in the preceding paragraphs why the Southern cotton-mill workers had so long remained inarticulate in the face of inordinate industrialism. Surely the absence of labor unions has never been proof that they were not needed.

The American Federation of Labor, at its convention in Toronto in 1929, resolved to throw its weight behind a united drive along the entire Southern front.[7] In January, 1930, a plan for organizing the workers of the South was adopted at Charlotte, North Carolina.[8] At that time, except for unions in the building trades and printing trades and some few thousands of textile workers, there were few trade unions in the South.[9] Inasmuch as relentless opposition to organized labor in that section is grounded in his-

[7] In 1929 there were three organizations in the textile industry. The United Textile Workers, the constituent union of the American Federation of Labor, had a voting strength of 30,000. Its rival, The American Federation of Textile Operatives, continued as an independent organization of 6,000 members. A new group, of "left wing" inception, was the Communist National Textile Workers' Union (membership not reported) which appeared to be drawing upon the disaffected elements of the others. See U. S. Bureau of Labor Statistics, *Bulletin No. 541*, p. 394 (Dec., 1931).

[8] See Louis Stark, "Labor Advances South for a Great Campaign" in *New York Times*, Jan. 20, 1930.

[9] See Dowell Patterson, "Organization Possibilities in South Carolina", *American Federalist*, vol. 36, p. 673 (1929).

toric reasons, infiltration would seem to be a better policy.[10]
What is needed at first is recognition and establishment of
confidence. This can probably be achieved more successfully by organizing a few mills at a time with little said
about demands. The necessary approach is one of orderly
cooperation in composing differences and bringing about
improvements in the interest of both labor and capital.

But what has the state done in an effort to preserve a
fair balance between these two groups and to reap the
wholesome benefits of industrialization for all of its citizens? It goes without saying that the state government
has a tremendous responsibility with respect to the topics
that form the subject of law-making in this sphere.

The first textile legislation in South Carolina was passed
by the Tillman Legislature, limiting the hours of labor in
cotton mills to 66 hours per week.[11] In 1922, this was reduced to ten hours a day or fifty-five hours per week.[12]
Not much can be done toward shortening the hours further
in South Carolina until surrounding states agree to do
likewise.[13] Without concerted action, a competitive hard-
ship would fall on local industry. It is hoped that the leading cotton manufacturing states of the South will enact the
uniform rule of 40 hours per week as provided in the
Textile Code under the N. R. A.

[10] For a discussion of this policy, see Mitchell and Mitchell, *op. cit.,*
pp. 20-23.

[11] See Simkins, *Tillman Movement in South Carolina,* p. 176.

[12] In 1916 the limit had been placed at 11 hours a day or 60 hours per
week. *Code 1932,* sec. 1466; *Acts of 1916,* p. 937; *Acts of 1922,* p. 1011.

[13] The legal limit in both North Carolina and Georgia is 60 hours.
In 1930, the average full-time hours per week in the five leading Southern
states were 55.26 as against 51.6 in the five leading New England states.
The average full-time weekly earnings of the first-named group were
$15.25 as against $20.06 of the latter. In South Carolina the average
was $15.02 for a week of 54.8 hours. U. S. Bureau of Labor Statistics,
Handbook of Labor Statistics, 1931, p. 753.

Women and children form a separate division of the working class and should be safeguarded by law in accordance with the nature of the industry. Night work is forbidden in most progressive states, and nearly all states prohibit the employment of minors under a certain age.

The census reports on cotton manufacture show that in the twenty-year period, 1880-1900, there was an increase in the South of nearly 600 per cent in textile operatives and a proportionate increase in the number of children employed. In 1903, Governor McSweeney pointed out the fallacy in the argument that legislation on this subject was an interference with family government and urged both a child labor law and compulsory education.[14] In 1907, a farcical child-labor restriction was enacted, with no machinery to enforce it. In 1911, the minimum age was fixed at twelve years, and in 1916 it was raised to fourteen.[15] The following year the law was amended to require a permit for any child between fourteen and sixteen years of age.[16] Governor Blackwood recommended that no minor under eighteen years be permitted to do night work and that no one under sixteen years, by permit or otherwise, be allowed to work in textile plants or cotton mills.[17] The recommendation was a progressive one, but an age limit fixed at a reasonable minimum is not a sufficient guarantee that the child is able to work in industries. A physical test in addition would be better calculated to protect children. More-

14 "Annual Message", *Reports and Resolutions*, 1903, vol. ii, p. 288.

15 *Code 1932*, sec. 1469; *Acts of 1916*, p. 655.

16 *Code 1932*, sec. 1473; *Acts of 1917*, p. 170.

17 *Inaugural Address*, 1931, p. 9. See U. S. Department of Labor, "Standards for Child Labor Legislation", *Bulletin No. 390* (1933). These standards relate to occupations other than agriculture and domestic service and are based on a child labor draft approved by the Association of Government Labor Officials.

over, an educational requirement would indirectly raise the school-leaving age.[18]

The hours for women in mercantile establishments of South Carolina are limited to sixty per week, not to exceed twelve in any one day, and they are not allowed to work later than ten in the evening.[19] Certain provisions are made for their health and comfort. The Factory Inspection Act, passed in 1909 and amended from time to time, seeks to provide sanitary conditions for all employees in industrial and mercantile establishments. Whatever may be said of the regulatory legislation, it is ridiculous to expect its en-

---

[18] In 1933, representatives from five Southern states—Alabama, Florida, Georgia, South Carolina and Tennessee—met in Atlanta to study the problem of uniform labor legislation, with particular emphasis upon a higher standard for minors. Among other things agreed upon as a goal were: (1) a minimum age of 16 years, a physical examination, and an educational requirement equivalent to a grammar school education—for all industrial employment of minors; (2) a minimum age of 18 years for night work. None of these proposed standards prevailed in the five conference states by state law at that time.

With respect to education, an eighth grade requirement became effective in Alabama in 1934. Georgia requires ability to read and write simple sentences. Florida, South Carolina and Tennessee have no requirement.

Alabama, Georgia and Tennessee require physical examinations of minors under 16. In Florida the test is optional. South Carolina has no provision.

[19] *Code 1932*, sec. 1478. During 1933 seven states enacted minimum wage laws for women and minors. A majority of these were based on a "standard" minimum wage bill, designed to meet a constitutional objection raised by the Court in *Adkins v. Children's Hospital*, 261 U. S. 525 (1923). The standard bill does not attempt to regulate wages generally but creates a wage board with authority to investigate wages in any occupation, upon complaint of less than a subsisting wage, and to recommend to the industrial officer of the state the establishment of a minimum fair wage standard for such occupation. The labor official depends upon public opinion to enforce his minimum wage orders. See U. S. Department of Labor, "Memorandum on Industrial Legislation", *Bulletin No. 4050* (1934); Bureau of Labor Statistics, "Handbook, 1931", *Bulletin No. 541*, pp. 445-449.

forcement by only two inspectors " assigned to manufacturing plants and all matters connected with the employment of labor.[20]

Since about 1910 there has been a movement to shift the burden of accidents from the victims to the industry itself. South Carolina, Florida, Mississippi and Arkansas were the only states in 1934 that had no workmen's compensation law, setting aside or materially modifying the doctrine of the common law in respect to damages or accidents in industry.　In other words, South Carolina is one of four states in the Union where the official attitude is that the individual must gamble with the lawyer to recover.[21]

As Professor Munro has written: " The principle at the basis of these laws is that when an employee is injured in the course of his work the burden should not be placed wholly upon himself, or upon his family, or upon the employer; it should be included in the cost of production and thus borne by the entire consuming public.[22]　That is to say, the employers are expected to regard this as an item of expense like taxes, fire insurance, or replacement of machinery—an expense of production.　This principle recognizes the well-known fact that every consumable commodity has a definite cost in human suffering and seeks to distribute these unavoidable losses over society at large.　Its soundness is accepted by students of political science and by the general

[20] During 1933 the state board of health conducted a special investigation of health conditions in textile mills.　See *Report of the State Board of Health*, 1933, p. 13.

[21] It is estimated that over one-third of the amount paid by employers in South Carolina in the form of damages to injured employees goes to lawyers.

[22] W. B. Munro, *The Government of the United States* (N. Y., 1929), p. 498.

public, and the constitutionality of such laws is generally conceded.[23]

Governor Manning recommended as long ago as 1916 that a workmen's compensation law be enacted.[24] For a number of years the advisability of such legislation has been discussed in the legislative halls of the state. Governor Richards urged enactment as "not only wise, but necessary to place South Carolina in line with her sister States".[25] Governor Blackwood made like recommendations, both in 1931 and 1932.[26]

A number of different laws have been proposed during the past few years, two of which will command our attention. The "Aycock Bill" (H. 299) of 1931, providing for the creation of a "Commissioner of Workmen's Compensation", would have required employers to bear the expense of insurance administered by the state sinking fund commission. County and municipal corporations, domestic and farm employers, and employers "wholly or partly engaged in interstate commerce" were excluded from its provisions.[27] A senate bill (S. 1124) introduced in 1932, was modeled after the Virginia compensation law.[28] Like the "Aycock Bill", the sinking fund commission would have carried all insurance taken under the proposal, but it

[23] Experience has shown that workmen's compensation laws have been a tremendous stimulus to accident prevention and organized safety work. See H. A. Hatch, "Workmen's Compensation Will Benefit South Carolina", *American Labor Legislation Review*, vol. xix, p. 383 (December, 1929).

[24] *Reports and Resolutions*, vol. iii, 1916, p. 338.

[25] *Annual Message*, 1930, p. 9.

[26] *Inaugural*, 1931, p. 10; *Annual Message*, 1932, p. 12.

[27] See "Workmen's Compensation" (ed.) in *The People*, vol. i, no. 7, pp. 17, 18, 21; *House Journal*, 1931, pp. 161, 892, 2310; *News and Courier*, Feb. 11, 1931, and March 5, 1931.

[28] *Senate Journal*, 1932, pp. 178, 737; *News and Courier*, Feb. 26, 1932.

would have been administered by the attorney general, the insurance commissioner, and the commissioner of the Department of Agriculture, Commerce and Industries.

The principal objection to both of these is the proposed administrative machinery. In neither case is it a proper one, for an *ex officio* personnel is totally unsuited for the task to be performed. An industrial commission of three members should be set up in a well-organized department of labor. However, the financial arrangement, the source of contribution, and the operation by a state fund without competition, are to be commended.[29]

A compensation law is favored both by labor and the textile industry in South Carolina. The chief opposition has been expressed by the lumber interests.[30] Passage has also been made difficult by the presence of a large number of lawyers in the General Assembly. It is likely, however, that some type of workmen's compensation will be enacted in the near future.[31] This state should be greatly benefited by the passage of the proper law, for there is little doubt that the absence of such is retarding industry.

[29] Insurance of the employer's liability to pay compensation may be effected through private insurance (stock or mutual companies), by self-insurance (proof of solvency, with or without the giving of a bond or other security), or by insurance in state funds which may be exclusive or competitive. Of the 19 states having state fund insurance systems in 1931, 7 were exclusive, whereas in 12 the state funds were in competion with private insurance companies.

Of the 44 state workmen compensation laws, 12 were compulsory and 32 were elective. It is the opinion of the writer that such laws should be compulsory.

For an outline of workmen's compensation in the United States, see U. S. Bureau of Labor Statistics, *Bulletin No. 541*, pp. 891-909 (1931).

[30] *Ibid.* Saw-mill owners are probably able to settle for damages with their negro laborers for very small amounts.

[31] See open letter of a prominent group of South Carolinians in *Charleston Evening Post*, Jan. 7, 1932. A workmen's compensation law was confidently expected in 1935.

The uncertainty created by a continued agitation of the tax question is another retarding influence upon healthy industrial growth. Governor Richards was of the opinion that the variable tax policy " not only seriously affects the business interests already established, but tends to drive away capital that might otherwise be invested in our midst ".[32] The effect of such policy is argument in itself in favor of biennial sessions of the General Assembly. South Carolina allows the legislature to meet annually, with the result that a manufacturer can scarcely adjust himself to one legal situation before other proposed laws are upon him.[33] Biennial sessions will not solve the tax question but they will add stability to policy.

Practically all states today have made some provision for mediation and arbitration of labor controversies. In 1916, South Carolina created the Board of Conciliation " for the investigation and arbitration of disputes ".[34] This board is composed of three members, appointed by the governor for overlapping terms of six years. In constituting its membership, the law provides: [35]

One of the members of said board of conciliation shall be an employer of labor in behalf of any incorporated company; one to be a member of a recognized labor union; the third member to be appointed on recommendation of the two appointed as aforesaid: *Provided*, That in case the two members appointed as aforesaid do not agree on a third member within thirty days

[32] *Annual Message*, 1929, p. 11.

[33] Only five states have annual sessions: South Carolina, New York, New Jersey, Massachusetts and Rhode Island. Proposals to amend the constitution to effect biennial sessions have been submitted to the electorate four times, receiving a favorably majority vote in each instance. The legislature has refused to ratify. The last effort was lost in 1932. *House Journal*, 1932, pp. 27, 32.

[34] *Code 1932*, secs. 6353-6357.

[35] *Ibid.*, sec. 6360.

after their appointment, then the Governor shall use his discretion in the appointment of a third member without recommendation, so that at least one member shall be neither an employer of labor in behalf of an incorporated company nor an employee of any such company.

It is the duty of this board to report their findings of fact to the governor, and to attempt to persuade the parties of the dispute to reach a voluntary agreement or to submit the issues to arbitration. In this way the pressure of public opinion is brought to bear on the contestants. This agency has met with good results on the whole.[36] Practical difficulties and constitutional restraints prevent the state from taking more drastic measures.[37]

The enforcement of legislation regulating industries and labor conditions in South Carolina is a part of the duties of the Department of Agriculture, Commerce and Industries. Two inspectors are assigned by the Labor Division of this department to manufacturing plants and to matters connected with the employment of labor. The inadequacy of such limited administration is too apparent to call for discussion.

In 1929, a committee was created by the house of representatives to inquire into allegations that statutes seeking to regulate textile manufacturing corporations in respect to hours of labor, and chain stores in regard to their methods of operating, were ignored. This committee reached the unanimous conclusion " that the allegations in the premises of the Resolution are well taken ". Indeed, a most severe

[36] However, it failed to compose differences in the prolonged textile strike in Horse Creek Valley of Aiken County in 1932.

[37] See experience of Kansas in attempting to make arbitration compulsory and the awards of a court of industrial relations mandatory, *Wolff Packing Company v. Court of Industrial Relations*, 262 U. S. 525 (1923).

indictment of the department was returned. The investigation revealed practically no prosecutions of reported violations of the criminal laws of the state in regard to the regulation of working conditions, in spite of the fact that there had been " flagrant violations of the Labor Laws " at the factories where strikes had occurred. The committee found, " as a matter of fact the Commissioner is quite indifferent to the industrial situation in the State, and frankly admits that he knows nothing of the methods adopted in the adjoining states where the Department of Agriculture is separated from the Department of Labor ". In conclusion, it was charged that the administration of the office of Commissioner of Agriculture, Commerce and Industries was in " a state of inertia and lethargy".[38]

Although the report of the investigating committee dealt principally with the administration of this office, the legislature should not lose sight of the fact that it has failed to provide sufficient and adequate machinery to serve the state.

RECOMMENDATIONS

If South Carolina is to keep its industries abreast and properly protect both labor and capital, a department of labor must be organized on a plane adequate to meet the new requirements. The industrial development requires an effective administrative equipment to deal with the problems connected with the safety and welfare of employees and the maintenance of just and amicable relations between labor and industrial elements. It is in the public interest that the proper machinery for this purpose be established without further delay.[39]

[38] *House Journal*, 1930, pp. 12-17. The commissioner resigned in 1932.

[39] A bill to create a department of labor (H. 1782) was overwhelmingly passed by the house during the closing days of the 1932 session but was not considered by the senate. Record vote was, 57-7. *House Journal*, 1932, pp. 836, 1257, 1273.

For the purpose of performing the usual functions of inspection of industrial establishments, enforcement of labor laws, collection of industrial statistics, mediation and arbitration of disputes, and making awards in compensation cases (when the General Assembly has enacted a workmen's compensation law), the following administrative organization is suggested:

Department of Labor
1. Bureau of Inspection
2. Bureau of Employment and Statistics
3. Industrial Commission.

The department should be in charge of a commissioner of labor, appointed by the governor with consent of the senate. His office would be the administrative unit of the department and he would be empowered to appoint the directors of the bureau of inspection and the bureau of employment and statistics. It is also desirable that the department head should have authority, with consent of the governor, to re-arrange the bureau structure as the needs require.

The industrial commission would be composed of three members appointed by the governor with consent of the senate for overlapping terms of six years.[40] It would be the duty of the commission to perform the quasi-judicial function of making awards under the provisions of the Workmen's Compensation Act, and to arbitrate industrial disputes.[41] The commission and the commissioner, acting together, would exercise the supplementary legislative power of making regulations as to safety and sanitation in industrial establishments.

[40] See J. D. Barnett, "Representatives of Industry in Administration", in *National Municipal Review*, vol. xii, pp. 347-349; also, J. P. Chamberlain, "Democratic Control of Administration", in *American Bar Association Journal*, vol. xiii, pp. 186-188.

[41] The present board of conciliation would be abolished.

CHAPTER VII

Public Health

WHILE it is true that local initiative and interest must always remain important factors in this vital function of the state government, individual communities are no longer left independent to make and apply their own regulations. It is generally recognized that public health is chiefly a matter of state concern, requiring coordinated supervision of its needs. Over fifty years have passed since South Carolina took definite steps towards central health administration. As conservation of health has become a greater problem with the increase of population, the activities of the State Department of Health have expanded until it is now recognized as one of the most useful in the state administration.

In 1878, South Carolina established the state board of health as "the sole adviser of the State in all questions involving the protection of the public health within its limits ".[1] This board was, and still is, composed of the South Carolina Medical Association, the comptroller general, and the attorney general. Like other state boards of that time, its powers were limited to making investigations, publishing reports, and offering advice to local authorities.

The legislature in 1892 directed the South Carolina Medical Association, at its first meeting after the first day of January, 1893, and every seven years thereafter, " to elect seven members, to be recommended to the Governor, who

[1] *Code 1932*, secs. 4997, 4998; *Acts of 1878*, p. 729.

shall appoint them to cooperate with the State officers above named, to constitute an executive committee, having power to act in the intervals of the meeting of the State Board of Health ". It further provided that " members of this committee shall be removable by and at the pleasure of the Governor, upon the request of the State Board of Health, or for neglect of duty, or other causes set forth by the majority of the members of the executive committee ".[2]

By 1892, the law had materially increased the supervisory and advisory control of the central agency over the local boards. The executive committee was authorized and empowered to divide the state into health districts and, in those districts where no boards of health existed, they were required to appoint " sub-boards of health " to consist of two practicing physicians and one layman. The original statute as amended, provided: " Local boards of health . . . shall be subject to the supervisory and advisory control of the State Board of Health, through its executive committee. They shall pass no ordinances, nor consider any such of force, which are repugnant to the rules and regulations of the State Board of Health ".[3] In 1899, the board was given power to order and enforce vaccination " of all such persons as it may consider necessary for the preservation of the public health ".[4]

It was in the attempted enforcement of the last-named provision that the need of positive central control manifested itself. The local health agencies had not yet been subordinated. By reason of lack of power, the state board was

---

[2] *Code 1932*, sec. 4999. Since 1893, the membership of the executive committee has been increased to nine, viz: appointment of a pharmaceutical member in 1908, and a dentist in 1927.

[3] *Acts of 1883*, p. 291; *Acts of 1885*, p. 319; *Acts of 1892*, p. 20.

[4] *Acts of 1899*, p. 104. In 1905, local school authorities were forbidden to admit any pupil not properly vaccinated, *Acts 1905*, p. 871.

unable to cope with an epidemic of smallpox in 1899. Governor W. H. Ellerbe, in his annual message, urged that the board's authority be enlarged. Likewise the South Carolina Medical Association at its annual meeting held in Spartanburg, April 17, 1900, presented a memorial to the legislature.[5] Accordingly, in 1901 the General Assembly vested in the state agency the power to remove the members of the local boards " upon refusal or neglect to execute the orders of the State Board of Health ".[6]

The spirit of the twentieth century had won a signal victory over the individualism of the preceding one. It was destined to move on to further triumphs. Through legislation approved February 12, 1905, each incorporated village, town and city of the state was required to have and maintain a board of health, and definite duties were vested in the local boards in regard to quarantine against contagious diseases.[7]

The powers and duties of the state board were increased considerably by the statute enacted in 1912, and amended in 1926. It follows, in part:

The executive committee of the State Board of Health shall have the power to make, adopt, promulgate, and enforce reasonable rules and regulations from time to time requiring and providing for the thorough sanitation and disinfection of all passenger cars, sleeping cars, steamboats, and other vehicles of transportation in this State, and also all convict camps, penitentiaries, jails, hotels, schools and other places used by or open to the public; to provide for the care, segregation, and isolation of persons having or suspected of having any communicable, contagious, or infectious disease; to regulate the methods of

[5] See "Report of State Board of Health, 1900," *Reports and Resolutions*, 1901, pp. 1480-1482.

[6] *Acts of 1901*, p. 733; *Code 1932*, sec. 5015.

[7] *Acts of 1905*, p. 903; *Code 1932*, secs. 5005, 5006.

disposition of garbage or sewerage or any like refuse matter in or near any incorporated town, city, or unincorporated town or village of the State; and to abate obnoxious or offensive odors caused or provided by septic tank toilets by prosecution, injunction or otherwise; to provide for the thorough investigation and study of the causes of all diseases, epidemics or otherwise in this State, and the means for the prevention of contagious disease, and the publication and distribution of such information as may contribute to the preservation of the public health, and the prevention of disease; to make separate orders and rules to meet any emergency not provided for by general rules and regulations, for the purpose of suppressing nuisances dangerous to the public health and communicable, contagious and infectious diseases and other dangers to the public life and health.[8]

In general, the State Board of Health is charged with all the duties pertaining to organizations of like character. The law provides:

. . . It shall be the duty of the State Board of Health, through its representatives, to investigate the causes, character and means of preventing such epidemic and endemic diseases as the State is liable to suffer from; the influence of climate, location, and occupations, habits, drainage, scavengering, water supply, heating and ventilation; and shall make inspection annually, or oftener if necessary, of the sanitary condition of all institutions provided as State charities or supported at the public expense.[9]

To promote and to carry out properly the policies of the state board of health as formulated by its executive committee, the legislature in 1908 created the office of state health officer, the occupant of which was to serve as the

---

[8] *Acts of 1912*, p. 744; *Acts of 1926*, p. 1015; *Code 1932*, secs. 5002, 5003. It was made a misdemeanor to violate the rules of the Board.

[9] *Code 1932*, secs. 4998, 5001.

secretary and executive officer of the state board of health.[10] This officer is appointed by the governor upon the recommendation of the executive committee. The law provides that he " shall be a graduate of a reputable medical college and a physician, skilled in hygienic and sanitary science ". As secretary, it is provided: " He shall be custodian of books, papers, instruments or appliances belonging to the State Board of Health, or that may be entrusted to him. He shall summon the board to meetings, and shall attend all meetings of the board, and discharge the duties pertaining to the office of secretary ".

Since the establishing of this office, the State of South Carolina has rendered a constantly increasing service in the effort to conserve the health of its citizenry. Dr. James A. Hayne has been state health officer since 1911 and during his incumbency the administrative service has increased from two to eight divisions. He is in charge of all health work, with an assistant in charge of each division. A brief examination of the activities of these divisions will indicate something of the character of the public service in this important field at the close of 1932.

The Division of Administration is headed by the state health officer who exercises general supervision of the work done throughout the department. It is through this division that the rules and regulations promulgated by the executive committee are enforced. Among the activities of this office are the administration of all funds and the distribution of biological products. Not the least of its functions is the waging of a campaign to enlighten the people of the state

---

[10] *Code 1932*, secs. 5053, 5054, 5056, 5057. Dr. T. Grange Simmons, chairman of executive committee, 1897-1907, had urged creation of this office, *Reports and Resolutions*, 1906, vol. ii, p. 39. Dr. Robert Wilson, chairman from 1907 to 1931, made like recommendation, *Reports and Resolutions*, 1908, vol. ii, p. 813.

upon matters of sanitation and prevention of disease. To this end pamphlets and other literature are distributed and lectures are delivered in the interest of health education and the betterment of health conditions. This campaign is based upon the realization that, before intelligent and adequate cooperation of the citizens of the state with the agencies which they have set up for their own protection along health lines can be had, the people must understand the public health program.[11]

The Division of Sanitary Engineering gives valuable service in securing pure drinking water, clean milk, and proper sewage disposal. All new water plants and sewerage plants have to be passed upon by this department before they can be installed, and it is the duty of the field workers to see that they are properly maintained. Health conditions have improved a great deal in the towns and villages of the state as a result of these inspections. Quarterly reports on the chemical analysis of water furnished the public, either by municipalities or by corporations, are required. It is unfortunate that, due to lack of funds in 1931, it was impossible to carry out the scheme of town sanitary inspections and school inspections begun in 1930. The sanitary engineer reports that the county health units, wherever they exist, are attempting to supplement the efforts of this division in this matter. He adds, however, "The reports submitted so far show a very bad condition existing in the

[11] See "Available Sources in Planning, Promoting, or Carrying Out a Health Program in South Carolina", a pamphlet issued by the state board of health in 1931, *passim*. Also, the valuable analysis of South Carolina's health problem by the South Carolina Council's pamphlet report, "Health" (Cheraw, 1931). The state department is ably assisted in its educational work by such organizations as the South Carolina Tuberculosis Association, and the South Carolina Federation of Women's Clubs.

rural schools, particularly along the lines of drinking water supply and toilet facilities ".[12]

There are only sixteen cities in the state which have their dairies controlled by the Standard Milk Ordinance. However, in 1931, " cooperation with several county health authorities has been had in the inspection of private dairies not coming under the Standard Milk Ordinance; also an arrangement has been made with the Clemson authorities to inspect and advise along sanitary lines of other dairies throughout the State." [13]

One of the most important activities of the Division of Sanitary Engineering is its cooperation in controlling malaria and the mosquito pest by engineering advice as to drainage and other control measures. One has but to travel through the coastal section of South Carolina to appreciate the devastating effect of malaria and the problem that attends the efforts to eradicate it. The reason why these fertile counties are not thickly populated is not far to seek. In recent years, however, this malady has decreased at a rapid rate. The annual death rate from malaria per hundred thousand was reduced from 17.8 in 1919 to 6.2 in 1925, as a result of an intensive campaign waged during those years. Systematic control work of a permanent nature was done in certain towns under an agreement with the U. S. Public Health Service and the International Health Board.[14] Inasmuch as effective control measures involve a considerable outlay for drainage, the program is being retarded by the present condition of the state's finances. The

[12] *Report of State Board of Health*, 1931, p. 60. The position of sanitary engineer was abolished by the legislature in 1933. *Acts of 1933*, p. 623. By law, the state chemist has charge of the periodical analysis of the water supplies of all cities, towns, mills, etc.

[13] *Ibid.*, p. 59.

[14] See *Report of State Board of Health*, 1926, p. 72; *idem*, 1921, p. 29.

control of malaria remains one of the major health problems in South Carolina.[15]

The Division of Epidemiology seeks protection against diseases of an epidemic nature by acting with the local authorities in an advisory capacity, though South Carolina has no epidemiologist in the strict sense of the word. This office tabulates the reports of communicable diseases submitted weekly by the physicians of the state, and transmits them to the Surgeon General of the U. S. Public Health Service. Part of the duties of the assistant in charge of this division is to make a personal survey, annually, of the penal, educational, and charitable institutions of the state.[16]

One of the useful services performed by the Division of Hygienic Laboratory is the distribution of biologics. South Carolina was the first state in the Union to commence free distribution of diphtheria antitoxin (1908), and to give innoculation against typhoid (1910). Before vaccine was distributed the mortality from diphtheria was forty per cent, while now it is about four. The record for typhoid in 1915 was 35 deaths per 100,000 inhabitants; in 1931 it had been reduced to 15.[16] It is through this division that the state undertakes to furnish free Wassermans to all citizens of the state and also free treatment for those who have been bitten by rabid animals.[17]

---

[15] Splendid work was done in 1931 in the region of Murray Dam, near Columbia. The effective spraying, oiling and general control of mosquito breeding places attracted considerable attention in the outside world. See *Report of State Board of Health*, 1931, pp. 17, 18, 61-63. This division was discontinued April 1, 1933. The director was retained, however, and designated sanitary inspector. See *Report of State Board of Health*, 1933, pp. 10, 51-53.

[16] Under the provisions of the Appropriation Act of 1933, the office of epidemiologist was abolished Dec. 31, 1933.

[17] *Report of State Board of Health*, 1931, pp. 12, 18, 76. Antirabic treatment was furnished to 1235 persons during 1931.

Of course, the principal purpose of this division is "to aid in the preservation of public health by the performance of accurate scientific laboratory tests".[18] With only four people actually engaged in laboratory work, the amazing number of 83,410 diagnostic tests were made during 1931, compared to 37,215 in 1926. In its annual report for 1931, the state board expressed the belief that a great deal more is accomplished with the small personnel employed "than has been shown in the reports of other states".[19]

The Division of Vital Statistics was established in 1915.[20] Since then certificates of every birth have been required to be filed each month in the central office by the local registrars, but enforcement of this provision is not easy. As is the case with all states having a large negro population, it is a difficult matter to persuade physicians to maintain a complete record. To meet the minimum requirements of the U. S. Census Bureau, it is necessary to collect ninety per cent of the births and deaths occurring in the state each year. South Carolina failed in that from 1925 to 1927, inclusive, and consequently dropped from the Registration Area during those years. Having been readmitted, it is tremendously important that the state shall not again be dropped. As the state health officer has remarked, "it is the bookkeeping of the State Board of Health so far as health is concerned and without it we would be groping in the dark to know whether our efforts to protect the health of the citizens of the State are successful or not".[21]

The purpose of the Division of Child Hygiene is to reduce infant and maternal mortality and to secure better care for the pre-school child; this is one of the most serious prob-

[18] *State Board of Bealth,* "Health Program", p. 6.
[19] *Report of State Board,* 1931, p. 12.
[20] *Code 1932,* secs. 5130-5135.
[21] *Report of State Board of Health,* 1931, p. 13.

lems that confront the people of the state, for South Carolina has the largest maternity and infant death rate in the United States. In the face of that fact, the staff of this bureau consists of only two nurses and a clerical worker. That this agency should be expanded and its efforts given more liberal support from the people of South Carolina is a proposition not open to debate. It is true, nevertheless, that in 1931 the house eliminated the appropriation for its services and considerable lobbying was necessary to have it restored by the senate and the free conference committee. Nor is that all; in 1932 the amount appropriated was about fifty per cent of the previous year.[22]

According to the statement issued by the Children's Bureau, U. S. Department of Labor, South Carolina had a maternity death rate for the year 1929 of 114 per 10,000 live births, as compared with a rate of 70 for the Registration Area. While it is true that a large negro population in South Carolina materially affects the rate, the South Carolina Council has shown through a comparative study of the rates of the Southern States that the negro will not serve as an alibi. Indeed, this comparison shows that relatively the situation in South Carolina is worse with respect to white mothers than to negro mothers.[23] In regard to infant mortality, it is pointed out that the rate in this state for 1929 was 91 infant deaths for every 1,000 live births, as compared to 68 in the Registration Area. It is true, furthermore, that only two states in the Registration Area had a higher rate than South Carolina, namely, Arizona and New Mexico, while Colorado had the same.[24] What is South Carolina going to do about this appalling situation? [25]

[22] See *Report State Board*, 1931, p. 47; *Acts of 1931*, p. 428; *House Journal*, 1932, p. 1371.

[23] South Carolina Council, "Health", pp. 7-13.

[24] *Ibid.*, p. 8.

[25] For recommendations and suggestions, see *ibid.*, pp. 8, 9.

The Division of Child Hygiene was established in 1919 and, as already indicated, continues today as a skeleton bureau. Its function is to get information to the public that will result in the reduction of the amount of illness and the number of deaths among infants and mothers. Its work has to be largely educational. The staff paid directly by the state operates in collaboration with local services financed by such cooperating agencies as several of the counties, the American Red Cross, Metropolitan Life Insurance Company, cotton mills, chambers of commerce, and women's clubs. In 1931 there were fifty-five nursing services reporting to the central office, twenty-five of which were county services.[26] The state bureau promotes joint projects with such organizations as the South Carolina Public Health Association, the South Carolina Graduate Nurses' Association, and the Child Educational Service of the South Carolina Tuberculosis Association. At present, only four pre-natal clinics are operating in the state.[27] The establishment of a greater number of these clinics, in charge of competent pediatricians, should no longer be postponed.

One of the principal causes of the high rate of maternity and infant mortality is the widespread practice of midwifery. Of the 3,000, or more, practicing this profession, the larger number of them are among the negro population. The prevalence of ignorance and incompetency among this group is a problem to which the state bureau is constantly addressing its attention. During 1931, approximately 1150 of this group were taking the required course of instruction.

[26] *Report of State Board of Health,* 1931, p. 49.

[27] See *Report of State Board of Health,* 1931, pp. 47-50. The clinics are at Columbia, Florence, Sumter, and Kingstree. There are four colored nurses working under grants from the Rosenwald Fund and the Harmon Foundation.

The Division of Child Hygiene was discontinued May 15, 1933.

The Division of Rural Sanitation and County Health Work is doing a valuable work for the people of South Carolina. Inasmuch as the census of 1930 indicated that 78.7 per cent of the people dwell in the rural districts, it is not surprising to find that the principal work of the state board of health is performed there. In its effort to safeguard the health of the rural communities, this division has striven continuously to demonstrate to the several counties the value of a properly organized health department. It has urged the necessity of a well-developed unit in each of the counties through which the health laws of the state be carried out. In 1931, the International Health Board contributed $18,000 to carry on this work. The increase in the number of counties maintaining full-time county health officers appears to be constant during the past decade. There were eight in 1921; 16 in 1926; and 24 in 1931. It is believed that the time has now arrived when all the counties should have county boards of health similar to the city boards as already provided by law.[28]

In each of the twenty-four counties maintaining health units, a systematic program of public health is being carried on. The expense of this work is defrayed by the counties, the Rockefeller Foundation, and by the state and federal governments. In those counties where sufficient funds are not available for a county office, a public health nurse performs the services of the state bureau.

Over twelve per cent of all deaths and a great proportion of sickness are due to communicable disease. Hence, one of the most useful phases of the county health work is in popular education.[29] The majority of the people are not

[28] *Code 1932*, sec. 5005. See *Report State Board of Health*, 1931, p. 16. A single unit serves both Charleston County and the City of Charleston with marked success.

[29] See *ibid.*, pp. 64, 65. Through cooperation of the U. S. Public Health Service in 1931, approximately $30,000 was provided specifically to aid and encourage sanitation in South Carolina. *Ibid.*, p. 66.

acquainted with many of the elementary principles of health, and there are none who are more eager to learn than those unfortunates living in certain sections of rural South Carolina. That this is a fact beyond peradventure is evidenced by the number of those who attend and listen attentively to the lectures given by the public health officials. Much constructive work is being done, and much more can be done through the local health units in collaboration with local educational facilities.[30]

In 1933, the South Carolina Sanitorium was made a separate unit to operate independently under its superintendent. During the preceding period, its management was one of the most important official duties of the executive committee of the state board of health. This institution, for the treatment of tuberculosis only, was established for whites at State Park in 1914. Six years later a negro department, known as the Palmetto Sanitorium, was added.[31] Through the generosity of the Masonic Order of South Carolina, a building was erected in 1928 for incipient cases of tuberculosis, and an infirmary for white women in 1930.[32] The superintendent reports the need for more infirmary wards and additional provision for negroes, while the present capacity for white children and for incipient cases appear adequate to meet the needs of the state. The population, of October 1, 1931, totaled 246: white adults, 187; negro adults, 21; white children, 38.[33]

[30] See *Report of State Board of Health*, 1931, p. 69. A dental division operates within this department. There are 13 white dental clinics in the state. The first negro dental clinic was inaugurated during 1931, in the colored schools of Columbia.

[31] See *Report of State Board*, 1921, p. 108.

[32] *Idem*, 1928, p. 4; *idem*, 1930, p. 9.

[33] *Idem*, 1931, p. 88. See report of Field Secretary Tuberculosis Work, *ibid.*, pp. 98, 99.

The State Sanitorium is of inestimable value. However, the plant will have to be expanded to take care of the long waiting list of some 800, or the number of county sanitoria increased. Great advances have been made in South Carolina against tuberculosis, but it is still giving considerable concern—especially among the negroes.

It has been suggested that the management of the sanitorium be transferred to the board of public welfare " because it has the same business and maintenance problems " as the institutions now under their control.[34] While this point is well made, it is believed that this institution should be under the control and supervision of the agency in the state government responsible for all health activities.[35] And, as Dr. Williams has pointed out, its connection with the Department of Health makes its educational value very great.[36] Only under that arrangement can the management of the sanitorium and the work of the department in the tuberculosis field be closely correlated. To this end, a bureau of tuberculosis should be set up in the Department of Health and the extension work of the institution should be expanded through local clinics as rapidly as finances will permit.[37]

The total number of deaths in South Carolina from October 1, 1930 to September 30, 1931 was 21,407. While this was the lowest mortality record for some years, the rate was extremely high. The state board of health made the following analysis:

[34] See *Report of Committee on Economy and Consolidation*, 1922, p. 71.

[35] See Brookings institution, *Survey of North Carolina*, pp. 182, 186. In 1925, over 30 state health departments had assumed definite responsibilities in connection with control and prevention of tuberculosis.

[36] Williams, *Social Problems*, p. 76.

[37] For nature and extent of field work being done by S. C. Sanitorium, see *Report of State Board of Health*, 1931, p. 99.

The percentage death rate in South Carolina for the year was 12.2, 9.5 for whites and 15.0 for colored. The percentage for whites is one of the lowest in the United States and that of the colored is in marked contrast to the high death rate found among negroes in the northern states. Were it not for this high colored death rate, which is gradually being reduced, it having come down from 17.4 in 1915 to 15.0 in 1931, South Carolina would have one of the lowest death rates of any State in the United States. The white death rate in 1915 was 12.2 as compared with 9.5 for the year 1931.[38]

The main causes of deaths in this state may be cited in the following order: diseases of circulation, 4,995; infant mortality, 3,292; kidney diseases, 2,176; pneumonia, 1,848; tuberculosis, 1,211; influenza and la grippe, 1,180.

The Health Department has recently devoted much attention to pellagra. Since this is a disease of deficiency of diet, it was feared that it would increase as economic distress became greater. With aid of the U. S. Public Health Service an intensive campaign was conducted. Clinics were held in 24 counties where 1000 patients were seen and instructed. This disease which annually affects over 20,000 persons was prevented from following the curve of the depression. Indeed, a noteworthy reduction in deaths resulted, e. g., 637 in 1931 as compared to 811 in 1930. During 1931, this office distributed at cost 23 tons of yeast in five-pound packages.[39]

The apparent indifference to the prevalence of venereal disease in South Carolina is amazing. The knowledge that this devastating form of disease is contributing greatly to the institutional population is a commonplace, and the South Carolina Council reports that it " is reliably informed by

[38] *Report of State Board of Health*, 1931, p. 15.

[39] See *ibid.*, p. 14; also report of sub-committee on nutrition of the South Carolina Council, "Health", pp. 15-18.

those in position to know that a large part of the still-birth rate is due to syphilis ".[40]   But it is a fact that the state makes no provision against it, as its program against venereal disease was stopped in 1924 by the refusal of the General Assembly to appropriate funds.[41]   Dr. C. V. Akin of the U. S. Public Health Service, who was directing the program in South Carolina, estimated the value of work done during 1921 (at lowest professional rates) at more than two million dollars.[42]   He added: " It is impossible to state the value of the work in terms of disease prevention and in the saving of life, and the increased productiveness of the individuals benefitted "

PROPOSED ADMINISTRATIVE REORGANIZATION

The act of the General Assembly in constituting the South Carolina Medical Association in its corporate capacity as the State Board of Health is fundamentally unsound. In the first place, an unofficial organization should never serve as the controlling force of a governmental agency. The public has no way of holding such a body responsible for formulating and administering the policies of such a highly important state department.   In the second place, the Medical Association is naturally restricted in the breadth of its vision by its professional training.   Consequently, it is not likely to appreciate all of the several aspects of the broad problem of the public health.   Finally, there is no

[40] South Carolina Council, " Health ", p. 11. The state does not even require a medical examination before issuing a marriage certificate.

[41] There are five locally-supported clinics in the state: in Charleston (Roper Hospital, out-patient work), Columbia, Spartanburg, Florence, and Orangeburg.

[42] See *Report of State Board of Health*, 1921, pp. 84, 85. The total expense of the work, including administration, operation and maintenance of nine clinics, and cost of medical and surgical supplies and equipment was $64,170.70. Of this amount, the state appropriated $33,886. 31,717 cases were treated at a per capita cost of $2.02.

more reason why the Medical Association should appoint and control the state health officer than, for example, that the State Teachers' Association should be empowered to appoint and control the state superintendent of education. It is therefore suggested that the State Board of Health, as now constituted, be abolished.

A Department of Health should be created under a commissioner of health, appointed by the governor with the consent of the senate.[43] This mode of appointment is designed to destroy the present anomalous relationship in which the state health officer is held responsible to a board not even of the chief executive's own making. The law should, by all means, require specific qualifications of the commissioner. He should be one who is schooled and experienced in the administration of public health work and sanitary science.[44]

To maintain continuity of policy and to provide for such quasi-legislative functions as may be required in adopting health regulations, an unpaid, advisory health board or council should likewise be appointed by the governor with consent of the senate. Since the governor's term is for four years, it is recommended that this council consist of seven members appointed for seven-year overlapping terms. It is further suggested that it should represent the medical, engineering, legal, educational, and welfare interests of the state, with no one group dominating.[45]

[43] This is the current practice in a number of the states that have reorganized their state administration.

[44] See National Institute of Public Administration, *Survey of Arkansas*, p. 145. It might well be required that the appointment shall be made from a qualified list of public health officers, certified by the U. S. Public Health Service.

[45] See New York Bureau of Municipal Research, *Survey of New Jersey*, p. 245. Also, Brookings Institution, *Survey of North Carolina*, p. 185.

In conclusion, it is understood that the purpose of the council is to advise with the commissioner on any phase of departmental work, but to have no administrative duties whatever. This position should be made perfectly clear in the statutes.[46] On the administrative side, bureau organization should be left to the judgment of the commissioner who should have the power to appoint the directors of the divisions.

The following internal units are suggested:

1. Office of Commissioner
2. Bureau of Local Health Work
3. Bureau of Sanitary Engineering and Inspection
4. Bureau of Epidemiology
5. Bureau of Laboratories
6. Bureau of Maternity and Child Hygiene
7. Bureau of Vital Statistics

It will be observed that the proposed bureau structure is similar to the organization under the state board of health before the recent cut in appropriations.[47] It contemplates, however, a needed augmentation of services along the lines stressed in the discussion of that organization.

[46] See National Institute of Public Administration, *op. cit.*, p. 55.

[47] It is assumed that the state intends to restore at the earliest possible moment the essential services that were discontinued in the "reorganization" of 1933. Therefore, the writer has allowed the description of 1932 to stand and has made suggestions on that basis—without comment on the unfortunate results that would necessarily attend permanent curtailment.

CHAPTER VIII

PUBLIC WELFARE

THE general field of public welfare is usually recognized as one of the largest single problems in state administration. Vast sums must necessarily be invested in social welfare to help the unfortunate elements in a state's population. These needs naturally increase and a benevolent state is constantly required to find more and more money to perform this service. Wise expenditure is essential in order that as great a measure of good as possible may result.

Welfare institutions and services are costing the state government of South Carolina today about fifteen per cent of the total amount appropriated each year.[1] This does not take into account permanent improvements, which are greatly needed but cannot be provided at this time. The state suffers not only from a lack of funds but from the absence of centralized supervision and control of her charitable, penal and correctional institutions, which practically operate independently of each other. An integrated agency must be created to make possible an intelligent and informed institutional planning.[2] Uniformity in the organization and administration of welfare institutions is desired, to the end that there may be a standardization of services, salaries, accounts, methods, and reports. It is submitted that the

[1] The General Assembly in 1932 appropriated around $1,285,000 for the operation of these services. No permanent improvements were provided. Appropriations for 1934 amounted to $1,270,526.

[2] A state board of public welfare is known to the law, but no appropriation is made for the operation of its field services.

establishment of responsible supervision, with a centralization of the purchase of supplies, would promote economy
and efficiency. Several of the more progressive states have
achieved this result through such organization.

Before undertaking to suggest further what changes
should be made in the state's administration of its public
welfare services, the several penal, correctional and charitable institutions and agencies now operating will be outlined.

I. PENAL INSTITUTIONS

1. State Penitentiary

The general penitentiary and prison of the state is located
in the City of Columbia on the Congaree River.[3] Two
prison farms, the De Saussure Farm and the Reid Farm,
are maintained in Sumter and Kershaw Counties by the
penitentiary and are worked by negro convicts. Although
these two farms adjoin, until 1933 they operated under separate management—for no apparent reason.

The State Penitentiary is in charge of a board of directors consisting of five members, appointed by the governor
with consent of the senate for overlapping terms of five
years. This board has exclusive power to appoint and remove the superintendent.[4] Prior to 1923, divided control
and responsibility resulted from the legislature electing both
the directors and the superintendent,[5] but this fundamental
defect was corrected at that time.[6]

---

[3] The buildings in Columbia have an estimated value of $600,000. See
J. Wilson Gibbes, *Legislative Manual*, 1934, p. 237.

[4] *Code 1932*, sec. 1962.

[5] See *Report of Joint Legislative Committee on Economy and Consolidation*, 1922, p. 61; *Report of Special Joint Legislative Committee to
Investigate Conditions at State Penitentiary*, 1923, p. 7.

[6] *Acts of 1923*, p. 224.

The question of employment of the convicts has long been a problem to the penitentiary authorities. The system of hiring them to private employers was still in vogue in 1900. For example, the services of both men and women were sold in 1891 on contract to a hosiery mill. When the contract expired in 1911, it was renewed for an additional period of five years.[7] This practice was not conducive to the best interests of those so employed. Indeed, Governor Blease used the alleged inhumane conditions in the penitentiary as an excuse for pardoning about 1700 convicts during his tenure of office, 1911-1915.

The administration of Governor Richard I. Manning was responsible for what was styled " a transition period in the history of the institution " [8]—as indeed it was in the history of the entire state government of South Carolina.

Following the expiration of the hosiery mill contract, a profitable industry was set up in the manufacture of fibre-craft furniture. It operates as a separate and distinct business from the penitentiary. Not only does it finance itself but it serves as a source of revenue.[9] However, its greatest recommendation is its contribution to the solution of the problem of providing prisoners with activity. During 1930, the license plate factory for the manufacture of license tags and road signs for the Highway Department was installed. In 1932, the board of directors completed negotiations for the establishment of a men's underwear manufacturing plant

[7] *Report of State Penitentiary*, 1910, *Reports and Resolutions*, 1911, vol. v, p. 340.

[8] See *Reports and Resolutions*, 1916, vol. i, p. 924. The " War Governor ", as Governor Manning was known, is generally regarded as South Carolina's ablest governor since the adoption of the constitution of 1895. His constructive leadership was reflected particularly in the field of social welfare.

[9] The furniture factory was destroyed by fire in the spring of 1932, but has been rebuilt.

at the prison. Since then a vegetable cannery has been added as an industry within the walls.[10]

Several official investigations have been made of the penitentiary within the past decade and the burden of the several reports has been the need of an entirely new plant.[11] The Special Joint Legislative Committee to Investigate Conditions at the State Penitentiary, 1923, was of the opinion that " immediate difficulties encountered by the management and about which conflicts centered are due to the need of adequate buildings ".[12] Most of the buildings were described as poorly designed and constructed. With reference to the main cell building where most of the white and negro male prisoners are housed at night, this committee had the following to say: " All cells were full at the time of our visits and in many of them two prisoners were confined where the quarters are very cramped for one. Two men spending from twelve to fourteen hours a day in a space 4½ by 7½ and seven feet high, and sleeping together in a bed two and a half by six and a half in a building that is cold in winter and often hot in summer is a condition that threatens the health of any but robust men, and many inmates are far from robust ".[13] The installation of completely new equipment was regarded as the only satisfactory remedy.[14]

[10] See *Report of Penitentiary*, 1934, p. 6.

[11] However, the Joint Committee on Economy and Consolidation, 1922, devoted its attention to criticism of the management. See *Report*, p. 61.

[12] See Report of Special Joint Committee, 1923, especially pp. 16, 18, 22, 24, 40-50. This report is very comprehensive and equally convincing. Photographs, showing the structure and operation of the plant, are printed throughout.

[13] *Ibid.*, p. 13.

[14] The superintendent and members of the board visited several penal institutions during 1923, both North and South, and were impressed by the lack of equipment in South Carolina. *Report of Penitentiary*, 1923, p. 8.

Another legislative investigation was made in 1926.[15] It brought out the same story of dilapidated and antiquated buildings, of obsolete equipment, and the lack of sanitary facilities. In addition, this committee made specific recommendations concerning possible funds for the establishment of a new plant.[16] During the same year a special committee of the state board of health returned a detailed condemnation, with this concluding statement: " It seems to us that the recommendations can all be included in one, viz., an entirely new plant ".[17] The legislature was moved to action. A bill was passed authorizing the penitentiary authorities to borrow $300,000 from the sinking fund commission for the purpose of commencing a new institution on state-owned land. But when the commission reported to the penitentiary board that the money was not available, the situation was left unchanged.[18]

The condition at the state's prison is deplorable and continues to grow worse. Experts in fire prevention and fire fighting proclaim it is a fire trap. The necessity of immediate steps looking toward the abandonment of the present plant and the establishment of a modern up-to-date prison has been urged by various officials and organizations, including the governor, the state board of public welfare, all of the investigating committees during the past decade, the American Legion, the American Legion Auxiliary, and the

[15] Gov. Thos. G. McLeod urged remedial legislation, *Inaugural Message*, 1923, p. 6. He suggested a bond issue of $10,000,000 for the purpose of financing permanent improvements at the educational, penal and charitable institutions. See his special message of Feb. 23, 1923, *House Journal*, 1923, p. 424. The state board of public welfare endorsed the governor's recommendation of a new prison, *Report*, 1925, p. 14.

[16] See *Report of Special Joint Committee to Investigate Penitentiary*, 1926, p. 6.

[17] *Report of State Board of Health*, 1926, pp. 31, 32.

[18] See *Report of Penitentiary*, 1926, p. 4.

South Carolina Federation of Business and Professional Women's Clubs.[19]

A new cell block of 102 cells, which is portable and can be transferred in the event of a new prison, was constructed in 1931. Still the population increases so rapidly that the authorities are unable to house the inmates properly. Indeed, the situation as of June 30, 1932, was worse than before the additional cells were added during the previous year. The crowded condition of the prison may be understood when it is realized that at that time it was necessary to place 960 men in 364 cells, each of which was supposed to accommodate two prisoners.[20]

It is hardly necessary to suggest that it is the experience of prison authorities that idleness and crowded conditions are the breeders of revolt. So desperate was the situation that the governor resorted very freely to his power of executive clemency. Unfortunately, a new plant cannot be had until economic conditions improve. Temporary expedients must necessarily be the order of the day. In 1933, the legislature authorized the governing board of the State Penitentiary to permit the use of convict labor on state highways and other public projects.

---

[19] See *House Journal*, 1924, pp. 1495, 1496; *idem*, 1927, pp. 422, 423.
On Feb. 21, 1935, a newly appointed state prison committee went on record as favoring the construction of a new penitentiary outside the city of Columbia and began preparation of a program to be submitted to the legislature.

[20] See *Charleston Evening Post*, June 30, 1932. The total number of convicts was 1,242. Of these, 71 were women: 15 whites and 56 negroes. Of the 1,171 men, 543 were white and 628 colored. There were 211 negro men on the two prison farms. The crowded condition caused the legislature to refuse to admit federal prisoners in 1931. *Acts of 1931*, p. 420. The average number in the prison at Columbia during 1934 was 1,021. In his *Inaugural Address* (Feb. 15, 1935), Governor Johnston suggested that the congestion be removed by transferring " prisoners with good records to the state farms, or to concentration barracks located one to each of the six congressional districts where they might aid in the work of reforestation, soil erosion, or the building of rural electric lines."

II. JUVENILE CORRECTIONAL INSTITUTIONS

Dr. G. Croft Williams, the distinguished sociologist of the University of South Carolina, has written: "At first the convicts of the penitentiary were leased out, later they made brooms and shoes within the walls, but under contract. In 1885, the county chain-gang was established. Then came the reformatories for boys, which were succeeded by the industrial schools for boys and girls. An understanding of our penal institutions cannot be had unless we take this development into consideration." [21] And, as he further observes, "not many years ago there were no separate institutions for children, so these youths roamed the streets or were caged with common criminals ".[22] Today there are three state institutions for juvenile offenders.

1. *State Reformatory for Negro Boys* [23]

This institution, located about six miles from Columbia on the Broad River Road, was established in 1900 under control of the penitentiary authorities. All negro boys, between the ages of eight and seventeen who are legally convicted of any criminal offense and are punishable by imprisonment in the state prison, are committed to the reformatory.[24]

For two decades this institution was administered as a juvenile penitentiary, but its management was greatly improved when turned over to the state board of welfare in 1920.[25] It is probably not too much to say that a transfor-

[21] Williams, *Social Problems of South Carolina*, p. 172.

[22] Williams, *op. cit.*, p. 65.

[23] The title was legally changed in 1930 to "The John G. Richards Industrial Training School for Negro Boys", but the institution is seldom referred to as such. *Acts of 1930*, p. 2160.

[24] *Code 1932*, sec. 2021.

[25] *Ibid.*, sec. 1996; *Acts of 1920*, p. 999.

mation was effected in the treatment of the inmates. New guards were installed and different methods were applied under the changed type of discipline. Superintendent S. A. Lindsay, though trained as an administrator of penitentiary discipline, quickly fell in line with the new spirit of the Board's policy.

Since the majority of the boys are under fourteen years of age, this institution could hardly be expected to be self-sustaining. Discipline is mild and an effort is made to have it conform to that of a public school. All small boys are required to attend four hours of school each day to be instructed in the rudiments of academic education. The larger boys are also taught shoe-making and carpentering. The farm consists of 603 acres, of which 425 are under cultivation of vegetables and fruits.[26]

2. *South Carolina Industrial School for Boys*

This school, established by statute in 1906 for the reformation of white boys, is located at Florence.[27] These boys had previously been housed in a separate building on the grounds of the penitentiary.[28] Like the Reformatory, this institution has been under the management and control of the state board of welfare since 1920. In addition to those legally convicted of crime, provision is also made for voluntary commitment of boys under seventeen years of age, upon request of parents or guardian and with the approval of the court. Consequently, all classes of the neglected and delinquent are received. The population as of December 31, 1930, was 214.

[26] See *Report of State Board of Welfare*, 1926, pp. 57, 58. Also, Gibbes' *Leg. Manual*, 1934, p. 238.

[27] *Code 1932*, secs. 2014-2020; *Acts of 1906*, p. 133.

[28] See "Report of State Penitentiary", *Reports and Resolution*, 1906, vol. ii, p. 542. Also, Governor Ansel, "Annual Message", 1909, *Reports and Resolutions*, 1909, p. 1035.

The state board of welfare, in reporting the last year in which funds were appropriated for the operation of its field services, set forth the purpose of this institution as being that of endeavoring to equip the inmates " with the rudiments of a common school education, the ability to pursue a useful occupation, and a well-developed character ". That this was not being realized was indicated, however, as it reported " an inadequate teaching force, cramped and unsuitable school quarters, and a lack of necessary articles of school equipment which would make toward greater effectiveness in school work ".[29] The Joint Legislative Committee on Economy and Consolidation of 1922 found conditions bad both from social and business points of view.[30] We are told by the state board of health that the health of the boys is at stake. The report of the sanitary inspection made in 1931 reads: " Again the attention is invited to the urgent need for hospital quarters or a hospital building. And attention is invited to the fact that in violation of the laws of the State there are no fire escapes. The whole plant is in need at many places of overhauling and repairing and in some instances of entire replacement." [31]

3. *State Industrial School for Girls*

This institution was established in 1918 and placed under the control of the board of correctional administration. For the first two years of its existence, it was carried on in an old hotel at Campobello. In February, 1920, it was moved to a new plant near Columbia and placed under the management of the state board of public welfare. White girls, under twenty-one years of age, are legally committed

[29] *Report of Board of Public Welfare*, 1926, pp. 54, 55.

[30] *Report*, pp. 54, 55.

[31] *Report of State Board of Health*, 1931, p. 39. The school has a capacity of 200.

for incorrigibility, immorality, or such crime as would otherwise imprison them in the penitentiary.[32]

The school was designed not only as a correctional institution, but also as a place for training in domestic and farm work. The girls do the light work on the farm and care for the school grounds. They are also required to attend school for one-half of each day for ten months of the year. Their general health is reported to be good, though many of the girls are in a deplorable physical condition when they enter.[33]

It appears, however, that this institution has suffered terribly within the past five years, since the virtual abolition of the central agency of supervision and control. The Special House Committee, appointed in 1932 to investigate the present operation, returned a severe indictment, containing, among others, the following particulars:[34] (1) Inefficiency of management under a superintendent unfitted for her job; (2) Inadequacy of medical attention; (3) Insufficient protection against fire; (4) Operation of the institution as a penal institution—title misleading; (5) Lack of real board control—the honorary board functioning in a perfunctory manner. In 1933 no appropriation was made for the operation of this institution.

Fairwold School

The State of South Carolina makes no provision for delinquent negro girls. When one of these commits an offense

[32] *Code 1932*, secs. 2024-2036.

[33] See *Report of State Board of Public Welfare*, 1926, pp. 49-51.

[34] *House Journal*, 1932, pp. 1197-1199. The legislature changed the title of the institution to, The South Carolina Reformatory for Girls, *ibid.*, p. 1506. In 1934 the legislature vested the control of this institution in the Superintendent of the State Training School and authorized him, in his discretion, to transfer inmates of the industrial school to the school at Clinton. *Acts of 1934*, p. 1655. For an account of the reorganization of the industrial school, see *Report of State Training School*, 1934, pp. 27-30.

or is a menace to the morals of the community, she is sent to jail or left to roam at large. Fairwold School is a private school for negro girls which the negroes of the state have conducted for over a decade. As one writer has said, " there is no reason why delinquent colored girls that are sentenced by regularly constituted courts should fall to the care of a few public-minded but poor members of their race ".[35] The state dropped its small contribution to this institution in 1927, on the plea that public money should not be given to a private institution.[36]

III. CHARITABLE INSTITUTIONS AND AGENCIES

1. State Hospital

In 1821 the General Assembly appropriated $30,000 for the founding of the South Carolina Lunatic Asylum, for lunatics and deaf and dumb persons.[37] The original building, erected on a square of four acres in the City of Columbia, was not completed until 1828. This building, designed by the celebrated South Carolina architect, Robert Mills, is still standing and is perhaps the oldest one in use in this country for the insane.

No State except Virginia had undertaken the care of the insane, and for several years the institution was regarded

[35] Williams, op. cit., p. 178. The state board of public welfare has recommended a state industrial school for negro girls. See its Report, 1925, p. 13.

[36] This item in the appropriation bill was vetoed by Governor Richards. House Journal, 1927, p. 1668.

[37] An account of the laying of the cornerstone of the " Lunatic Asylum and School for the Deaf and Dumb " in the Charleston Courier, August 3, 1822. It is reprinted in Report of State Hospital, 1923, p. 9. That these two classes of unfortunates should have been grouped together is not surprising, for in early years insane persons and paupers were handled together. A separate institution for the deaf and the blind was founded in 1849. See Chapter IV.

as an experiment. At first, advertisements for patients were placed in the newspapers of South Carolina and of adjoining states. However, after the General Assembly in 1830 made it obligatory to send lunatics, idiots and epileptics to the asylum, the institution made steady growth in numbers and in usefulness.[38] It was not until 1870 that its operation became a direct charge on the state treasury.[39]

From the beginning, applications for the admission of negro patients were received but they were not admitted until 1848, when it was ordered by the General Assembly that they be received upon the same terms and conditions as white patients. Though the question of segregating the races was agitated for forty years or more, the same basis for admission has remained a fixed policy to this date.[40]

It has been aptly suggested that the evolution of the name of the institution indicates the development of its attitude toward its inmates. The original title of Lunatic Asylum was changed by the constitution of 1895 to State Hospital for the Insane. The adoption in 1915 of the title of State Hospital seemed to tell the story of a new vision acquired. "From being a place of custody for maniacs", writes Dr. Williams, "it has become a hospital for the care of the mentally sick."[41]

The State Hospital has had only five superintendents in its history. For the purpose of the present study, attention is confined to the administrations of the last two, i. e., Dr.

---

[38] For an explanation of the rapid growth, see Governor M. B. McSweeney's "Annual Message", 1901, *Reports and Resolutions*, 1901, vol. ii, pt. 2, p. 1428.

[39] See *Report of State Hospital*, 1900, *ibid.*, p. 1428; *idem*, 1903, vol. ii, pp. 1269, 1270.

[40] "Report of Regents of State Hospital for the Insane, 1902", *Reports and Resolutions*, 1903, vol. ii, p. 1271.

[41] William, *op. cit.*, p. 111.

J. W. Babcock (1891-1914) and Dr. C. Fred Williams (1915-   ).[42]   Governor B. R. Tillman brought Dr. Babcock, a recognized alienist, to the superintendency in 1891. The story of his career in South Carolina is a pathetic one. Though cognizant of the needs of such an institution, this shy individual took orders from the dominating Tillman to economize. Consequently, he did not insist upon sufficient appropriations and the condition of the hospital became deplorable.[43]

For several years prior to 1915 there had been a growing belief among the people of the state that the treatment of the insane was not in accordance with modern ideas and methods. Noticeable agitation resulted from the legislative investigations of 1909 and 1914.[44]   Before his inauguration, Governor Manning sought advice from Dr. Thomas W. Salmon, Medical Director of the National Committee for Mental Hygiene. Following his induction into office, he caused an investigation to be made by Dr. Herring, Secretary of the Lunacy Commission of Maryland, which helped to crystallize sentiment in favor of improvement in equipment and reform in the administration of the institution.[45]

A new board of regents, appointed by Governor Manning, qualified March 8, 1915. Dr. C. Fred Williams, previously vice-president of the board of regents and state health officer, was appointed superintendent. The legislature at the same time appropriated $150,000 to inaugurate a projected

[42] Dr. T. J. Strait was acting superintendent during the reorganization, March 8 to May 1, 1915.

[43] See " The State Board of Health and the State Hospital for the Insane, 1880-1906 ", *Reports and Resolutions*, 1910, pp. 184-231.

[44] See Report of Regents, *Reports and Resolutions*, 1915, vol. iii, p. 212.

[45] See Governor R. I. Manning, *Annual Message*, 1919, pp. 6, 7. The recommendations made by Dr. Herring were substantially the same as those previously made by Dr. Babcock.

four-year program of reorganization.[46]   Dr. Williams, who made no claim as an expert, has apparently proven himself an excellent administrator.

The constitution of 1895 provided that the governor, with the consent of the senate, should appoint both the board of regents and the superintendent.   Obviously, such a division of responsibility for the management of the institution was likely to prove unsatisfactory.   This defect was corrected in 1918 by an amendment which provided: " The Board of Regents shall have exclusive power to appoint and, in its discretion, remove one Superintendent thereof ". The board consists of five members with overlapping terms of five years, appointed by the governor with consent of the senate.[47]

A very serious handicap to the effective operation of the State Hospital is the lack of accommodations for the number to be treated.   Since the commencement of the period of its rapid growth the hospital has been taxed beyond its capacity.   For many years, all classes of defectives—idiots, epileptics, inebriates, dotards, the homeless and friendless— were forced upon it.   There was no redress until the state could provide accommodations elsewhere.   Finally, it was enacted in 1920 that the institution should be maintained " solely for the support and treatment of persons with mental diseases ".[48]   Even so, the main problem of administration continues to be the need of adequate buildings; it is the urgent cry year after year, the principal burden of each annual report.

In 1920, the board of regents adopted the program of remodeling the main plant in Columbia, with the view of

[46] See "Report of State Hospital", 1915, *Reports and Resolutions, 1916*, vol. iii, pp. 347, 361-365.

[47] *Constitution*, art. xii, sec. 2; *Code 1932*, sec. 6222.

[48] *Code 1932*, sec. 6227; *Acts of 1920*, p. 704.

segregating all negro patients at State Park, about seven miles from that city.[49] Overcrowding in the colored male department was overcome to a great extent in 1927 by the completion of three buildings at State Park. By 1931, all negro patients had been transferred except 345 colored women.

In its report for 1931, the board of regents wrote: " If the hospital is to continue to accept patients, it must have additional quarters in which to place them. Otherwise the time will shortly come when the hospital will not be justified in continuing to accept patients except when vacancies occur through death or discharge ".[50]   However that may be, the fact is inescapable that someone is going to care for them and that in the last analysis the burden falls upon the people. And it might be added that this care is not only an act of charity, but also a protection to the state. Moreover, a natural and normal increase of patients each year may be expected. The following table speaks for itself.

Year	Value of Plant	Total Expenditures	Daily per Capita Cost	Population
1920	$2,454,895.89	$1,035,052.86	$0.8658	2,205
1921	2,505,314.49	746,448.65	.7735	2,354
1922	2,467,974.22	652,407.28	.7218	2,399
1923	2,457,127.30	776,060.48	.7880	2,421
1924	2,546,392.33	857,566.32	.7981	2,527
1925	2,668,110.24	821,688.70	.8580	2,532
1926	2,642,048.01	944,040.37	.8986	2,558

[49] The board of public welfare described the housing facilities of the negroes as " shockingly inadequate " at that time, *Report*, 1921, p. 53. Also, see *Report of South Carolina Mental Hygiene Survey*, 1922, pp. 63, 64.

[50] *Report*, 1931, p. 6.   See *Report of State Board of Health*, 1931, p. 39.

In 1934 the legislature authorized the State Hospital to borrow $500,000 from the Public Works Administration of the U. S. Government. This amount, together with the related grant of $150,000, should relieve the crowded condition to a considerable extent. *Acts of 1934*, p. 1204. See *Report of State Hospital*, 1934, p. 6.

1927	2,820,369.13	1,127,499.66	.8980	2,709
1928	3,048,086.37	1,057,681.83	.8997	2,884
1929	2,859,819.94	1,056,098.90	.8956	3,029
1930	2,945,900.67	1,045,613.55	.8171	3,166
1931	2,951,025.47	979,416.49	.7735	3,273

The appropriation for 1932 was $800,000, as compared to $948,268 for the previous year. On July 1, 1934, there were 3461 patients and county commissioners were being urged to send only violent cases to Columbia.

One of the specific needs of the institution is special buildings for the criminally insane of both races. There is no place in the penal system of South Carolina for them, where they can be securely held for their own care and treatment, as well as for the protection of the general public.[51]

It was the opinion of the Committee on Economy and Consolidation in 1922, that the hospital was " one of the best managed institutions of the kind in the South or indeed in the whole country ". In 1931, the state board of health described it as being " excellently kept and managed ", but added, " the plant can be much improved by replacing some of the very old buildings and adding to the others ".

2. State Training School

This institution was established in 1918 at Clinton for feebleminded persons of the white race. Though separate both in location and management, it was originally placed under the control of the board of regents of the State Hospital. Supervision was transferred to the state board of welfare, however, when that agency was created in 1920.[52]

[51] See Williams, *op. cit.*, p. 179; and, *Report of State Hospital*, 1931, p. 25.

[52] *Code 1932*, secs. 1996, 6250-6269. There is no provision in South Carolina for the care of the feeble-minded of the negro race.

This governing body selects a superintendent and also appoints an advisory committee of three women.

The cost of maintenance for 1931 was $128,834.37, or a daily per capita cost of 72.4 cents, which is said to be far below the general average cost of state institutions of this kind throughout the United States. Located on a tract of land of about twelve hundred acres, the plant has an estimated value of $350,000. With a capacity of only 430, the daily average enrollment was 487, and demands upon the institution are greater than ever. Indeed, according to the superintendent, " the institution finds it impossible to give serious consideration to any except the most urgent applications." [53]

It is believed that the school is being run as efficiently and effectively as may be reasonably expected. While citing the need of better accommodations, " if the school is to function properly ", the board of public welfare found no fault with the work that was being done under the administration of Superintendent B. O. Whitten.[54]

Reference to a study of fairly recent date will indicate the need of additional provision for the care of mental defectives.

In 1921, the National Committee for Mental Hygiene conducted a survey under the auspices of the South Carolina Mental Hygiene Committee, money being made available through a special appropriation of the Rockefeller Foundation. Aside from a study of the facilities of the various state, county, and city institutions, private agencies, and public schools, the survey included a careful examina-

---

[53] *Report*, 1931, pp. 5, 6. See *Report of State Board of Health*, 1931, p. 38. At the close of 1934, the application of the State Training School for a loan and grant, totaling approximately $165,000, had not been approved by the Public Works Administration. See *Report of State Training School*, 1934, p. 9.

[54] *Report*, 1926, p. 71.

tion of the inmates of a number of these institutions and agencies. The following are some of the startling facts revealed by that survey: [55]

1. Public schools — approximately 13,000 feeble-minded children: 5,000 whites and 8,000 negroes.
2. State Penitentiary:
   a. Insane: 8.6% whites; 9.8% negroes.
   b. Feeble-minded: 5.2% whites; 18.2% negroes.
3. County jails — feeble-minded: 10.5% whites; 15.2% negroes.
4. Juvenile delinquent institutions—feeble-minded: 19.7% whites; 20.6% negroes.
5. Almshouses:
   a. Inmates suffering from mental diseases—45.7%.
   b. Feeble-minded—34.5%.

The information gained from this survey reveals an appalling condition that has not yet received from the state the consideration that its relative size and seriousness demand. The State Training School is not able to care for one-tenth of the feeble-minded persons of the state who are in desperate need, nor will the public ever bear the expense of giving custodial care to all of them. While it is elementary that all other state machinery, intended for the solution of this problem, must revolve around the state institution, some plan will have to be devised whereby the vast majority of this enormous number of defectives can be cared for outside. As yet there are few public school classes for the feeble-minded and no community or colony care for them. There should be clinical facilities for the diagnosis of all problem cases. As the state board of public welfare advised

[55] *Survey*, pp. 17, 63. This survey was conducted in cooperation with State Board of Public Welfare, State Board of Health, State Hospital, and State Superintendent of Education.

in its report for 1920, " As there are county agents for farm demonstration work and for health advancement, there should be field workers to look after the mentally deficient ".[56]   The proper supervision and correlation of the work of such mental clinics, the State Hospital and the State Training School, through a central state agency, is a service South Carolina owes to her schools, her courts and the general community.   And as Dr. Williams has counselled, " . . . We can never come near dealing with this problem adequately or worthily if we eliminate the negroes from our program.   This is not a question of charity, but of economic and social necessity whose neglect will bring only hurt to all the people of the state ".[57]

3. John de la Howe Manual Training School

Founded in 1797 under the terms of the will of Dr. John de la Howe, a native of France, this is said to be the oldest manual training school in America.   It is located in McCormick County, and was taken over by the state in 1918 to be operated for normal destitute children of South Carolina. The school is under the administration of seven trustees, appointed by the governor with the consent of the senate for overlapping five-year terms.   An advisory board of three women is also provided.   The state board of public welfare, likewise, acts in an advisory and investigational capacity.

This school has about two thousand acres of land, on which the inmates assist in cultivating vegetables and other crops.   The industrial building was destroyed by fire in 1929, and its replacement is urgently needed.   The children enjoy the advantage of an accredited school of eleven grades.

[56] *Report of State Board of Public Welfare*, 1920, p. 15.

[57] Williams, *op. cit.*, p. 95.   For a keen analysis of the problem of South Carolina's defectives, see *ibid.*, pp. 90-95.   Also, see *Mental Hygiene Survey*, 1922, pp. 71, 72.

In 1932, the legislature appropriated $58,000 for maintenance of the 231 inmates.[58]

4. Confederate Home

The Confederate Home, located at Columbia, is for infirm or destitute Confederate soldiers or sailors and their wives, widows, unmarried daughters, and sisters over seventy years of age. On April 20, 1932, there were 55 inmates; 22 veterans and 33 women. For their maintenance during the year, the General Assembly appropriated $26,000. The plant is valued at about $60,000.

Established as the Confederate Infirmary in 1908, its title was changed in 1915. The home is managed by a commission of five members, appointed by the governor for overlapping terms of nine years.[59]

5. Children's Bureau of South Carolina

The child welfare work of the South Carolina Children's Home Society, an organization financed by private resources, was taken over by the state board of public welfare in 1920. When the board ceased to function in 1927, for want of an appropriation, this work was transferred to the state board of health. The present independent bureau emerged in 1930. There is no justification for the independent position of this " political football " other than this—the absence of an integrated department of public welfare.

The supervisor is appointed by the governor for a term of six years. The law provides that the Children's Bureau is authorized " to place out in free family homes for adoption destitute, delinquent, neglected and dependent children

---

[58] *Code 1932*, secs. 5676-5683; *House Journal*, 1932, p. 1358; *Report of John de la Howe School*, 1931, pp. 4-6. *Cf. supra*, p. 151.

[59] *Code 1932*, secs. 2244, 2245. See Gibbes, *Legislative Manual*, 1931, p. 232, and *House Journal*, 1932, p. 1501.

committed to their care ".[60] It is further provided that defective and otherwise handicapped children committed to the care of this agency " shall be placed in such institutions as are provided by the State for their care as may appear advisable for the best interest of the child ". On June 30, 1931, there were 163 children in the care of this agency, with requests on hand from 500 families in which there were 989 children.[61]

Development of Public Welfare Supervision

Social welfare reform did not begin to crystallize in South Carolina until the beginning of the second decade of the twentieth century. About that time, the desirability of a central agency to supervise and direct the administration of all the state's welfare institutions and services became apparent to some, at least. The Conference of Social Workers, called by Governor Ansel, endorsed the establishment of a board to perform that function. However, this matter was not pressed during the Blease administration which followed, 1911-1915.

Governor Manning appeared to recognize the social needs of the state as no other governor had, for he urged that something be done without further delay. Accordingly, the state board of charities and corrections was created under an act, approved February 20, 1915. The duties of this board were strictly visitorial and advisory, without administrative or executive powers. It had jurisdiction over all state, county, municipal and private institutions and associations that were of a charitable, correctional or reformatory character.[62] In 1918, the state board of correctional

[60] *Code 1932*, sec. 4989.

[61] See *Report of Children's Bureau*, 1931, p. 4. Also, radio address of the supervisor, printed in *News and Courier*, Nov. 17, 1930.

[62] *Acts of 1915*, Act no. 100. For an account of function and accomplishment, see Governor Manning, *Annual Message*, 1918, p. 10.

administration was created to pay particular attention to the administration of the three juvenile correctional institutions. In 1920, both of these boards were abolished and their duties and powers devolved upon a single agency, the state board of public welfare, then created.[63]

The state board of public welfare consists of seven members, as follows: the governor, as *ex officio* chairman, and six others appointed by him with the consent of the senate for overlapping terms of six years. It is required to hold quarterly meetings, and to meet oftener if necessary. The board is empowered to make such rules and regulations as it may deem advisable and necessary " for the government and control of all penal and charitable institutions and activities of the State ". It appoints the superintendents of the three juvenile correctional institutions and of the State Training School, to serve at its pleasure. The functions of this governing body may be divided into the three classifications of supervision, investigation, and control.[64]

The creation of such an agency, with vast potentialities for constructive achievement, reflected a decade of reform and promise for the future. But, sad to relate, the people did not appear to understand or appreciate its services. It was impolitic to sponsor its activities. The Cooper and McLeod administrations contributed little more than lip-service—certainly no aggressive support. The Joint Committee on Economy and Efficiency of 1926 recommended its abolition.[65] This was decidedly a backward step, showing a lack of appreciation of the need of institutional planning

---

[63] *Code 1932*, secs. 1993, 1995; *Acts of 1920*, p. 999.

[64] *Ibid.* For detailed outline of functions under this classification, see *Report of Board of Public Welfare*, chap. iii, pp. 7-12 (1926). For an appraisal of accomplishments, see *Report of Joint Committee on Economy and Consolidation*, 1922, p. 71.

[65] *Report*, pp. 7, 8.

and coordinated effort in the scientific solution of the state's social needs. Governor Richards, militantly antagonistic, applied the torch of destruction by vetoing the item for the expense of the board in the appropriation bill of 1927.[66] Thus a very valuable agency which had given splendid service was virtually destroyed. Such an agency let in the light, the greatest remedy for corruption, wrongdoing, inefficiency and neglect. Reform had been given a definite backset.[67]

Social welfare work has never been deeply implanted in South Carolina; it has always been under continuous attack, because it has never been regarded by the masses as a proper state function. In a word, the populace has not yet become socially-minded. However, it is believed that if this matter is clearly put before the people, they will respond. The social workers have held steadfastly to their course, against handicaps and discouraging conditions, and should be commended for rendering an unselfish service to their state.

Proposed Department of Public Welfare

Proper coordination of effort on the part of all welfare institutions and agencies is essential. Haphazard institutional planning and the lack of any definite and integrated welfare program in South Carolina are to be deplored. Formulation of policy with a view to the future needs of the state as a whole is out of the question with each insti-

[66] *House Journal*, 1927, pp. 219, 1668. This was perhaps about the worst act of his administration. It is probably true that this agency would have fared better had it been made an executive department from the beginning.

[67] See James C. Derieux, " Crawling toward the Promised Land ", in *Survey*, vol. xlviii, pp. 175-180 (April 29, 1922).

In view of congressional plans for a federal social security program requiring state cooperation, the South Carolina Senate in February 1935 created a special committee to formulate the necessary legislation.

tution a more or less autonomous and isolated unit, operating under the independent board system of management with its own individual interest paramount. And, what is perhaps of equal importance, there is no state supervision of the local charitable and correctional institutions. A well-organized department of welfare must be created to meet these needs. Such a department should coordinate all institutional activities, establish general policies, supervise institutional management, prepare all budget requests, and supply the necessary staff service for the state institutions.[68] Acting in an advisory and investigational capacity, this central agency would supervise the local almshouses, hospitals, jails, and chain-gangs. Much constructive aid and advice could be given on the numerous problems of treatment, care, and training of inmates.

It is generally admitted that the present system of pardon investigations and parole work is most unsatisfactory. The board of pardons has no means of performing its task in a desirable fashion. It should be abolished and its duties devolved upon the board of public welfare. This agency should make all field investigations concerning pardons and paroles for the governor. Moreover, a system should be set up whereby the case of every person in a correctional institution would automatically come before the board at the end of some fixed period. Furthermore, it is very necessary that a bureau in the Department of Public Welfare should be staffed with a sufficient number of field workers to supervise those paroled from the penal and correctional institutions.[69] In this connection, all juvenile delinquents should be committed to this central agency to be given a

---

[68] See Brookings Institution, *Survey of North Carolina*, pp. 284, 285.

[69] See *ibid.*, pp. 288, 289; *Report of North Carolina Advisory Commission to Governor Gardiner*, 1930, pp. 7, 8; *Report of (S. C.) Joint Legislative Committee on Economy and Consolidation*, 1922, pp. 60, 61.

thorough physical and psychiatric examination before being placed in an institution.

The Children's Bureau of South Carolina should be abolished and its work transferred to a bureau in this department.

In the organization of departments of welfare the present tendency seems to be toward the adoption either of the unified board of control type or of the single commissioner type. It is forcefully contended by many students of administration that the lines of responsibility should run directly from the superintendents of the institutions to the director of welfare and thence to the governor.[70] It is believed, however, that the former type better adapts itself to the political situation that obtains in South Carolina at the present time.

It is suggested, therefore, that a Department of Public Welfare be created under the management and direction of an unpaid board of seven members appointed by the governor with the consent of the senate for seven-year overlapping terms, and that this board be empowered to appoint a commissioner of welfare to serve at its pleasure. It is to be understood that the board would determine the general policy of the department but would have no administrative duties whatsoever.[71] The commissioner should have full charge of the administration of the services.[72] While the

[70] For able argument in favor of the one-man type of control, see C. E. McCombs, "State Welfare and Consolidated Government", in *National Municipal Review*, vol. xiii, pp. 461-473 (1923). For contrary opinion, see Gertrude Vaile, "An Organization Problem of Public Welfare Departments", in *Annals*, vol. cv, pp. 144-148. Also, see White, *Public Administration*, pp. 171, *et seq.*

[71] The duties of the board functioning as a board of pardons are here interpreted as advisory to the governor. "Administrative duties", involving investigation and supervision, would be performed by the commissioner through the bureau of pardons and paroles.

[72] He should have authority, with approval of the governing board, to re-arrange the bureau structure as the needs require.

present governing bodies would be abolished, the board of public welfare might find it helpful, as an aid to the formulation of the proper policies in institutional planning, to appoint an advisory committee for each of the several institutions under its control.

The following suggestions, in summary, are submitted:

Present Organization	*Proposed Reorganization*
I. Board of Public Welfare	Department of Public Welfare
II. Independent boards of institutions	I. Board of Public Welfare
III. Board of pardons	II. Administrative organization
IV. Children's Bureau of South Carolina	1. Office of Commissioner
	2. Bureau of Institutional Supervision
	3. Bureau of Pardons and Parole
	4. Bureau of Child Welfare
	5. Bureau of Mental Hygiene
	6. Bureau of City and County Organizations

CHAPTER IX

BUSINESS REGULATION

THE proper agencies for the enforcement of regulatory laws affecting banks and other financial institutions, insurance companies, and public utilities should be of tremendous concern to the people of South Carolina. It is our intention to examine briefly the functions of each of the agencies organized for that purpose, with the view of determining whether the state might be able to exercise more effectively and more sufficiently its police power in this field through administrative reorganization.

I. REGULATION OF PUBLIC UTILITIES

The General Assembly of South Carolina enacted a railroad regulation bill in 1892, creating a railroad commission of three members to be popularly elected for overlapping six-year terms.[1] This law was not unlike those already enacted in certain of the Western states. The constitution adopted three years later provides: " A commission is hereby established to be known as the Railroad Commission, which shall be composed of not less than three members, whose powers over all transporting and transmitting corporations, and duties, manner of election and term of office shall be regulated by law ".[2] In 1910, a public service commission was created of three members, appointed by the governor with consent of the senate for overlapping six-year terms. This agency was authorized to fix reasonable and

[1] For a discussion of the opposition to its creation, see Simkins, *Tillman Movement*, p. 174; also, *News and Courier*, Dec. 8, 1892, and Dec. 13, 1892.

[2] *Constitution*, art. 9, sec. 14.

just rates and charges for water, gas and electricity furnished the cities of the state.[3] But upon the recommendation of the Joint Committee on Economy and Consolidation of 1922, the General Assembly of that year abolished this regulating agency, devolving its duties and powers upon the railroad commission.[4]

The fact is there had been no real regulation of public utilities in South Carolina in the period before 1922. The railroad commission, which had been forced to rely almost entirely upon statements of the utilities because of the absence of a technical staff, was then reconstructed and given vastly more power. The consolidating statute provided for a commission of seven members, one from each congressional district, to be elected by the General Assembly for two-year terms.[5] To the former general supervision of all railroads and railways, express and telephone lines in the State, the following powers were added:[6]

The railroad commission is hereby vested with power and jurisdiction to supervise and regulate the rates and service of every public utility in this State and to fix such just and reasonable standards, classifications, regulations, practices and measurements of service to be furnished, imposed or observed and followed by every public utility in this State.[7]

[3] *Code 1922*, secs. 1045, 1047; *Acts of 1910*, p. 564. The organization of the public service commission was not completed until 1919. According to Governor Cooper, "its services were not required before that date". *Annual Message*, 1920, p. 13.

[4] See Committee, *Report*, 1922, p. 63.

[5] *Code 1932*, sec. 8244; *Acts of 1922*, p. 956. The original members were to serve 1, 2, 3, 4, 5, 6, and 7 years, respectively.

[6] *Code 1932*, sec. 8248.

[7] The term "Public Utility" was defined as including every corporation or person furnishing or supplying in any manner gas, electricity, heat, electric power, water and street railway service to the public. *Ibid.*, sec. 8252.

The authority of the commission was not extended to the supervision and regulation of motor carriers in South Carolina until 1925.[8] The increasing use by motor transports of the splendid highway system nearing completion in the state has focused public attention in that direction. In 1931, a commission of five members was created for the purpose of determining the practicability and justice of increasing the tax levied on motor transportation.[9] This committee, consisting of two members from the state highway commission, two from the railroad commission and one from the state tax commission, made its report to the General Assembly in 1932, with its recommendation in the form of a proposed bill upon which action was not taken.[10]

One of the recommendations made by the Special Committee on Industrial Investigation in 1923 was " that our people and our Legislature be brought to realize that the possession of cheap, abundant, reliable hydro-electric power is the greatest asset that any State can have and that the Legislature be urged to do everything possible to foster and encourage such development."[11] In 1931, the General Assembly created the South Carolina Power Rate Investigating Committee and vested in it the power " of investigating rates charged consumers of electric current, and whether or not public utilities and power companies are receiving a fair, equitable and reasonable income upon its, or their investments ".[12] Constituted of a strong personnel with Dr. John

[8] *Ibid.*, secs. 8516-8528.

[9] *Acts of 1931*, p. 1086.

[10] See "Report of Motor Transportation Committee", *House Journal*, 1932, pp. 44-59. The investigation was partly inspired by protests of railway organizations. See communications and resolutions printed in *ibid.*, 1931, pp. 325, 327. While there is no question that motor transports should be taxed, they should not be penalized because they compete with railroads.

[11] *Report, 1923*, p. 12.

[12] *Acts of 1931*, p. 463.

Bauer, economist of New York, as consultant and adviser, this committee performed an unusually constructive piece of work in the interest of the state.[13]   On the basis of its study, the committee came to the conclusion that the five electric utility companies, which generate 95.6 per cent of all the electric power produced in the state, were making more than a fair return on the present fair values of their properties. Among its definite conclusions were: [14]

1. That the valuations of their physical properties as submitted by the appraisal engineers exceed their present fair value.
2. That each of the companies has issued securities in excess of the actual values represented in their properties.
3. The earnings from operations have produced a return sufficient to pay all operating expenses, bond interest and dividends on preferred stock and still allow for dividends on stocks issued on inflated values.

The committee recommended to the General Assembly and to the Railroad Commission the following methods to be used in readjustment of rates and rate schedules: [15]

1. Proceed immediately to readjust rates on the basis of maximum present fair values that the Committee has found; and,
2. After making such adjustments, proceed to make for each company a scientific valuation based upon detailed procedure, including hearings to permit the companies to present their cases in an orderly manner under rules of evidence.

With the view of giving the regulatory body ample authority to carry out its recommendations, the committee

---

[13] See Governor Blackwood's special message, *House Journal*, 1932, pp. 404-409.
[14] *Report of Rate Investigating Committee*, 1932, p. 20.
[15] *Ibid.*, pp. 21, 22.

drew up a model regulatory Act and attached it to its report.[16] With minor changes it was enacted into law, and immediately a staff of engineers, statisticians, accountants, and advisory counsel were selected to carry out its provisions.[17]

One of the purposes of the Rate Committee's investigation was to ascertain whether or not electric power is available to the industries of South Carolina, including agriculture, in sufficient quantities at reasonable cost. The nature of the problem of rural electrification, and its importance to the state in its need to transform agriculture from a predominant cotton to a diversified system, was set forth in the report in considerable detail.[18] The committee urged the need of " State leadership " in the solution of this problem and strongly recommended the creation of a bureau of rural electrification in the regulatory body.[19]

Mention should be made of the state's policy in taxing electric public utilities. Great care should be had in taxing " power " which industries require and which they must have as cheaply as possible, if the state is to have increasing investment by outside capital in the various manufacturing industries.[20] The Rate Investigating Committee did not

[16] For a summary of the principal provisions of proposed legislation, see *ibid.*, pp. 36-41.

[17] *Acts of 1932*, pp. 1497-1522. See Bonbright and Company, *Survey of State Laws on Public Utility Commission Regulation* (New York, 1928), *passim*. A " Uniform Public Utilities Act " has been approved and promulgated by the National Conference of Commissioners on Uniform State Laws. *Ibid.*, p. 7.

[18] *Report of Investigating Committee*, 1932, sec. I, pp. 446-480. See " South Carolina Electrified ", in *South Carolina* (Handbook, 1927), pp. 42-54. For comparison of States, see *Bonbright Regulation Chart*.

[19] *Report of Rate Investigating Committee*, pp. 42-43, 449-450. The regulatory statute of 1932 created such a bureau.

[20] See editorial in Columbia *State*, Feb. 28, 1931.

feel that " the percentages of taxes to gross revenues, even with the addition of the one-half mill kilowatt hour tax" are excessive.[21] It did feel, however, that the desired development of hydro-electric plants in South Carolina " could never materialize so long as the generating tax applies to export power ".[22]

1. The Railroad Commission

As already indicated, a railroad commission of seven members regulates public utilities in South Carolina. In 1932, the chairman received a salary of $2,664, while $12,-000 was appropriated for the remaining six members on a basis of eight dollars per diem. All members receive travel expense while engaged in official duty. A technical staff is headed by the secretary, a rate expert, a technical engineer, the superintendent of motor transportation and the chief engineer of the electrical utilities division.

The original field of activity of the railroad commission has largely been taken over by the National Government and the importance of this work has declined in proportion. Particularly has this been true in recent years since the Supreme Court has sustained the Interstate Commerce Commission in compelling state agencies to raise intrastate rates to the level of the interstate basis.[23] Not only was the South Carolina agency forced to raise its rates in one case during 1932,[24] but it may be noted that the Andrews Branch of the Seaboard Air Line was abandoned over its protest.[25]

[21] *Report of Rate Investigating Committee*, p. 28.

[22] *Ibid.*, p. 30. *Acts of 1931*, p. 357.

[23] *Houston Railway v. United States*, 234 U. S. 342 (1914) ; *Wisconsin v. C. B. & Q. R. R.*, 257 U. S. 563 (1922). Forty-two states joined Wisconsin in fighting this test case.

[24] Docket 21377, *Report of Railroad Commission*, 1932, p. 6-A.

[25] *Ibid.*, p. 8-A.

The motor transportation division was established under the Motor Transportation Act.[26] While more than twelve thousand letters and notices were sent out by this office and nineteen public hearings were held by the commission in connection with motor transportation matters during 1934, it must be said that the regulation of this traffic is likewise destined to be definitely circumscribed by the federal agency. Perhaps the state should attempt only a minimum degree of regulatory control, sufficient to secure reasonable convenience and comfort, and a secured indemnification of persons and property against injury or damage.

The scope of the duties of the railroad commission was more than doubled recently with the creation of the electrical utilities division, under the executive control of a chief engineer. This division was charged with the duty of investigating the electrical utilities operating a seventeen million dollar power business in South Carolina, and of recommending to the commission the readjustment of rates. Also, it was its task to put into effect the various regulatory features of the law.

The commission had previously approved rates without investigating because it had had neither the funds nor the staff necessary to probe the rate basis. Such approval, therefore, had generally been made entirely on an *ex parte* showing of the power and light companies concerned. Now with a force of about fifteen men it commenced the tremendous undertaking of determining whether the rates charged consumers of electricity in the state produced more than a fair profit for the companies.[27] In conducting the investi-

---

[26] The law provides that the expense of this division shall be paid by the motor transport carriers for hire subject to regulation by the commission. The levy is upon gross revenue and is in addition to all other taxes or license assessed. *Acts of 1932*, p. 1607.

[27] It continued the work of the rate investigating committee of 1931, whose report was suggestive rather than informative. For the purpose

gation, the commission based its appraisal of electric properties on estimated replacement costs, i. e., value based on reproduction cost (new), less depreciation of properties used and useful to South Carolina.

With the view of readjusting rates charged, analyses were made of the consumption and cost of electricity supplied to more than 80,000 customers in the state. In this connection, the rate division made the following report:

Considerable research and study have been made by the department into the forms and styles of rates and rate schedules used by companies throughout the country. In this connection, available data and information of a statistical character have been studied and analyzed from many sources in an effort to apply later scientific developments in rate-making to the South Carolina situation.[28]

A 2300-mile rural electric survey was made in the state during 1932. Information was gathered from reports of county agents and demonstration agents under the direction of the extension agricultural engineer of Clemson College, and from investigations made by the division of rural electrification under the supervision of the railroad commission. In 1933 the division of electrical utilities rendered substantial assistance to the highway department in its study of the social and economic desirability of rural electrification on a state-wide basis. FERA funds made it possible for the railroad commission to seek additional information in 1935. If rural electrification can be made possible at such rates as

of the previous study, each company investigated had been required to appraise the value of its own property at an average cost to itself of $75,000. In addition, the companies had been assessed on their gross income to bear the cost of the survey made by the committee.

[28] *Report of Railroad Commission,* 1932, p. 11-A. For an account of increased activities, due to the influence of the Tennessee Valley Authority, see *Report of the Railroad Commission,* 1934, pp. 9-13.

will be profitable to the farmer, rural life will be made more attractive and agriculture will be rendered a much needed service.

2. Recommendations

An up-to-date regulatory law benefits both the public and the companies regulated. South Carolina would do well to follow as a guide the model law prepared by the National Association of Railroad and Utilities Commissioners, which can be adapted to this state. But it must be remembered that the law does not administer itself. Not only is the highest type of administrative ability required to cope with the intricacies of regulating utilities, but a public service commission must be adequately equipped with competent accounting and engineering staffs and sufficient funds to discharge their complicated duties effectively.

Nor is that all. These regulatory bodies are constantly involved in difficult and expensive litigation over rates and valuations with powerful corporations. If South Carolina expects to protect properly the interests of its citizens, all of whom are affected directly or indirectly, generous financial support must be given the commission to combat extensive propaganda and to meet the highest legal talent.

A Public Utilities Commission Proposed

A public utilities commission may be of tremendous service to the public. However, if it is not composed of specialists of uncommon ability, it is likely to do almost unlimited harm. Such an agency should be composed of men of business, legal and engineering training, and of judicial temperament, if it is to deal fairly and equitably with complex problems that affect every citizen of the state. Qualifications of a very high standard should be set forth in the law and salaries should be paid that command a high order of talent.

The present railroad commission should be abolished. In its place should be created a public utilities commission of three members, appointed by the governor with consent of the senate for terms of six years, one to expire every two years. A long tenure of office is wise in order to employ the special knowledge and to make the members reasonably independent of politicians and corporations.[29]

II. BANKING AND INSURANCE

1. *Insurance Department*

The Insurance Department of South Carolina is headed by the insurance commissioner who is elected by the General Assembly for a term of four years. He is charged with supervision and regulation of every class of insurance as transacted by all companies doing business in the state. Licensing insurance companies and their agents, collecting the fees and taxes, and adjusting differences that arise in the insurance field, constitute only a part of the duties to be performed. This office is directed to audit every domestic company at least once in every two years, and is authorized to examine into the condition of any company doing business in South Carolina. As a closely related function, the commissioner is charged with the administration of the " Blue Sky Law ", regulating the sale of securities.[30]

The duties assigned in many states to a state fire marshal are required of this department. Though handicapped by

[29] Commissions in most states have three members, and are appointed by the governor in 26 states.

In 1935 the name Railroad Commission was changed to Public Service Commission by an amendment to the constitution, approved February 11, 1935.

[30] *Code 1932*, chap. 157, art. 1. There were more than 450 insurance companies of various sorts doing business in South Carolina in 1931. See *Report of Insurance Commissioner*, 1931, pp. 115-121.

reason of insufficient appropriations, it is expected to inspect and remove fire hazards in municipalities and public buildings and to investigate all fires suspected of incendiary origin.

Due to the entry of new companies and to the imposition of new fees and taxes, revenues have steadily increased during the twenty-five years the Insurance Department has functioned. From a total collection of $48,707.30 in 1908, the amount had reached the figure of $597,506.73 in 1932. During the same period the cost of operating this agency of insurance control and fire protection increased from $4,647.18 to $20,818.78.[31]

One of the remarkable features of the insurance business in South Carolina is the growth of domestic companies, whose total assets in 1909 of $224,366 had increased to $7,064,020 in 1931. While this expansion may be gratifying as a development of home industry, one wonders to what extent it may result from laxity in the insurance laws. Should investigation reveal the need of raising the requirements for entrance into this field, the insurance laws of New York State which are known to provide a sound system of supervision might well serve as a guide.[32]

2. Office of State Bank Examiner

From 1906 to 1933, the state bank examiner was appointed by the governor, to serve at the pleasure of the appointing officer. The law provided that the selection might be made upon the advice of the executive committee

[31] *Report of Insurance Commissioner*, 1932, p. 11.

[32] The demand in recent years that all insurance companies doing a general business should be brought under federal control is not without reason. Perhaps it is unfortunate that the Supreme Court should have ruled that insurance is not interstate commerce. *Paul v. Virginia*, 8 Wallace 168.

of the South Carolina Bankers' Association.[33] It was the duty of the bank examiner to examine semi-annually " into the affairs and the condition of all banks and banking institutions conducted by corporations in the State ". He was also required to audit the books of state offices, educational, charitable and penal institutions of the state. Upon the written request of the grand jury of the county, he might be required to audit the books of county officers who are charged with the receipt and expenditure of public funds.[34]

The law provided that no person should be appointed to the office of state bank examiner unless he was an expert accountant and had had practical experience in the banking business. For the performance of his banking duties, he was provided with a field staff of eight or ten associate and assistant examiners. Fees, graduated according to the capital of the several banks, were collected for the support of this office. The examiner was required to make a full and detailed report of his findings and to file the same in the office of the state treasurer. The law stipulated that this report should set forth " all violations, if any, of the banking laws of the State, and also such a full summary of the affairs of the bank as shall be necessary for the protection of the depositors, stockholders and creditors of such bank ". In the event that a bank closed on account of insolvency, the state examiner was directed to publish an audit within ninety days. With the view of protecting the interests of all concerned, he was authorized to take control of a bank for a period of thirty days upon the request of a majority of the directors of the said bank.[35]

[33] *Code 1932*, sec. 7843.

[34] *Ibid*, sec. 7846. The office of the state bank examiner was investigated by a legislative committee in 1932, which recommended his removal.

[35] *Code 1932*, secs. 7843-7848.

The state auditor and two assistants were employed by the bank examiner to perform the auditing of state institutions and state offices. The auditor was empowered and directed to require the installation and adoption of an adequate system of accounts.

During the national banking crisis of 1933, the office of state bank examiner was abolished and the governor was given " plenary power and control" of all state banking institutions for a period of eighteen months.[36] The governor was " authorized and empowered, in his discretion, to appoint a board of bank control to advise and consult with him and to vest them with such power and authority " as he deemed necessary to carry out this statute. Under the provisions of this and supplementary legislation a bank-examining department was established under the direction of the state board of bank control, and the position and duties of state auditor were placed under the supervision of the state budget commission.[37]

That the banking laws of South Carolina could be materially improved is a proposition that will not admit of debate. The experience of 1933 emphasized the fact that double liability of bank stockholders furnishes small relief to depositors in closed banks. Moreover, the Federal Banking Act of 1933, which removed this liability from all national bank stock issued after the date of its enactment, practically forces the state to take similar action if state banks are to compete. It is hoped that the legislature will not delay ratification of the repeal amendment which was approved by the electorate in 1934. Probably the best guarantee of solvency

[36] Act approved March 9, 1933, *Acts of 1933*, p. 1174. In 1934 the legislature created the State Board of Bank Control composed of seven members for a period of two years, beginning July 1, 1934. *Acts of 1934*, p. 2275.

[37] *Acts of 1933*, pp. 296, 1177.

would result from a requirement that all South Carolina banks insure deposits in conformity with federal regulations under the plan that is being administered by the Federal Deposit Insurance Corporation.

A Department of Corporations Proposed

A Department of Corporations is suggested as an integrated agency through which the state might properly exercise its police powers in safeguarding the channels through which private individuals invest their savings.[88] Those duties and powers which clearly belong to this class should be grouped together as a single administrative department. Consequently, the examination of and supervision over banks, trust companies, building and loan associations, insurance companies, and concerns engaged in the issuance and sale of securities, are consolidated under this suggested arrangement. Inasmuch as the same basic qualifications in training are essential in the members of the staff performing these closely allied services, it should lead to certain economies as well as to increased efficiency and flexibility of administration. Auditors could be used interchangeably in the general auditing work. The proposed department should be built around the present Department of Insurance, with the expense of operation placed upon the agencies regulated.

The head of the Department of Corporations should be the commissioner of corporations, appointed by the governor with the consent of the senate. The department might advantageously be organized into three bureaus, as follows:

[88] A number of states have agencies similar to the one here proposed. See recommendations of Institute of Public Administration for the State of Arkansas, *Survey of Arkansas*, p. 44. Also, see Brookings Institution, *Survey of North Carolina*, p. 314.

1. Bureau of Insurance
2. Bureau of Banking
3. Bureau of Securities.

In addition to administering general supervision over the department, it might be well for the commissioner to exercise direct supervision over either the bureau of insurance or the bureau of banking.[39] In any event, he should be empowered to appoint the directors of the bureaus not under his complete direction. The commissioner should also be given the power to distribute the functions of this department among the established bureaus as may seem most advantageous to him from an administrative standpoint.

Of course, the suggested establishment of the Department of Corporations contemplates the abolition of the Department of Insurance and the State Board of Bank Control. It is suggested that the powers and duties of these two agencies devolve upon the proposed department, with the following exceptions:

1. The inspection of buildings to remove fire hazards and the examination of suspicious fires, devolve upon the Bureau of Inspection in the proposed Department of Labor.

2. Collection of taxes on gross premiums of insurance companies, devolves upon the proposed Department of Revenues.

3. Prosecution for arson, devolves upon the proposed Department of Law.

4. Examination of the financial affairs of state and county offices, devolves upon the proposed Department of Audit.

[39] This suggestion is made in the interest of economy. It is strongly urged that the director of the bureau of banking be not appointed on the recommendation of the South Carolina Bankers' Association.

In addition to the powers and duties of the Insurance Department and of the State Board of Bank Control, with exceptions noted, the Department of Corporations would supervise the issuing of charters of incorporation. To that end, all the powers and duties with reference to domestic and foreign corporations invested in the Secretary of State would be transferred to this department.[40]

[40] For recommendations in regard to the assignment of the powers and duties of the Insurance Department and the State Examiner's office, see *Report of House Committee on Consolidation of State Offices*, 1932, in *House Journal*, 1932, p. 1291.

CHAPTER X

Highway Administration

At the beginning of the year 1917, South Carolina was one of six states still following the system of county or local road management. Approximately a million dollars was being raised each year by county taxation to be expended on road building entirely through county agencies.[1] The inauguration of the system of federal aid, however, brought a new incentive. A state was not eligible to receive its apportionment until it established a state highway department and provided the necessary machinery. At the urgent insistence of Governor Manning, the State Highway Department was created under an Act approved February 20, 1917.[2] A commission of five members, established as the governing body, was composed of the professors of civil engineering at The Citadel, Clemson College, and the State University, together with two other members appointed by the governor for terms of two years.[3]

In 1920, under Governor Cooper's administration, the department was reorganized with a more comprehensive program, but it continued to operate largely on a county basis. The legislation of that year created a commission of seven members, one from each congressional district, ap-

[1] It is interesting to note that the first mountain-to-the-sea highway, known as the "State Road", had been built a century earlier under legislation of 1818, appropriating $100,000 for that purpose.

[2] *Annual Message*, 1917, pp. 8, 9. *Acts of 1917*, p. 320.

[3] Department was originally created to cooperate with local road authorities in the counties, and to comply with requirements of Federal Highway Act of 1916, 43 *U. S. Stat. at Large*, 653.

pointed by the governor with consent of the senate for overlapping terms of four years.[4]   The new body was authorized to select a highway engineer and an executive secretary.   The scope of the work contemplated was reflected in the provision that directed the commission to lay out a system of highways throughout the state, " connecting every county seat within the State and covering such main avenues of travel and traffic as said Highway Commission may deem advisable ".   The license tax accruing to the county, together with the proceeds of the two-mill tax levied under the law, was to be used by the county " for the construction of highways in the state system in the respective county, under the general supervision of the Highway Department ".   It is obvious that under such an arrangement it was yet impossible to execute a consistent plan of road building.

The organization under which a statewide system of highways has developed dates from 1924, when the " Pay-as-you-go Plan " was enacted.[5]   This law created a statewide system of hard-surfaced, topsoil and other types of public roads " which shall be constructed by the State of South Carolina, and ever after maintained as highways ".   The legislature designated the specific routes to be taken over and maintained by the Highway Department.[6]   Funds for this purpose were provided " from any amount which might be made available from the automobile tax, federal aid, and gasoline tax ".[7]

For the administration of this system there was created a commission of fourteen members, one from each of the

[4] *Acts of 1920*, p. 1072.

[5] *Code 1932*, chap. 126, art. 1.

[6] See *ibid.*, art. 2, for a list of roads added to the system and confirmed by the General Assembly in 1927.

[7] *Code 1932*, sec. 5929.

judicial districts of the State, to be appointed by the governor with consent of the senate for four-year overlapping terms.[8] The commission was authorized to appoint a state highway engineer and a chief highway commissioner.

The Highway Department, under control of fourteen commissioners, is directly administered by the chief highway commissioner. This executive officer is assisted by a staff consisting of the secretary-treasurer, the auditor and the superintendent of purchase.

The engineering organization is headed by the state highway engineer. In addition to the assistant highway engineer, the staff consists of the following: bridge engineer, construction engineer, maintenance engineer, office engineer, chief of surveys and plans, testing engineer, ad four division engineers.

The administration of the laws relating to motor vehicles is under the direction of the motor vehicle division. Motor vehicle licenses and drivers' licenses are issued through this office. The highway patrol, the field personnel of this division, was created by law in 1930. The law enforcement officers in 1932 consisted of the following: chief of law enforcement, assistant chief, eleven license inspectors, seven lieutenants of patrol, and fifty patrolmen.

The efficient regulation of traffic in the interest of safety on South Carolina's rapidly expanding system of highways is very necessary. It would be a serious mistake to rescind the driver license law or to take the patrol off the highways, as has been attempted in the General Assembly. Instead of weakening the effect of this legislation, efforts should be made to strengthen it. In the first place, very strict examinations should be given those seeking a license to drive, instead of the perfunctory tests now so common. Secondly, the law should be revised to require the publication of the

[8] *Ibid.*, secs. 5867-5869.

reason for revocation of licenses. An average of a hundred licenses are revoked each month in South Carolina for drunkenness. An automobile driven by an inebriate is a deadly weapon and sufficient publicity would be the most effective means of curbing this practice. Finally, some scheme should be worked out for the requirement of general liability insurance. An adequate safety responsibility law should be tied to the driver license law as a necessary supplement.

The State Highway Department has been investigated practically every year since 1924. Although no evidence of dishonesty has been brought to light, there is no department of the state government that is criticized so much nor one that is so greatly distrusted. This may be accounted for in a large measure by its seemingly detached position, as it operates under a fund separated from that of other general state purposes, and by the enormous amount of money that passes through its hands. If the administration were somewhat simplified and its accountability more definitely fixed, it is likely that the public's confidence would be more firmly established.

HIGHWAY FINANCE

The Reimbursement Act of 1926, amending the law of 1924, made further provision for road construction by counties.[9] Provision was made for reimbursement of the counties for the cost of hard-surfaced roads prior to incorporation in the state system, and conditions were laid down as a basis upon which counties could float bonds for continued construction of those roads designated as state highways, the counties later to be reimbursed according to agreements entered into.

Highway building in the state made its greatest single forward movement with the passage of the $65,000,000

---

[9] *Code 1932*, chap. 126, art. 3; *Acts of 1926*, p. 1001.

State Highway Bond Act of 1929.[10] This financing plan provides for the capitalization over a period of twenty-four years of the revenues derived from a gasoline tax levied at the rate of five cents per gallon and from motor vehicle license fees.[11] It was estimated that these revenues would be sufficient during the life of the bonds to pay the principal and interest, as well as retire the outstanding obligations of counties and road districts.[12] The governor and the state treasurer are authorized to issue state highway certificates of indebtedness and notes, to the maximum amount of $20,000,000 within a single year, and the state's taxing power is pledged in payment.

Before such certificates of indebtedness may be issued, however, the law requires the state highway commission to transmit to the governor a written request for the issuance thereof. This request must embody a statement showing the following: [13]

(a) The principal amount of the certificates of indebtedness proposed to be issued, the maximum rate of interest to be paid thereon, and the times of payment of such principal and interest;

(b) The amount of revenues derived in the next preceding calendar year from the entire gasoline tax and motor vehicle license fees, except such portion, if any, of the gasoline tax as shall have exceeded the amount of a gasoline tax levied at the rate of five cents per gallon;

[10] *Ibid.*, chap. 127.

[11] A tax of six cents is charged, but one cent is returned to the counties for the upkeep of county roads. North Carolina likewise has a six cents tax, while the tax in Florida is seven.

According to the census of 1930, there were only four states with a smaller number of automobiles for total population than South Carolina. In the U. S. the ratio was one motor car for every 4.6 persons; in South Carolina, one car for every 7.9 persons.

[12] Alternate unit plans of financing are provided, viz: State Unit Plan and the District Unit Plan. *Code 1932*, chap. 127, art. 2.

[13] *Code 1932*, sec. 5947.

(c) The amount, as estimated by the State Highway Commission, to be derived from said gasoline tax and motor vehicle license fees, with said exception, in each year during the term for which the proposed State Highway certificates of indebtedness are to run. In estimating these revenues, the State Highway Commission shall not assume that prior to the year 1939 the revenues of any year will be more than five *per centum* in excess of the actual or estimated revenues of the next preceding year, nor that in 1939 or later years there will be any increase in such revenues over and above the revenues of the year 1938;

(d) The amount as estimated by the State Highway Commission, which will be required in each year during the term of the proposed State Highway certificates of indebtedness for the payment of the principal and interest of all such certificates of indebtedness issued or to be issued pursuant to previous requests made by the State Highway Commission, as provided in this section, the administration and operation of the State Highway Department, the maintenance of all highways in the State Highway System, the payment of accident claims (as hereinafter defined), and the payment of the amount required to be paid to counties or highway or bridge districts by the provisions of this Chapter.

Supplied with this statement of facts and estimates, the governor exercises his discretion. It is generally conceded that, because of the contract between the state and the purchasers of the bonds, the vehicle revenues may not be diverted from the purpose of highway construction and maintenance to any other purpose.[14] Moreover, it is a sound principle of highway administration and finance that the state should be the sole agency to levy these special taxes upon motor vehicle or highway users and that these funds should be used exclusively for highway purposes.

[14] But, see effort made (H. 1072), *House Journal*, 1931, p. 30, and again in 1932 (H. 24), *House Journal*, 1932, p. 447.

Of the authorized issue of $65,000,000, only $20,000,000 in bonds had been sold at the close of the year 1931.[15] In addition, however, the Highway Department in 1931 issued $5,000,000 in highway notes to be refunded in bonds later. The state treasurer estimated that, if no more were issued, constant revenue would give a balance of about $32,000,000 in 1953, the last date of the period of capitalization.[16] It was the opinion of W. H. James and Associates, who audited the department in 1931, that an aggregate issue of $45,000,000 of certificates of indebtedness was the limit warranted under then present conditions.[17]

Highway finances appeared to be sound at the end of the year 1932, even under unfavorable economic conditions. Funded debts of the department, which had increased from $61,226,861 in 1930 to $63,280,195 in 1931, actually decreased by $3,157,395 during the year.[18] Of the approximate $60,000,000 outstanding at that time, reimbursement highway agreements accounted for about $36,000,000 of the total. In spite of the general business trend during these years, fortunately there was no alarming loss in the general revenue scale of the department. It should be remembered that the department's credit is the credit of the state and extreme care should be taken to protect it.

[15] An advertised sale of $10,000,000 in highway bonds was cancelled in the last week of 1931. The reason given by Governor Blackwood was that the market was "unfavorable".

[16] See *News and Courier*, June 28, 1932. On June 30, 1934 bonded indebtedness amounted to $24,771,000 as follows: bonds, $24,412,000; notes, $359,000. *Report of Comptroller General*, 1934, p. 44.

[17] *Audit Report*, 1931, pp. 3, 4.

[18] According to the *Audit Report*, 1932, as released to the press. The report was unavailable at this writing, due to the failure of the General Assembly to provide funds for printing.

The condensed statement that follows is based upon the department's "General Balance Sheet" of September 30, 1932.[19]

RESOURCES

Cash:

Deposit	$ 124,538.99	
State Treasurer	1,764,573.00	$1,899,111.99
Suspended Banks		1,313,576.18
Sinking Fund		201,816.89
Accounts Receivable		226,138.35
Materials and supplies		310,873.63
Property and Equipment		1,289,089.91
Roads and Bridges		
Completed Projects	77,708,205.02	
Projects in Progress	16,763,572.35	
		94,471,777.37
Total Resources		$99,702,384.32

LIABILITIES

Accounts Payable		$91,117.41
Accrued and Deferred Items:		
Interest Accrued	$785,467.14	
Premium Certificates of Indebt	373,243.50	1,158,710.64
Special Fund Accounts		70,333.89
Funded Debt:		
Reimbursement Certificates Payable:		
Counties	7,978,829.34	
State of South Carolina	25,000,000.00	
Reimbursement Agreements Payable: ..	28,490,173.28	
Written Evidences of Obligations	2,039,400.00	
		63,508,402.62
Total Liabilities		$64,828,564.56
Net Investment of State		34,873,819.76
Total		$99,702,384.32

[19] *Report of Highway Department*, 1932, p. 14.

All funds of the department, with the exception of a revolving fund which is held for emergencies, are deposited with the state treasurer. All bank deposits are protected by securities, required by law.

Net investment represents the cost to the state of the highways and properties under the control of the department.

Accrued and deferred items consist of accrued interest on the funded debt and that portion of the premium received from the sale of certificates of indebtedness which is applicable to future periods.

The State Highway Fund is the general cash account of the department. All revenues are accredited to this fund and the cost of operating, interest on obligations, amounts due to counties under reimbursement agreements, and certain construction expenses are paid therefrom. During the year 1932 the department's receipts exceeded its matured obligations and the sum of $4,800,000 was transferred to the Highway Bond Fund and used for the construction of highways.[20]

HIGHWAY SYSTEM

The State Highway System consists of the highways specifically named in the provisions of the Highway Act of 1924, together with such roads as have been added from time to time by the highway commission with approval of the General Assembly. Its development is indicated by the following comparative statement: [21]

	Miles, Dec. 31, 1924		Miles, Sept. 30, 1932	
Completed:				
Standard pavement	228.25		2,380.4	
Bituminous surfacing	———		796.2	
Improved earth types	2,848.42		1,662.0	
		3,076.67	———	4,838.6
Uncompleted:				
Standard pavement	34.70		———	
Bituminous surfacing	———		337.7	
Improved earth types	198.63		28.8	
		233.33	———	366.5
Unimproved	1,430.00	1,430.00	758.7	758.7
Total		4,740.00		5,963.8 [22]

[20] *Ibid.*, p. 11. During the fiscal year ended June 30, 1934, the receipts exceeded the disbursements by $1,233,199.63. *Report of Highway Department*, 1934, p. 10.

[21] State Highway Department, *Report*, 1924, p. 23; *Report*, 1932, p. 116.

[22] This total includes the Federal Aid System of 3,246.7 miles, *ibid.*, p. 119. The State Highway System contained 5,999.22 miles on June 30, 1934. *Report of Highway Department*, 1934, p. 126.

Roads under maintenance in 1932 averaged 5,680.9 miles. Some idea of the extent to which operations were curtailed during the year is reflected in the approximate 30 per cent reduction in the cost of this activity. Of course, the reduction is partly explained by the decreased cost of labor and material. The total cost in 1932 was $1,297,372.18, as compared to $1,976,747.99 for the fiscal year 1931.

There is a growing sentiment for the idea of placing all county roads under the State Highway Department, as has recently been done in North Carolina and Virginia.[23] The arrangement in these two states appears to be working satisfactorily and it might be well for South Carolina to consider seriously the advisability of taking such a step. Before any action is taken, however, it is essential that an engineering survey be made. Such a survey is likely to sustain the belief that the county roads could be constructed and maintained by the Highway Department far more economically than by the forty-six county units. On the other hand, the state may regard it a matter of sound policy to complete her present road-building before transferring the financial burden of the counties to the state.[24]

---

[23] In 1931, North Carolina took over approximately 45,000 miles of county roads to be added to the 10,000 miles of state highways, creating a reorganized state system of 55,000 miles—the largest in the United States. It was to be maintained entirely from the proceeds of a six cents gasoline tax, relieving property of all road tax burden. Incidentally, all county prisoners and chain-gang camps were transferred to the state to be used for road work. See Gardner, in *Saturday Evening Post*, vol. 204, no. 27, pp. 72, 73 (Jan. 2, 1932). One difference between the situation in North Carolina and that in South Carolina is that the latter, under the Funding Act, assumed all county bonds issued in favor of road building and such roads as were built from the sale of these bonds have not been taken over by the state.

For Virginia, see H. A. Byrd, "Better Government at Lower Cost", in *Yale Review*, September, 1932, pp. 73, 74.

[24] See Governor Blackwood's *Annual Message*, 1932, p. 11.

RECOMMENDATIONS

For the present, the Highway Department should continue to be headed by a commission. However, the present body of fourteen members, representing each of the judicial districts, should be abolished. If the desired well-knit system is to be attained, a smaller group with a state-wide rather than a district point of view must be created to administer its affairs. It is therefore proposed that a commission of five members be appointed at large by the governor with consent of the senate for overlapping terms of five years.

In this connection, attention should be called to the law governing the expansion of the State Highway System. The designated system of roads is fixed and is changed from time to time by the legislature, the commission being authorized to add not more than twenty miles to the system each year.[25] This matter should be in the hands of the Highway Department, to remove it from politics. The basis for distribution of funds should likewise be eliminated from the law. They should be distributed where traffic needs warrant, not on a county basis.

The present arrangement whereby the chief commissioner and the highway engineer are both appointed by the commission and appear to have authority and responsibility of equal rank tends to create unnecessary and unfortunate administrative division. Two executive officers should not be authorized by statute. The chief highway commissioner should have authority to appoint his chief engineer, and to reorganize the department as needs of highway work dictate.

In regard to the internal reorganization of the Department, the following suggestions are made:[26]

---

[25] *Code 1932*, sec. 5873.

[26] See recommendations of the National Institute of Public Administration, *Survey of Arkansas*, pp. 55-58.

1. That the administration and collection of motor vehicle license fees be transferred to the proposed Department of Revenues. Revenue work has nothing to do with engineering problems.

2. That highway patrol duties be transferred to the proposed bureau of state police in the Executive Department.

3. That, when a central accounting system has been developed, most of the accounting be transferred to the proposed Department of Finance, where the audit of highway bills before payment would follow the same routine as bills of other departments. Cost accounting is practically all the Highway Department needs to do.

4. That post-auditing be made by the proposed Department of Audit, under the direction of the state auditor elected by the legislature.[27]

In several of the states today highway work is closely associated with the other public works activities, all being under one department head. When the present highway program, as contemplated by the Bond Act of 1929, is completed and the highway work becomes one largely of maintenance, South Carolina might properly combine all her engineering work under a single department.

When that time arrives, the highway commission should be abolished and the department should then be headed by a commissioner of highways and public works. In the merger of all engineering activities, the duties of the bureau of buildings and grounds would be transferred from the proposed Executive Department. And, by all means, there should be a state architect to prepare plans and designs of all state buildings and to supervise their construction. There is no doubt that considerable economy would accrue from such service rendered.

[27] The Bond Act of 1929 incorporated a provision that the affairs of the Highway Department be audited annually by certified public accountants, appointed by the governor. *Acts of 1929*, p. 670. Prior to that date, the books and records were audited occasionally by the state bank examiner.

CHAPTER XI

Executive Direction

With the exception of the governor's office and the office of the attorney general, the plan of reorganizing the present administrative machinery of the state government of South Carolina has been outlined in some detail. The writer has not hesitated to suggest a thorough overhauling, requiring rather extensive constitutional changes, so convinced is he that a comprehensively integrated reorganization is necessary. The plan seeks unity of purpose and coordinated effort through singleness of direction and responsibility. This would be achieved by making the governor the actual and responsible head of state administration. He would direct and control a small number of departments, organized on a basis of closely related functions or of major purpose of activity.

If the governor is to fill the role of general manager, it is essential that the heads of the administrative departments should have a subordinate legal status. Only when they are appointed by the governor and are subject to his general supervision is it possible to hold the chief executive responsible for the efficiency with which the administrative affairs of the government are conducted.

I. EXECUTIVE DEPARTMENT

The position of the governor as chief magistrate of the State of South Carolina has been described in the first chapter of this study and need not be repeated here. In addition to his constitutional and statutory duties as chief executive, the governor serves in an *ex officio* capacity as a member of the following boards and commissions:

1. State Board of Education (Chairman)
2. State Finance Committee (Chairman)
3. Sinking Fund Commission
4. State Board of Public Welfare (Chairman)
5. Budget Commission (Chief Budget Officer)
6. State Service Commission (Chairman)
7. Board of Trustees, University of South Carolina
8. Board of Visitors, The Citadel
9. Board of Trustees, Winthrop College
10. Board of Trustees, State Medical College
11. Board of Trustees, State Colored College

At the present time, the governor's office is only a small establishment handling for the most part routine matters. Since it is the purpose to suggest the expansion of this office into a real executive department, similar to those established in New York and Virginia, attention will now be given to those agencies now performing services that will be included in the proposed Executive Department.

1. Secretary of State

The secretary of state, a constitutional officer, is popularly elected for a term of four years. He has charge of all property of the state, the care and custody of which is not otherwise provided for by law, and is custodian of the state archives and state seal. He countersigns proclamations and commissions issued by the governor, issues certificates of incorporation to corporate bodies, and performs a variety of miscellaneous duties required by law. The primary function of this office is to keep the records of the state.[1]

---

[1] *Code 1932*, chap. 114, art. 3.

In addition to the aforesaid duties, the secretary of state is *ex officio* a member of the Board of Claims, the Commission on State House and State Grounds, the State Board of Canvassers, and the Board of Trustees for the State Library.

2. Adjutant General

The adjutant general, another executive officer known to the constitution, is likewise elected by the qualified electors of the state for a term of four years. He has the rank of brigadier general and is chief of the governor's military staff. As such, he is responsible for the handling of the military funds, property and records of the state. As adjutant, he causes to be executed the commands of his commander-in-chief.[2] This official is also a member of the State Service Commission and the Board of State Canvassers. In addition, he is an *ex officio* member of the Board of Visitors of The Citadel.

An inspector general is appointed by the governor, upon the recommendation of the adjutant general, to serve as assistant to the adjutant general and to perform such duties as may be assigned to him by this officer.

On the recommendation of the adjutant general and subject to the approval of the Secretary of War, the governor designates an officer of the National Guard as the Property and Disbursing Officer of the United States. It is the duty of this officer to receipt and account for all funds and property belonging to the United States in possession of the National Guard and to make such returns and reports concerning the same as may be required by the Secretary of War.

The National Guard, organized under the terms of the National Defense Act, and the Naval Militia are collectively

[2] *Code 1932*, secs. 2900-2901.

known as the Organized Militia of South Carolina and are subject to call by the Congress for United States service. The militia of the state not in the service of the United States is governed and its affairs administered pursuant to law by the governor through the office of the adjutant general.

3. State Service Officer

For the purpose of assisting ex-service men in securing benefits to which they are entitled under the provisions of federal legislation and under terms of insurance policies issued under the federal government for their benefit, the governor appoints the state service officer on recommendation of the American Legion, Department of South Carolina. This officer is in charge of the State Service Bureau which is under the direct supervision of a commission consisting of the governor as chairman, the attorney general and the adjutant general.

4. Commission on State House and Grounds

The secretary of state, the comptroller general and the state librarian constitute the Commission on State House and State Grounds, " for the purpose of their proper keeping, landscaping, cultivation and beautifying ".[3] This *ex officio* body is directed to employ all help and labor in policing, protecting and caring for this property and has full authority over the same.

5. State Electrician and Engineer

Electrical and engineering service for all state buildings and property in Columbia is under the direction of the state electrician and engineer who is appointed by the governor and is subject to removal by him.

[3] *Code 1932*, sec. 2242.

6. Board of State Canvassers

The Board of State Canvassers, of course, is active only in election years. It is an *ex officio* body consisting of the secretary of state, the comptroller general, the attorney general, the adjutant general, the state treasurer, and the chairman of the committee on privileges and elections of the house of representatives. It is the function of this board to determine and to declare those duly elected. In performance of this duty, they decide contested cases on appeal from the decisions of the county boards of canvassers.

Proposed Executive Department

The suggested creation of this department contemplates bringing together directly under the governor certain activities which should be attached to his office. The following units of internal organization are recommended: [4]

1. Office of Governor
2. Bureau of State Records
3. Bureau of Military Affairs
4. Bureau of State Police
5. Bureau of Buildings and Grounds.

The governor's office would be in charge of his executive secretary and would serve as the clearing house for the chief executive. Through this office he should be kept informed of the work being done by the proposed administrative departments. It would serve as his constant liaison agency

[4] The Joint Committee on Efficiency and Economy, 1926, recommended the creation of a mixed executive and legislative administrative board, the governor to act as chairman. See its *Report*, p. 6.

In 1932, the House Committee on Consolidation of State Offices recommended the creation of a State Board of Control, to consist of the governor, the state treasurer, the comptroller general, the attorney general, the state superintendent of education and the chairman of the state tax commission. *House Journal*, 1932, pp. 1289, 1290.

and any unusual condition that required his personal attention could be readily made known to him.

The bureau of records would keep all records now kept by the secretary of state, except those relating to charters which would be transferred to the proposed Department of Corporations. This bureau would also perform, in collaboration with the attorney general, the work of the state board of canvassers. The director might continue to be called the secretary of state, but he should not be a constitutional officer.[5]

The bureau of military affairs would exercise the functions of the adjutant general, but that officer should be appointed by his commander-in-chief, the governor. The constitutional office should be abolished. The state service officer would continue to be attached to the division headed by the adjutant general, and there would be no need of the state service commission should the bureau of military affairs be established under the Executive Department. The legal advice of the attorney general would continue to be available.

The creation of a bureau of state police contemplates the merger of the patrol work of the present highway patrol with that of the state constabulary and the elimination of county rural policemen. The South Carolina Council in a recent report estimated that the taxpayers of the state spend approximately $1,000,000 a year for an "elaborate and decentralized" police system which it described as "utterly inefficient".[6] In the place of five or six varieties of state

[5] This office requires little exercise of discretionary authority and there is no good reason for it to continue on a "constitutional pedestal".

[6] As a remedy, the Council suggested the establishment of a state police system with a superintendent to be appointed by the governor. See its report, *Police* (Cheraw, 1932), *passim*.

The state constabulary was formed in 1893 to regulate the liquor dispensaries and has seen service intermittently ever since. See Governor

and county police, limited in their particular fields, the state police would be vested with general police power to be exercised in any part of the state. This arrangement should not only result in a material reduction in the cost of maintaining police protection, but should also prove an effective instrument for securing a better and a more uniform enforcement of the laws of the state.[7]

Local police agencies are unsatisfactory for enforcing state law because they are elected or appointed by the community in which they operate. And certainly the state militia is of no value in the performance of minor police duties or in apprehending ordinary criminals. Nor is it likely to be effective in major police duties, because of the slowness with which it is mobilized, the expense involved, and the danger of its using too little or too much force.

The bureau of buildings and grounds is designed to perform the functions of the commission on state house and state grounds and the office of the state electrician and engineer. These two agencies would be abolished, and the bureau would be directed by a state engineer.

It is to be understood that the heads of the bureaus would be appointed by the governor and would serve at his pleasure.

II. DEPARTMENT OF LAW

The attorney general, popularly elected for a term of four years, is the chief law officer of the state. He is assisted by a legal staff of two assistant attorneys general whom he is authorized to appoint.

It is the duty of this officer to protect the rights and property of the state; to appear for the state in the Supreme

Blackwood's plea in behalf of this force in special message to General Assembly, Feb. 5, 1932, *House Journal*, 1932, p. 364.

[7] See *Report of State Reorganization Commission of New York*, 1926, Legislative Doc., no. 72, p. 19.

Court to defend and prosecute all causes in which the state is interested or is a party, and in such causes in any court or tribunal when required by the governor or either branch of the General Assembly; to consult and advise with state officers on questions of law relating to their official business, when requested to do so, and to conduct litigations for them; to advise the General Assembly, upon request; to appoint all clerks and necessary help in the engrossing department and to have charge of the same during a legislative session; to sue for penalties incurred by any public officer or board of public officers; to consult with and advise the solicitors of the judicial districts in matters relating to the duties of their office and when, in his judgment, the interest of the state requires it, to assume the direction and management of any prosecution and suit in which the state is a party or is interested.[8]

In addition to the regular duties of his office, the attorney general is made by law a member of the following boards and commissions: Board of Claims, State Board of Health, Sinking Fund Commission, State Service Commission and the Board of State Canvassers.

During the year ending September 30, 1931, this department disposed of 256 of the 666 cases handled. One is impressed, however, by the considerable amount of time that is applied to the giving of opinions. Over one hundred pages of the annual report is devoted to opinions rendered to various officials and individuals during the year.

The recital of the powers and responsibilities of the attorney general indicates very clearly the fact that this official is extremely limited in actions which he may undertake of his own will. Too often his services are contingent upon requests made for them. This is true of legal advice given his associates in state office and of his office as a depart-

[8] *Code 1932*, chap. 114, art. 4.

ment of law enforcement. The Institute for Government Research of the Brookings Institution found like restrictions upon the attorney general of North Carolina and its statement, which follows, may be applied to this state.

In most instances, his services are called into play and utilized only after requests have been received for them. He is almost entirely limited to defending actions in the Supreme Court in which the state is a party, to prosecuting cases only when requested to do so by a state officer, and to giving opinions and advice when such are requested. A comparison of these circumscribed powers with those exercised by the United States Department of Justice, which is a well organized department of law enforcement, points emphatically to the conclusion that North Carolina is in need of a prosecuting agency that will enforce both substantive and administrative law and secure uniformity in methods of judicial administration throughout the counties of the state.[9]

The absence of uniform law enforcement throughout the state is due largely to the fact that there is no positive tie-up between the solicitors, or local prosecuting officers, and the state prosecuting agency. The constitution provides: " There shall be one Solicitor for each Circuit, who shall reside therein, to be elected by the qualified electors of the Circuit, who shall hold his office for the term of four years, and shall receive for his services such compensation as shall be fixed by law ".[10] Under such an arrangement, the local prosecutor naturally regards himself as being largely independent of central superintendence and responsible only to the local electorate. The solicitor resents intrusion and the attorney general seldom interferes. If the general public realized that the solicitor exercises more power over the

[9] *Survey of North Carolina*, p. 147.
[10] Art. 5, sec. 29.

administration of justice than does the judge, it would be understood why a great many of those who are apprehended for violations of law never come to trial.

As already noted, it is the duty of the attorney general to conduct litigations for the departments of the state government. Nevertheless, the state tax commission is furnished general counsel independent of the attorney general's office. While it is true that he has shown deference to the central legal authority in prosecuting his duties, the law does not restrain him. In the development of a strong and effective law-enforcement agency, all special counsel should be made subordinate to the central office. The first application of this sound principle by the legislature was in 1933 when it authorized special counsel for the electrical utilities division of the railroad commission. This legislation stipulated that the attorney general should be the legal head of all suits arising in the activities of this agency.[11]

Proposed Department of Law

With the view of meeting the need for a greater centralization in the state government of authority for the administration of law, the following organization is suggested:

Department of Law
    1. Office of Attorney General
    2. Bureau of Solicitors
    3. Bureau of Criminal Statistics.

Since the attorney general is the legal advisor of the governor and other state officers, it is generally contended that the desired cooperation between the Department of Law and other executive agencies can best be had through his appointment by the governor.[12]   The writer believes that

---

[11] *Acts of 1933*, p. 645.

[12] See,, for example, the opinion of the late Chief Justice Taft, speaking to the New York Constitutional Convention in 1915, Doc. no. 11, cited in *A Model State Constitution*, p. 29.

this method carries with it a distinct advantage in that it is calculated to create a desirable legal advisory establishment and that it more definitely places the responsibility for the administration of justice upon the governor.

The suggested bureau of solicitors would involve the appointment, direction and active supervision of the solicitors of the fourteen judicial districts by the attorney general. In this way the responsibility for law enforcement would be definitely fixed and the Department of Law would be, in fact, the central prosecuting agency of the state. No longer would the local prosecuting attorneys be free to prosecute or *nolle pros* at their will.

The function of the bureau of criminal statistics would be to conduct studies of crime, of criminal and civil procedures, and to collect such criminal statistics in general that would aid in the more effective enforcement of law. It should prove of particular value in coping with the problem of migratory criminals. In this connection the identification bureau now maintained at the penitentiary should be transferred to this department and should be operated in close touch with the cities of the state.

CHAPTER XII

Personnel Administration

I. ADMINISTRATIVE HEADS

BEFORE undertaking a discussion of methods of obtaining a greater degree of efficiency among the subordinate personnel of the state's administrative service, it may be well to examine briefly the quality of public servants that South Carolina has placed in charge of its agencies since the adoption of the constitution in 1895.[1] To that end, attention is directed to qualifications acquired by previous training or by experience in related activities. Tenure of service will also be noted.

Manifestly, it would be impossible within limited space to deal with all of the numerous agencies. Nor is that necessary. Fourteen sets of officials are selected and are grouped under the following classification: (1) chosen directly by the electorate; (2) selected by the General Assembly; (3) appointed by the governor with consent of the senate.

[1] Information was gathered largely from the following sources: *Cyclopedia of Eminent and Representative Men of the Carolinas of the Nineteenth Century* (Madison, Wis., 1892) ; J. C. Hemphill, *Men of Mark in South Carolina: Ideals of American Life* (Spartanburg, 1902) ; G. H. Crawford, *Who's Who in South Carolina* (Columbia, 1921); Yates Snowden, *History of South Carolina* (New York, 1920) ; R. E. Grier, *South Carolina and Her Builders* (Columbia, 1930) ; J. W. Gibbes, *Legislative Manual*, 12 editions, 1916-1931; *Reports and Resolutions of the General Assembly*, 1895-1920; *Reports of State Officers, Boards and Committees*, 1921-1933. Newspaper files were examined, and several individuals gave the writer the benefit of their memory.

1. Officials Popularly Elected

Governor. So long as this office was filled for a period of two years, the chief executives were invariably elected for a second term.[2] This practice was largely responsible for the constitutional amendment in 1926 which increased the term to four years and made the governor ineligible to succeed himself.

Eleven governors were elected during the period reviewed. One was a journalist, six were lawyers, and the remainder may be classified as planters and business men. All had had previous legislative experience except two of the planters, one of whom had served as comptroller general while the other had held no public office of any kind. One of the planters had also been a railroad commissioner. Three of the six lawyers had seen service as solicitors in the circuit court of the state.

Secretary of State. Prior to 1907, each of the secretaries of state served four years. Since that date the tendency has been to re-elect almost indefinitely. R. M. Mc-Cowan served for ten years, 1907-1917, and was followed by W. Banks Dove who held the office until his death in 1924. The latter was succeeded by the present incumbent, W. P. Blackwell, whose term expires in 1935.

Three of the six secretaries of state had previously performed the duties of chief clerk of that office. A governor's private secretary, a superintendent of public schools, and a farmer constituted the remaining number.

Attorney General. Since 1907 each of these officials has been elected for three terms. The ten-year tenure of the

[2] The only exception was John Gary Evens, the first governor under the present organic law, who did not seek re-election. William T. Ellerbe, 1897-1899, died in office during the first year of his second term. Miles B. McSweeney, who succeeded him, was later elected for a full term, 1901-1903.

present incumbent, John M. Daniels, represents one term of two years and two four-year terms. Five of the seven elected to this office since 1895 had previously been members of the law-making body. The other two had served as assistants to the attorney general. Oddly enough, only one of the seven had had the experience of state's attorney in the judicial circuits.

Comptroller General. In only two instances has the tenure of this office exceeded a period of four years.[3] A. W. Jones resigned after twelve years (1903-1915) to become chairman of the newly created State Tax Commission. The present incumbent, A. J. Beattie, has served since 1925.

Five of the seven comptrollers general had previous practical experience tending to fit them for the position. Two had served as assistant attorney general, two as county auditor and one as United States Internal Revenue agent. Of the remaining two, one was a World War veteran and the other a journalist.

State Treasurer. The first three to hold this office served six, four, and twelve years, respectively. The fourth died in office during the thirteenth year of tenure. The present incumbent, originally appointed to fill a vacancy for one year, is now serving a second elected-term of four years.

One of the five state treasurers had previously served for fifteen years as bookkeeper and chief clerk in this office. Two of the remaining four had been trained in medicine and two had engaged in business. State Treasurer Scarborough was a member of the legislature from 1921 until he was elected to this position.

State Superintendent of Education. Those who have directed the public school system of South Carolina have

---

[3] Carlton W. Sawyer died during his fourth year in office and Rut L. Osborne resigned at the end of his second year.

served four, four, six, fourteen, and twelve years, respectively. The present incumbent has been elected for two terms of two years each and for two four-year terms.

As might be expected, all who have filled this office had received college training and had been actively engaged in public education. Three of the five superintendents had had valuable administrative experience, viz., one had organized a system of graded schools and had established the first teachers' institute in the state; a second had served as school principal for ten years; a third had been superintendent of city schools for twenty years and county superintendent of education for five years.

Adjutant General. Each of the first four adjutants general served for four years. The next died in office during the seventh year of his tenure. Following a vacancy filled by appointment, the next elected to this position died during his second two-year term. General James G. Dozier is now serving his second four-year term.

There have been five war veterans in this group of seven. One of these veterans had also received formal military training at The Citadel and also had served as assistant in the office under discussion. Of the two who had had no war experience, one was a Citadel graduate and a former assistant adjutant general; the other had been an officer in the state militia for many years.

Commissioner of Agriculture, Commerce and Industries. Three commissioners have been elected for periods of fourteen, eight and eight years, respectively. Each of the first two died in office approximately a year before the expiration of his legal tenure. The third resigned (1932) about the middle of his second term of four years.

Two of the three were recognized leaders of the state in this field, viz.: one was the author of a number of monographs on agricultural and industrial subjects and an aggressive promoter in industrial development; the other, farmer and stockman, was a pioneer in breeding certain types of cattle and in advancing the interests of those engaged in cotton culture. The third commissioner had served for twenty years as county farm demonstration agent.

2. Officials Elected by the General Assembly

Chairman, Railroad Commission.[4] It has been customary for the commission to choose one of its members as chairman for a period of two years. The practice of rotating executive direction was departed from in only two instances, i. e., where the same individuals were retained in that capacity for six and eight consecutive years, respectively (1895-1901 and 1919-1927). It is true, however, that two other commissioners served as chairman for a second term, but in broken tenure.

Seven farmers, two lawyers, a county treasurer, and a former railroad employee make up the list of eleven chairmen of the State Railroad Commission. All but two had previously been members of the General Assembly.[5]

State Warehouse Commissioner. Three commissioners were elected by the legislature during the period (1914-1933) that the state warehouse system was operated as a separate unit. The first two served for three years each and the third died in office (1932) during the thirteenth year of tenure.

The first, lawyer and planter, had previously served the state as attorney general and had been a member of both

---

[4] The chairmen are surveyed as being representative of the commission that selects them from its own membership.

[5] In 1932 the commission was composed of four farmers, a lawyer, a merchant and a railroad man. All but one had previously served in the legislature.

houses of Congress. The second had been engaged in the textile industry and had promoted the interests of cotton planters. The third was a farmer and merchant. Two of the three were members of the General Assembly immediately preceding their election by that body to this office.

Insurance Commissioner. The present incumbent, elected in 1928, was re-elected in 1930 with the term increased to four years. His predecessors served for periods of ten, three and eight years, respectively. The brief tenure of the second commissioner resulted from his resignation to re-enter private business.

The following types of individuals have filled this position: (1) a lawyer and newspaper editor; (2) a merchant, accountant and manager of a loan and investment company; (3) a president of a realty company; (4) a former state superintendent of education. Three of the four had served in the legislature.

3. Officials Appointed by the Governor with Consent of the Senate

Chairman, State Highway Commission. The incumbent was chosen in 1931. The previous chairmen (since the Highway Department was reorganized in 1920) served in that capacity for periods of six, one and four years. All four of these officials had enjoyed substantial reputations as the following: lawyer and banker, lawyer and realty promoter, farmer and banker, and newspaper editor.

State Tax Commission.[6] Since its creation in 1915, this body has had only two chairmen. The first, who served until his death in 1922, was equipped with a business education and had served as a county auditor and as comptroller general of the state. The present chairman, a man

6 A full-time commission. Hence, all members are considered.

of considerable business experience, has been a member of the commission since its organization and is recognized as a capable financial administrator.

There have been three other members of this agency. A former county auditor and comptroller general has served since the beginning. Another, who had been attorney general and later special counsel to the commission, was a tax administrator for eight years. The third, a legislator for a dozen years, is now serving his first term of four years.

Board of Public Welfare. During the seven years in which this agency of six members received financial support (1920-1927), eleven individuals served for the following lengths of time: two for seven years, one for six, three for five, three for two and two for one year, each.

Four lawyers, two bankers, two industrialists, a planter and business executive, an educator, and a woman physician composed the membership of an unusually well qualified governing board. Practically without exception these individuals had been identified with public welfare work in South Carolina and were recognized leaders in the field.

Summary

The writer freely admits that the facts, concerning the quality of the selected groups of administrators, are superficially presented. It could hardly be otherwise. In a matter so personal it would be extremely awkward to allude more specifically and in more det..il. Even if that were not so, the varying needs a: d demands of the several positions reviewed would make it difficult to pass precise judgment upon the kind of men who have filled them. Nevertheless, a few general observations may be recorded.

The popularly elected group appear to have been of such quality as might have been expected. As a rule, the electorate has required no special fitness, congruous training, or experience for the position filled.

Convincing evidence is found in the characteristics of the group elected by the General Assembly to support the thesis that this body should not elect administrative officers, for here we find politics at its worst. The legislature is totally unfitted for the performance of this task which is distinctly non-legislative in character. It has been almost invariably the case that officials have been chosen from the membership of the law-making body itself. If it be argued that membership in the General Assembly should not necessarily preclude a choice, it may be replied that experience shows that it has often served as practically the only apparent prerequisite.

Appointment by the governor with consent of the senate has been the most satisfactory method of selection in South Carolina. The group of officers so chosen, as a whole, has unquestionably been superior in native ability and training and in the quality of service rendered. It is believed that if this method of selecting the administrative overhead is extended to a consolidated administrative machinery, sufficiently correlated on a functional basis, marked improvement may be expected in the public service of the state.

In regard to tenure, one is impressed by the inclination in recent years to retain the same individual in office over an extended period. The constitutional restriction upon the governor's term is the only noticeable exception. Fortunately, the people of South Carolina do not appear to subscribe to the idea that a public office should be passed around as a matter of course.

II. SYSTEM OF PERSONNEL CONTROL

Many years ago Woodrow Wilson wrote, " We have declined to provide ourselves with a professional civil service, because we deemed it undemocratic ".[7] Since then

[7] Woodrow Wilson, " Democracy and Efficiency ", in *Atlantic Monthly*, vol. 87, p. 291 (1901).

about one-fourth of the states have instituted the " merit " system and a number of others have adopted improved methods of personnel administration in some form.[8] In South Carolina, little attention has been given to the problem of establishing a personnel system to recruit the best qualified men and women for the public service and to assure them just salaries and reasonable opportunities for promotion.

The State of South Carolina has no centralized personnel supervision. Nor has there been any attempt to consider the state service as a whole. Appointments are made for the most part by heads of departments without check. Being a departmental matter, there are as many plans and policies for recruiting as there are state agencies. It is inevitable under this mode of procedure that many appointments are made through political considerations and that employees are often selected with little regard for their training and experience.

Under the present arrangement, the best talent is not likely to be recruited. Certainly, it is not conducive to economical and efficient administration. In the first place, administrative heads should be relieved of the burden of selecting personnel, as they have no protection against unwarranted political pressure and are embarrassed by requests for personal favors. Secondly, and of more importance, the departments have no organized method of getting in touch with properly qualified individuals. Employees should be recruited only after they have passed appropriate tests administered by a central personnel agency.

[8] For the best survey of recent trends in personnel management, see L. D. White, *Trends in Public Administration* (New York, 1933), chap. xviii. For a thorough analysis of the problems of public personnel and the most constructive program for its improvement, see the report of The Commission of Inquiry on Public Service Personnel, *Better Government Personnel* (New York, 1935), *passim*.

Recruitment is only a part of the problem. A practical basis for arriving at compensation requirements is of equal importance. Salaries cannot be standardized without standardizing qualifications according to a classification plan, which may be used as the foundation upon which an entire personnel system may be constructed. Without such a plan gross injustice is being done to many competent and faithful employees. Moreover, an adequate plan would greatly aid the General Assembly. As Mr. A. E. Buck points out, it removes from this body " the onus of considering multitudinous details in passing on the budget. It permits lump sum appropriations to be made for personal services with the assurance that proper control can be exercised over their expenditure ".[9] Incidentally, with the necessity of such detailed appropriations removed, the legislative sessions each year would be greatly shortened. As matters now stand, the chief hope of a salary increase for the individual employee of the state is often through bringing political influence upon members of the General Assembly.

It is common knowledge that employees performing similar work are receiving different salaries in the several departments of the state government. Without central determination, titles appearing in the appropriations do not necessarily indicate like service rendered. Yet, in most cases, this is the only possible guide of the appropriating body. The extent to which such titles are followed may be seen from the amounts appropriated in 1932 for payment of personal services in a selected group of agencies.

COMPTROLLER GENERAL		TREASURER'S OFFICE	
Chief Clerk	$2,304	Chief Clerk	$2,304
General Bookkeeper	2,064	Bookkeeper	1,980
Second Bookkeeper	1,860	Bookkeeper	1,824
Audit Clerk	1,680	Corporation Clerk	1,824

[9] *Public Budgeting*, p. 540.

Bond Clerk 1,680

Steno-clerk 1,680

Disbursing Clerk 1,344

TAX COMMISSION

Director of Division, each $2,712

Inheritance Tax Examiner . 2,304

Chief Auditor 2,064

Auditor, each 1,968

Corporation & License Clerk 1,860

Bookkeeper—Warrant Clerk 1,680

Inheritance Clerk 1,680

Gasoline License Clerk 1,608

Steno-Clerk 1,464

Field Agent, each 1,339

Stenographer, each 1,248

DEPT. OF AGRICULTURE, ETC.

Chief Clerk $2,304

Cashier 1,320

Steno-Clerk 1,320

Clerk 900

Bond Clerk 1,824

General Clerk 1,788

Disbursing Clerk 1,788

SECRETARY OF STATE

Chief Clerk $2,304

Auditor & Corp. clerk 2,304

File Clerk & Steno 1,788

INSURANCE DEPARTMENT

Chief Clerk 2,064

Actuary Examiner 2,064

Bookkeeper 1,248

Stenographer 1,248

RAILROAD COMMISSION

Secretary $2,304

Rate Expert 2,016

Steno. & Record Clerk 1,548

Reporter 1,248

While certain amounts recur more often than others, e. g.,
$2,304, $2,964, $1,860, 1,680, $1,248, it can hardly be said
that a classification plan exists. The General Assembly has
little information on the basis of which to apply the sound
idea that duties and responsibilities of the persons designated by similar titles should be comparable and should
command like compensation.

Intelligent and equitable treatment of employees can not
be expected so long as salaries are determined on the basis
of the present defective method of fixing rates of pay.
Consideration of the public interest alone is sufficient to
condemn this mode of procedure. The greatest incentive to
increased efficiency, in private business or in government
service, is to be found in the hope of advancement in salary
and in responsibility. There is no such hope for employees
as a class when there is no scientific or equitable plan for

advancements or promotions. And there is no plan when increases in compensation are matters to be considered individually by a legislative committee. To quote a recent study made in another state, " No other system has the vicious defects of this method ".[10]

The most important task of government is that of carrying out effectively, day by day, the actual work of administration. It is essential, therefore, that the clerical and ministerial officials who simply execute orders of their superiors shall be recruited, promoted and paid on a merit basis. It is likewise desirable that these technical subordinates and experts shall have a reasonable permanence of tenure, to the end that a maximum of efficiency may be attained. After all, expertness comes largely from long experience. As Professor Goodnow pointed out, " without it, it is true, the work of government can go on, but without it the cost of government is vastly increased, while the work is poorly done ".[11]

When the short ballot is adopted, it will be the function of the department heads, as representatives of the governor, to execute the policy or policies to which he has committed himself. In that role, they will be expected through their personal leadership " to mediate between the technician, the politician, and the public ".[12] There are many instances in which the administrators could not be well trained in all branches of work which they may be called upon to direct. But these administrators must have technically trained chiefs in charge of the technical divisions or bureaus if the policies are to be properly and effectively administered.

A recent writer has suggested the following three purposes of a personnel system: " (1) To prevent an elected

---

[10] Brookings Institution, *Mississippi Survey*, p. 464.

[11] F. J. Goodnow, *Politics and Administration* (New York, 1900), p. 87.

[12] See White, *Public Administration*, p. 16.

official from barricading himself in office for the rest of his life, be he good, bad, or indifferent; (2) to increase the efficiency of the public service; (3) to cut taxes ".[13] With the view of accomplishing these purposes, the bureau of personnel in the proposed Department of Finance would serve as the recruiting agency of the state service.[14] It would be its function to secure capable employees and to maintain them in the service of the state so as to prevent waste from large turnovers with each change of administration.

The bureau of personnel should be given power to determine the qualifications of applicants for positions by tests which should be competitive, free and open to all persons who are legally eligible; to classify positions according to the nature of the duties required and to their worth to the state; to establish fixed salary ranges and rates; to devise service ratings; to check payrolls before payment of salaries; and to make general employment regulations not inconsistent with law.[15] In the exercise of these powers and duties, it is essential that this bureau work in close collaboration with the director of the budget.

Entrance into the state service should normally be at the lowest salary rate and increases should be made only upon the performance of satisfactory service and after certain intervals have elapsed.[16] Periodic reports of the employees'

[13] Leroy Bartlett, "The Cost of a Personnel System", in *Tax Digest,* August, 1931, p. 272.

[14] Educational institutions face problems different from those of other organizations and should not be brought under this jurisdiction.

[15] For discussions of the function of a state personnel agency, see Institute of Public Administration, *Survey of Arkansas,* p. 17, and *Organization and Administration of the State Government of New Jersey* (Trenton, 1930), p. 83. Also, Brookings Institution, *Survey of North Carolina,* pp. 115-119, and *Survey of Mississippi,* pp. 465-467.

[16] See New York Bureau of Municipal Research (National Institute of Public Administration), *Organization and Management of the State Government of Virginia* (Richmond, 1927), p. 24.

ability, based upon standard specifications, are necessary. Otherwise, there can be no real personnel control and no equitable adjustment. Salaries should be fixed on the basis of responsibility, training and experience, with flexible scales.

The suggested arrangement would not deprive an administrator of his rightful and necessary discretion in directing his personnel. He would not have an employee forced upon him, for he would be free to select from a group of individuals certified as being competent to perform the duties of a position to be filled. The personnel agency would merely test applicants and establish an eligible register of those passing. Moreover, the executive or appointing officer of each department, institution or agency would have authority to remove any subordinate official or employee under his jurisdiction. Upon the written request of an employee so removed, however, the officer making the removal should be required to file with the director of personnel a statement setting forth the reasons for such removal and this statement should be open to public inspection.[17] It is believed that, so long as vacancies can be filled only by competitive examinations, removals without cause are likely to be few.

Discussing the establishment of a permanent technical staff for the detailed work of government, Professor W. F. Dodd has this to say:

Permanency of tenure for governmental employees, with permanent under-directors of departments, would establish a continuing expert personnel such as is necessary for the efficient handling of the technical side of any private business, while leaving to the political officers of the government a control of matters of policy. Such a change cannot be brought about merely by constitutional amendment or by legislation. It involves a fundamental change of attitude upon the part of the

17 See *Survey of Arkansas*, pp. 122, 123.

American people. So long as we regard government as an organization of little personal concern to ourselves, but as one through which the winners in a political game may legitimately gain private profit, we lack the essential element of efficient and permanent administrative policy.[18]

While it is quite true that the greatest need of government is a fundamental change in the attitude of the people, it is believed that the system of personnel control suggested here would unquestionably result in savings and better administrative service in South Carolina. It must be emphasized, however, that these desired results are entirely bound up with consolidation and internal reorganization of the departments, and with executive responsibility in the governor and control over economies by him through an executive budget system.

[18] Dodd, *State Government*, p. 576.

BIBLIOGRAPHY

I. Documents

Acts and Joint Resolutions of the General Assembly of the State of South Carolina.

Constitution of the State of South Carolina, ratified in Convention December 4, 1895. (Cited as *Constitution*.)

Journal of the Houes of Representatives of the State of South Carolina. (Cited as *House Journal*.)

Journal of the Senate of the State of South Carolina. (Cited as *Senate Journal*.)

Reports and Resolutions of the General Assembly of the State of South Carolina. Columbia, 1897-1920.

Reports of State Officers, Boards and Committeees to the General Assembly of South Carolina. Columbia, 1921 —.

South Carolina Code of Laws, 1932. 3 vols. (Cited as *Code 1932*.)

SPECIAL STUDIES IN SOUTH CAROLINA

Report of the Joint Special Committee on Revenue and Taxation, 1921.

Report of the Joint Committee on Economy and Consolidation, 1922.

Report of the South Carolina Mental Hygiene Survey, 1922.

Report of the Special Joint Legislative Committee to Investigate Conditions at State Penitentiary, 1923.

Report of the Special Joint Legislative Committee to Investigate the Penitentiary, 1926.

Report of the Joint Legislative Committee on Efficiency and Consolidation, 1926.

Report of the House Committee on Consolidation of State Offices, 1932.

SELECTED STUDIES IN OTHER STATES

Report of the Illinois Efficiency and Economy Committee. Springfield, 1915.

Report of the Kentucky Efficiency Commission: The Government of Kentucky. 2 vols. Frankfort, 1924.

Report of the (Massachusetts) Commission on State Administration and Expenditures. Boston, 1922. (The Webster Report.)

Reorganization Commission of Maryland, *Plan for the Reorganization of the Administrative Departments of the State Government of Maryland.* Annapolis, 1921.

Report of the Joint Legislative Survey Committee of New Jersey. Trenton, 1925.

Report of the New York Reconstruction Commission on Retrenchment and Reorganization in the State Government. Albany, 1919.

Report of the State Reorganization Commission of New York. Albany, 1926. (Hughes Report, *Leg. Doc. No. 72.*)

Report of the Ohio Joint Legislative Committee on Administrative Reorganization. Columbus, 1920.

Report of the Commission on Simplification and Economy of State and Local Government to the General Assembly of Virginia. Richmond, 1924.

Report on Organization and Management of the State Government of Virginia. Richmond, 1927.

United States Department of Commerce, Bureau of Census. *Financial Statistics of States,* 1929; *Fifteenth Census of the United States:* 1930, *Population Bulletin, Second Series, South Carolina.*

United States Department of the Interior, Office of Education. *Education in the United States,* 1927; *Biennial Survey of Education,* 1928-1930.

United States Department of the Treasury, Public Health Service. *State Laws and Regulations Pertaining to Public Health.* Published annually.

II. BOOKS AND PAMPHLETS

Andrews, Columbus, *Administrative County Government in South Carolina.* Chapel Hill, 1933.

Barth, Harry A., *Financial Control in the States with Emphasis on Control by the Governor.* Philadelphia, 1923.

Beard, Charles A., *American Government and Politics.* Sixth Edition. Chaps. XXV, XXVI, XXVII, XXIX. New York, 1931.

Bethea, Power W., "A Decade of School Progress, 1914-1924," *Bulletin No. 167, The University of South Carolina.* Columbia, 1925.

Betters, Paul V., *State Centralization in North Carolina.* Washington, 1932.

Bonbright and Company, *Survey of State Laws on Public Utilities Regulation in the United States.* New York, 1928.

Breckenridge, S. P., *Public Welfare Administration in the United States.* Chicago, 1927.

Brookings Institution, *Report on a Survey of the Organization and Administration of the State Government of North Carolina.* Washington, 1930.

——, *Report on a Survey of the Organization and Administration of State and County Government in Mississippi.* Jackson, Mississippi, 1932.

Buck, A. E., *Administrative Consolidation in State Governments.* Fifth Edition. New York: National Municipal League, 1930.
——, *Budget Making.* New York, 1921.
——, *Public Budgeting.* New York, 1929.
——, *The Budget in Governments of Today.* New York, 1934.
Butts, A. B., "Public Administration in Mississippi," *Mississippi Historical Society Publications, Centenary Series,* vol. iii. Jackson, 1919.
Childs, Richard S., *Short Ballot Principles.* Boston, 1911.
Cleveland, F. A. and Buck, A. E., *The Budget and Responsible Government.* New York, 1920.
Cleveland, F. A., "Constitutional Provision for a Budget", *Proceedings of Academy of Political Science,* vol. v, 1914.
Commission of Inquiry on Public Service Personnel, *Better Government Personnel.* New York, 1935.
Commons, John R. and Andrews, John B., *Principles of Labor Legislation.* Revised Edition. New York, 1927.
Cook, William A., *Federal and State School Administration.* New York, 1927.
Crawford, G. H., *Who's Who in South Carolina.* Columbia, 1921.
Croly, Herbert, *The Promise of American Life.* New York, 1909.
Dodd, Walter F., *State Government.* Second Edition. Chaps. VIII, IX, XVII, XXI. New York, 1928.
Donaldson, J. L., "State Administration in Maryland," *Johns Hopkins University Studies in Historical and Political Science,* Series XXXIV, 1916.
Forbes, Russell, *Governmental Purchasing.* New York, 1929.
Garlington, J. C., *Men of the Time, Sketches of Living Notables in South Carolina.* Spartanburg, 1902.
Gettys, Luella, *The Reorganization of State Government in Nebraska.* Lincoln: Nebraska Legislative Reference Bureau, 1922.
Gibbes, J. Wilson, *Legislative Manual.* Thirteenth Edition. Columbia, 1931.
Goodnow, Frank J., *Politics and Administration.* New York, 1900.
——, *Principles of Administrative Law in the United States.* New York, 1903.
Greer, Sarah, *A Bibliography of Public Administration.* New York, 1926.
Grier, Ralph E., *South Carolina and her Builders.* Columbia, 1930.
Griffenhagen and Associates, *Report on the Organization and Administration of the State Government of Maryland.* Annapolis, 1921.
Heer, Clarence, *The Post-War Expansion of State Expenditures.* New York, 1926.
Hemphill, J. C., *Men of Mark in South Carolina: Ideals of American Life.* Washington, 1909.

Holcombe, A. N., *State Government in the United States.* Third Edition. New York, 1931.

Kilpatrick, Wylie, *State Administrative Review of Local Budget Making.* New York, 1927.

Knight, Edgar W., *History of Public Education in the South.* Boston, 1922.

Lutz, H. L., *Public Finance.* Chap. XVIII. New York, 1924.

McBain, Howard Lee, " The Problem of Governmental Reorganization ", *Proceedings of Academy of Political Science,* vol. ix, no. 3, May, 1921.

McCrady, Edward, Jr. and Ashe, Samuel A., *Cyclopedia of Eminent and Representative Men of the Carolinas of the Nineteenth Century.* 2 vols. Madison, Wisconsin, 1892.

Magruder, F. A., " Recent Administration in Virginia ", *Johns Hopkins Studies in Historical and Political Science,* Series XXX, 1912.

Mathews, John M., *Principles of American State Administration.* New York, 1921.

——, *American State Government.* Chaps. VIII, IX, X. New York, 1924.

Mayers, Lewis, *Federal Service.* New York, 1922.

Meriam, Lewis, *Principles Governing the Retirement of Public Service Employees.* New York, 1918.

Meriwether, Colyer, *History of Higher Education in South Carolina.* Washington, 1889.

Missouri Association for Economy in Public Expenditures, *A Digest of Systems of Government Enacted in Thirteen States.* St. Louis, 1926.

Mitchell, Broadus and Mitchell, George S., *The Industrial Revolution in the South.* Baltimore, 1930.

Moley, Raymond, *The State Movement for Efficiency and Economy.* New York, 1917.

National Industrial Conference Board, *Cost of Government, 1923-1934.* New York, 1934.

National Institute of Public Administration, *Findings and Recommendations on a Survey of the Administrative Structure of the State of Arkansas.* New York, 1930.

——, *Organization and Administration of the State Government of New Jersey.* Trenton, 1930.

National Municipal League, *The Merit System in Government.* New York, 1926.

National Municipal League, Committee on State Government, *A Model State Constitution.* Reprinted with explanatory articles, 1927.

National Tax Association, " A Plan of a Model System of State and Local Taxation," *Proceedings of National Tax Conferences,* 1919, vol. xii.

New York Bureau of Municipal Research, *Organization and Management of the State Government of Virginia.* Richmond, 1927.

——, *Nevada and its Government.* Printed as a supplement to the Nevada State Journal, Reno, November 20, 1924.

——, *The Constitution and Government of the State of New York.* Bulletin No. 61, May, 1915.

Newcomer, Mabel, " Separation of State and Local Revenues in the United States," *Columbia University Studies in History, Economics and Public Law,* vol. lxxvi, no. 2, 1917.

Odum, Howard W., *An American Epoch.* New York, 1930.

Ogg, F. A. and Ray, P. O., *Essentials of American Government.* Chaps. XXVIII, XXIX, XXX. New York, 1932.

Recent Social Trends in the United States: Report of the President's Research Committee on Social Trends, 2 vols. New York, 1933.

Salley, A. S., Jr., " The Methods of Raising Taxes in South Carolina prior to 1868 ", *Bulletin No. 8 of the South Carolina Historical Commission.* Columbia, 1925.

Seligman, E. R. A., *Essays in Taxation.* Tenth Edition, New York, 1928.

Simkins, Francis B., *The Tillman Movement in South Carolina.* Durham, N. C., 1926.

Simkins, F. B. and Woody, R. H., *South Carolina during Reconstruction.* Chapel Hill, N. C., 1932.

Snowden, Yates, *History of South Carolina.* 5 vols. Chicago, 1920.

South Carolina, a Handbook Prepared by the Department of Agriculture, Commerce and Industries, and Clemson College, 1927.

South Carolina Council, *Agriculture; Education; Health; County Government* (Pamphlets). Cheraw, 1931.

Stewart, Frank M., " The Reorganization of State Administration in Texas," *Bulletin No. 2507, The University of Texas, 1925.*

Thomas, John P., *History of the South Carolina Military Academy.* Charleston, 1893.

Thomason, John F., *Foundations of the Public Schools in South Carolina.* Columbia, 1925.

Thompson, Henry T., *The Establishment of the Public School System in South Carolina.* Columbia, 1927.

Wager, Paul W., *County Government in North Carolina.* Chapel Hill, N. C., 1928.

Wallace, David D., *The South Carolina Constitution of 1895.* Bulletin No. 197, the University of South Carolina, 1927.

Wallace, Schuyler C., *State Administrative Supervision over Cities in the United States.* New York, 1928.

White, Leonard D., *Introduction to the Study of Public Administration.* Chaps. II, VII, VIII. New York, 1926.

——, *Trends in Public Administration.* New York, 1933.

Wiest, Edward, *Agricultural Organization in the United States.* Lexington, Ky., 1923.

Williams, G. Croft, *Social Problems of South Carolina.* Columbia, 1928.

Willoughby, W. F., *Principles of Public Administration.* Chaps. III, IV, V. Baltimore, 1927.

III. PERIODICALS

Bartlett, Leroy, "The Cost of a Personnel System", *The Tax Digest,* August, 1931.

Barnett, James, "Representation of Interests in Administration", *National Municipal Review,* vol. xii, 1923.

Breckenridge, S. P., "Summary of the Present State Systems for the Organization and Administration of Public Welfare", *Annals of American Academy of Political and Social Science,* vol. cv, 1923.

Buck, A. E., "Administrative Reorganization in Tennessee", *National Municipal Review,* October, 1923.

——, "Nebraska's Reorganized State Administration", *National Municipal Review,* July, 1922.

——, "The Illinois Civil Administrative System—What it has accomplished", *National Municipal Review,* November, 1922.

——, "Measuring the results of Government", *National Municipal Review,* vol. xiii, 1924.

Chamberlain, J. P., "Democratic Control of Administration", *American Bar Association Journal,* April, 1927.

Childs, Richard S., "New York State Reorganizes", *National Municipal Review,* May, 1926.

Coker, F. W., "Dogmas of Administrative Reform", *American Political Science Review,* vol. xvi, 1922.

Conover, Milton, "Merit Systems of Civil Service in the States", *American Political Science Review,* vol. xix, 1925.

——, "Centralized Purchasing Agencies in State and Local Governments", *American Political Science Review,* vol. xix, 1925.

Crawford, Finla G., "Administrative Reorganization in New York State", *American Political Science Review,* May, 1927.

Derieux, James C., "Crawling Toward the Promised Land", *II Survey,* April 29, 1922.

Dodd, Walter F., "Reorganizing State Government", *The Annals of American Academy of Political and Social Science,* vol. cxiii, 1924.

Edmonds, R. W., "The Workshop of the Carolinas", *Review of Reviews,* October, 1929.

Edwards, William H., "The State Reorganization Movement", *Dakota Law Review,* January and April, 1927, and February and April, 1928.

Engelhardt, Fred, "The Future School District", *American School Journal*, vol. lxxxi, July, 1930.

Fairlie, John A., "State Governor", *Michigan Law Review*, vol. x, March and April, 1912.

Gardner, O. Max, "One State Cleans House", *Saturday Evening Post*, vol. 204, January 2, 1932.

Googe, George L., "Union Progress in South Carolina", *American Federalist*, vol. xxxvi, June, 1929.

Hatch, H. A., "Workmen's Compensation Will Benefit South Carolina", *Labor Legislation Review*, vol. xix, December, 1929.

Jacobson, J. M., "Evaluating State Administrative Structure: the Fallacy of the Statistical Approach", *American Political Science Review*, vol. xxii, November, 1928.

Kilpatrick, Wylie, "State Supervision of Municipal Finance in New Jersey", *National Municipal Review*, vol. xiv, 1925.

Lancaster, Lane W., "Connecticut Consolidates State Financial Control", *National Municipal Review*, May, 1928.

Logan, Joseph C., "The Relation of Layman and Expert in Social Work", *Journal of Social Forces*, May, 1924.

Lowden, F. O., "Reorganizing the Administration of a State", *National Municipal Review*, vol. xv, January, 1926.

Lutz, H. L. ,"The Control of Public Expenditures", *Tax Digest*, November, 1931.

McCombs, C. E., "State Welfare Administration and Consolidated Government", *National Municipal Review*, vol. xiii, 1924.

Mathews, John M., "State Administrative Reorganization", *American Political Science Review*, vol. xvi, 1922.

Maxwell, A. J., "Complete Executive Control of the Budget", *Tax Digest*, November, 1931.

Mort, Paul R., "The Financing of American Schools", *South Carolina Education*, vol. xii, 1930.

Newcomer, Mabel, "Tendencies in State and Local Finance", *Political Science Quarterly*, vol. xliii, 1928.

Patterson, Dowell, "Organization Possibilities in South Carolina", *American Federalist*, vol. xxxvi, June, 1929.

Sly, J. F., "Administrative Reorganization Adopted in California", *National Municipal Review*, April, 1928.

Smith, Alfred E., "How We Ruin Our Governors", *National Municipal Review*, vol. x, 1921.

Smith, Clarence, "Control of Public Expenditures", *Tax Digest*, August, 1931.

Staples, Abram P., "Operation of the Segregation Tax in Virginia", *Manufacturers Record*, January 15, 1931.

The Annals, vol. cxiii, May, 1924. A valuable series of articles entitled " Competency and Economy in Public Expenditures ".

Tucker, Robert H., " The Virginia Reorganization Program ", *National Municipal Review*, November, 1928.

Turner, Jessie M., " Democracy in Administration ", *American Political Science Review*, vol. xvii, 1923.

Walker, Harvey, " Theory and Practice in State Administrative Reorganization ", *National Municipal Review*, April, 1930.

——, " Ohio Appraises its Reorganized State Government ", *National Municipal Review*, April, 1929.

Wells, Roger H., " The Item Veto and State Budget Reform ", *American Political Science Review*, vol. xviii, 1924.

Wicker, W. H., " Court Experience in South Carolina Shows Need of Accident Compensation ", *American Labor Legislation Review*, March, 1930.

Wilson, Woodrow, " The Study of Administration ", *Political Science Quarterly*, vol. ii, June, 1887.

——, " Democracy and Efficiency ", *Atlantic Monthly*, vol. 87, 1901.

INDEX